G000291653

Dear Theo,

I do hope you won't find this too "heavy going" — but knowing your love for detail, I hope you will find some enjoyment reading this book.

A very happy birthday to a darlin' brother.

Much love

Ibah

xxx

Tribute

A Salute to the
British Armed Forces
of the Second World War

Alwyn W. Turner

Lennard Publishing

First published in 1995 by
Lennard Publishing
a division of
Lennard Associates Limited
Mackerye End, Harpenden
Herts AL5 5DR

Produced in association with
Tribute Promotions Limited

© Alwyn W. Turner 1995

All rights reserved. No part of this publication may be reproduced,
stored in a retrieval system, or transmitted, in any form or by any
means, without the prior permission in writing of the publisher, nor be
otherwise circulated in any form of binding or cover other than that in
which it is published without similar condition including this condition
being imposed on the subsequent purchaser.

A catalogue entry is available from the British Library

ISBN 1 85291 129 8

Design by Design 2 Print
Editors: Elizabeth Pritchard, Jacky Cleaver
and Alison Bravington
Maps by Gordon Chambers
Reproduction by Leaside Graphics

Printed and bound in Great Britain by
Butler & Tanner, Frome and London

CONTENTS

THE ROYAL AIR FORCE

PREFACE

The Second World War was the first – and, mercifully, so far the only – global conflict in human history. During its course, the men and women of the British armed forces were involved in a huge diversity of struggles, from the fjords of Norway through the deserts of Africa and the Middle East to the jungles of the Far East, not forgetting the vast expanses of the oceans and the air.

Tribute is written in salute to those men and women.

It does not attempt a chronological narrative, but is rather a survey of the three major services: the Royal Navy, the Army and the Royal Air Force. In each, the structure adopted has been tailored as seemed appropriate to the particular service: the Royal Navy is approached through the major campaigns that it fought, the Army by description of the regiments and corps in the regular force, and the RAF by the command structure of the time.

This has resulted in an imbalance in favour of the Army and in particular of the 'poor bloody infantry', a fact which of course is not to be taken in any way as a judgement on the contribution that each service made to the war effort. Indeed this imbalance was probably inevitable, for not only did the Army absorb a disproportionate number of personnel, but it was also involved in a wider range of action.

It is hoped that as much of the variety of campaigning has been covered as possible, with as little repetition as is consistent with coherence. Throughout, the emphasis is on the unique or unusual role of each unit in an attempt to maximise the limited space available.

Thus, despite Churchill's famous comment that before Alamein we never had a victory and that after it we never had a defeat, equal weight has been given to such early successes as the battle of Keren and such later blows as the Dodecanese expedition. Believing that the serviceman's experience of war is not confined to the great, epoch-making battles, the assault on Madagascar is seen as being as valid as the assault on Normandy. And the 'forgotten army' of the Far East is duly acknowledged, along with such other forgotten servicemen as those in the RAF who suppressed the Iraqi rising of 1941.

The pressures of space have, however, imposed limitations. Chief amongst them have been the concentration on combat forces abroad, at the expense of the support mechanisms at home, and the restriction to the regular British services alone. These limitations are regrettable but necessary in a single volume: due apologies are therefore offered to those whose invaluable contribution was made in the field of training or of home defence or in the reserve forces, and to those volunteers from the Colonies and Dominions, whose involvement was so vital.

Finally, one more word of warning should be given. Every ship of the Royal Navy, every regiment of the Army, every squadron of the Royal Air Force deserves a volume of its own to cover its activity in the Second World War; here there can be room for only the briefest mention of the broadest outline.

ALWYN W. TURNER
MARCH 1995

ACKNOWLEDGEMENTS

Thanks are due to the staff and librarians of the various institutions visited during the writing of this book, particularly those at the National Army Museum. Gratitude is also expressed to Mr Nick Flower, on whose initiative this project was undertaken and whose continuing faith has been much appreciated. And finally I am indebted to Major (retd) Gordon Turner MBE, who rendered invaluable assistance in research and support during the writing.

In the interests of space and clarity, the footnote references at the end of each chapter do not give full publishing details; these can be found in the Bibliography.

The regiments and corps of the Army are in the order shown in the 1939 Army List, which gives separate sections for the Cavalry and for the Armoured Corps, thus producing the occasional variation in the more normal order of seniority. Units created during the course of the war are given in their appropriate seniority. The details of the raising of the regiment and the major battle honours at the beginning of each chapter are based on Mr David Ascoli's authoritative *A Companion To The British Army 1660-1983*, published by Harrap Ltd in 1983.

THE ROYAL NAVY

The Royal Navy

The Battle of the Atlantic

In the aftermath of Dunkirk, with mainland Europe either under occupation by the German war machine or at its mercy, the defiant decision that the struggle continued, that the British Empire and the Dominions would stand alone against Nazi aggression, was a desperate gamble. The long-term goal, the key to victory, was clearly the entry of the Americans into the war, but surviving until that point was dependent entirely upon the Royal Navy's ability to keep open the lines of communication bringing food and supplies into Britain.

Arguably the RN contribution in the Atlantic was the greatest made to the war effort, for if the German navy had established control of the seas, there is no doubt that Britain, starved of war materials and of the essentials of life, would have fallen. As Churchill was later to write: 'The Battle of the Atlantic was the dominating factor all through the war. Never could we forget that everything depended ultimately on its outcome.' [1]

The Battle of the Atlantic, though at its most acute for a period of three years to May 1943, in fact lasted for the duration of the war, the first sinking by a U-boat coming on 3 September 1939 and the last U-boat not surrendering until some days after the German capitulation. The geographical scale of the conflict too was huge: the Atlantic has an area nearly ten times the size of Europe, and of course the battle of supplies spread far beyond the ocean that gave it its name. The task was to protect a British merchant fleet that had by 1940 an average of 2,000 ships at sea each day.

The Royal Navy entered this epic and unrelenting campaign as numerically the strongest navy in the world, though many of its ships were old and unsuitable for the war that was to come. And it faced a more dangerous enemy than it might have anticipated. For more than a decade, Germany had regularly been flouting the various treaties and agreements that were supposed to limit the size and scope of its navy and to limit the size of warships for all countries; in particular it had been building U-boats, albeit in small numbers only at this point, but it was this weapon that was to wreak the greatest devastation. Britain, handicapped by its observance of international restrictions, was vulnerable to a swift offensive.

The first six months of the war gave an indication of what was to come. On 17 September a U-boat torpedoed the aircraft carrier *Courageous*, and in November another penetrated the defences of the Royal Navy's anchorage at Scapa Flow and sank the battleship *Royal Oak*. The propaganda blow of the latter was terrible, though the Admiralty could be grateful that, with most of the fleet at sea, the material price paid was no higher.

Of concern in the long-term was the assault on merchant shipping by the still comparatively small resources available to the German navy: by the end of March 1940, 46 U-boats had sunk 222 merchant ships, for a loss of just 17 vessels. The first victim was the liner *Athenia*, whose sinking on the day war was declared cost the lives of some 110 civilian passengers and 18 crew members. International conventions demanded that unescorted civilian ships be warned and crew and passengers taken off before the vessel was attacked; on this occasion, the safeguards were not undertaken and, though some on both sides tried to maintain the conventions, the pattern for the future of total war against the merchant navy was set.

Against this backdrop of aggressive action, the Royal Navy had two hopeful developments from which to take comfort. The first was the rapid adoption of the convoy system for merchantmen. During the Great War, U-boats had wreaked havoc on shipping and it was not until the Admiralty's introduction of convoys that the threat was reduced. In 1939 the lesson did not need to be learnt again: convoys were accepted as necessary from the outset.

Nonetheless, convoys were not universally popular. Ships had to travel at the speed of the slowest member, common routes had to be agreed upon, often to the detriment of individual requirements, and the congestion at ports slowed down the process of loading and unloading. As a result one third of Britain's cargo capacity was immediately sacrificed; even with the largest merchant navy in the world, it was a considerable loss. Against these objections could be placed the arguments that ships were less likely to be spotted in convoy and were easier to protect. The figures from the first months of the war at least demonstrated clearly that safety was greatly enhanced by the Admiralty's precautionary decision.

The second source of hope for the Navy in that early phase was the marginalisation of Germany's surface fleet in the war against merchant ships. The German military leadership, though far advanced in strategies and tactics when it came to land war, still saw a powerful surface fleet as a a symbolic statement of its power and was reluctant to jeopardize its capital ships.

A major exception was the *Admiral Graf Spee*, the so-called pocket battleship sent to terrorize the trade routes of the South Atlantic and the Indian Ocean. In December 1939 it was located and engaged by three RN ships: *Exeter*, *Ajax* and *Achilles*. Badly damaged and forced back into Montevideo, the *Graf Spee* was scuttled by its crew rather than face again a battle in which it was believed to stand no chance. The fact that this decision was largely based on a mistaken belief that more ships were closing in on the striken vessel was of less significance than the loss of such a prestigious symbol of the enemy navy: the German disinclination to risk its surface fleet in the uncertain waters of the Atlantic was reinforced. The

U-boats, however, remained and – in the aftermath of the Scapa Flow raid – were now actively celebrated in Germany as front-line weapons.

The opening of the land initiative in Europe – the invasions of Denmark, Norway and the Low Countries – took both navies away from the tussle over international trade. By the time the impasse of mid-1940 was reached, and the period commonly known as the Battle of the Atlantic commenced, the situation had altered in several crucial respects. Germany's land successes had gained its navy the French Atlantic ports and therefore a substantial increase in U-boat range, as well as coastlines on the English Channel and North Sea, rendering both dangerous for British shipping. With Ireland insisting that its neutral status precluded British use of its bases, access to British ports was ever more limited.

The fall of Scandinavia, on the other hand, had brought over to Britain the substantial Norwegian merchant navy and had led to the Allied occupation of Iceland as a forward base. Britain had also acquired some 50 destroyers from America: old ships, but still serviceable as escorts for convoys.

Despite these gains, and despite a German navy reduced to just 28 U-boats and a severely depleted surface fleet, the Royal Navy was clearly on the defensive. The re-opening of the campaign in May 1940 saw a single U-boat mission sink 11 merchant ships of some 44,000 tons. The following month 64 ships (260,000 tons) were lost to U-boats, all but one of them in the Atlantic. Eight had been travelling in convoy, 56 sailing alone, illustrating again the value of convoy, as well as the fact that it was still not universal.

In September 1940 the U-boats adopted the tactic that was to become known as the wolf-pack: submarines continued to patrol individually but signalled for others to join when a target was identified. It was a tactic long planned, but only now implemented, and one that reaped instant rewards with the sinking of 274 merchant ships in five months, a total of 1.4 million tons of shipping lost. During the same period, a similar loss was caused by enemy aircraft and mines. The most fearful development within this was the ability of the wolf-pack to strike at ships in convoy: some 24 were sunk in a single week in September, and of the 75 ships lost the following month, 60 had been in convoy.

The Royal Navy's response to the renewed onslaught was muted. Partly the problem was material: there was a shortage of ships that was only partly eased by the US destroyers and the earlier comandeering of private yachts and whaling ships; the technology available for detecting U-boats (the Asdic system) and destroying them (depth-charges) was inadequate; and there was a lack of money for the RAF's Coastal Command. But partly too there was an inappropriate approach to dealing with the U-boat menace – RN ships were all too often occupied in hunting the enemy, sweeping through vast expanses of ocean in a futile attempt to locate submarines that had no intention of engaging in direct combat.

The consequence of these separate factors was that while Allied convoys were escorted 200 miles out into the Atlantic, they remained vulnerable to German attack with U-boats operating up to 700 miles out.

1941 saw the losses continue, but the balance was shifting in the Allies' favour. Royal Navy ships had begun to focus more on escorting the convoys, effectively adopting a more defensive posture that waited for U-boats to identify themselves rather than trying to find them. Later in the year Support Groups were introduced; ships in addition to the escorts, which could remain behind after an incident and force the U-boats to the surface.

Convoys were also receiving more protection from the other side of the ocean. The Royal Canadian Navy was providing escorts for merchantmen, and the areas of protection were gradually extended far enough to overlap in the midst of the Atlantic: in May 1941 the first convoy sailed with a continuous armed presence.

The American navy too had become more active since the re-election of President Roosevelt, and had begun to provide ocean-going assistance for convoys containing US ships; in May 1941 it took over the bases in Iceland. By the autumn of that year America was sinking U-boats in the Atlantic – at war in all but name, at least so far as the sea was concerned. This support, together with the introduction of high frequency direction finding ('huff-duff' as it was inevitably abbreviated) and ship-borne radar that enabled U-boats to be tracked more effectively, helped bring sinkings under some control.

The battle, however, was far from over. In September 1941 53 merchantmen were sunk, a vast improvement on the previous year but still high. And the massive improvements in November (13 lost) and December (just four) were not solely due to Allied efforts – the departure of several U-boats for the Mediterranean had reduced the fleet available. The situation remained volatile.

It was transformed with the official entry of the US into the war with Germany. U-boats were now free for the first time to operate in US waters, and with many more vessels coming into service – 100 at the beginning of 1942, nearly double that by October – the danger was even greater than it had been in 1940. The American navy failed to provide the close escorts necessary and the western waters of the Atlantic became a happy hunting ground for U-boat commanders. It was as though the long experience of the Royal Navy in discovering the ways and means to combat the German initiative was discarded, as though all the early mistakes were destined to be repeated. In the first five months of 1942 the tonnage of merchant shipping lost equalled the total for the whole of the previous year, most of it on the American coast. In response, the United States navy sank just one U-boat.

The second half of 1942 also saw appalling losses, as well as greater numbers of U-boats hunting in larger packs: attacks by up to 20 at a time were not uncommon. The year as a whole cost seven and a half million tons of shipping, more than the entire total of the war thus far. Behind this catastrophic figure, however, the balance was again shifting. More ships were becoming available, Coastal Command of the RAF had begun to make a significant intervention into the struggle, America had learnt the hard way how to protect ships, and U-boat sinkings were increasing. There were some optimistic signs for the future, providing of course that the war was not lost beforehand.

Running parallel to these shifts in force was a technical battle to produce better equipment. On the Allied side, improvements for detection of U-boats were becoming more widely available with radar and 'huff-duff' on more ships, and Leigh lights on 'planes. German advances had also been made with tanker submarines that kept the U-boats supplied far away from their bases, and with anti-radar sets. But the ultimate hope of a vessel that could remain beneath the waves without needing to surface was still far away, and the increasing ability of the Allies to spot U-boats was causing concern.

All these factors played their part in the Allied victory of 1943. The sinkings were high in the first three months, with some of the worst figures of the war registered for March, but that shock seemed to provide the final impetus for change. America extended the scope and strength of its cover – both surface and air – and the gaps in the Atlantic were closed. April saw the number of sinkings cut by half, and in May for the first time the numbers of U-boats lost exceeded the numbers of merchantmen. With production of new vessels at home reduced by RAF bombing attack, Germany had no alternative but to abandon the field of battle.

The struggle was not yet over, and there were still encounters to be faced, but never again did U-boats seriously threaten the trade shipping across the Atlantic. By January 1944 only two merchantmen were lost to submarine attack. And the Royal Navy, now more often engaged in direct combat with U-boats, lost just one ship. At the same time, the Hunting Groups were scoring remarkable successes, most spectacular of all the Second Support Group of Captain John Walker that sank six U-boats in the space of a single five-week patrol.

Thereafter, despite the occasional blip in the figures, the relentless encircling of Germany made the war against merchant shipping impossible to restart with any conviction. The Allies' retaking of France deprived the Germans of their forward bases, and lack of resources delayed the building of the new U-boats, fitted with snorkling apparatus that enabled them to stay underwater almost indefinitely, thereby evading easy detection; the first such U-boat to be sent on patrol surrendered in May 1945 without having fired a shot in combat.

Convoys to the USSR

A subsidiary conflict ran parallel to the Battle of the Atlantic during 1941-2. With the entry of the Soviet Union into the war following its invasion by Germany, a new political demand arose of providing supplies to that country.

A sea route to Archangel and Murmansk was possible, but it required ten days of sailing to reach the destination, during which time the convoys were in continual danger. The return journey, of course, was equally hazardous.

Nonetheless the first convoys passed through without loss, before the German leadership became convinced that a British invasion of Norway was imminent and allocated ships to the area, most notably the battleship *Tirpitz* which proceeded to Trondheim.

The critical moment came with perhaps the most famous of all convoys during the war: PQ17. 35 ships were being escorted by the Royal Navy in July 1942 when the information, incorrect as it subsequently transpired, was received that the *Tirpitz* was at sea. The escort was instructed to withdraw and the merchantmen to scatter. Left to themselves, the merchant ships were at the mercy of enemy submarines and aircraft, and in the ensuing carnage, 24 of the ships were sunk. The scale of the convoys was drastically reduced.

In all, 811 merchant ships sailed for the USSR in 40 convoys. Nearly 100 were lost.

Tragically this terrible price was paid for very little. The tanks and aircraft despatched to the Soviet Union were largely surplus to requirements and many were never even unpacked, let alone employed in the war effort. The fact that they were desperately needed by Allied forces elsewhere, such as in Asia, simply made the sacrifice more appalling. And even when the USA began to provide the materials that the Russians truly needed, most of the supplies went by land through Iran.

The Command of the Seas

The fact that Britain has not endured a serious invasion for nearly a thousand years is often ascribed to its being an island; the corollary to this is of course that any military action by Britain is also dependent on control of the sea. The Royal Navy's tasks during the war, apart from protecting merchant shipping, were also to include denying the enemy its supply routes and facilitating land engagements with the enemy.

The first six months of the war might have been dismissively termed the 'Phoney War' on land, but at sea they were a time of continual activity on both sides, with successes to show for both. British ships, such as the armed merchant cruiser *Rawalpindi,* were sunk in waters that perhaps should have been safe, but the victory at the River Plate was a major boost to morale, reinforced by the capture of the *Altmark,* the *Graf Spee*'s supply ship, off the coast of Norway by the destroyer *Cossack,* when 300 prisoners were freed. Most important of all, the British Expeditionary Force was conveyed across the Channel unimpeded, the prime military objective at that time.

The return of the men of the BEF, of course, was to become one of the most critical moments of those first years. The evacuations from Dunkirk and elsewhere were accomplished, despite the presence of the legendary 860 small boats, for the most part by RN destroyers. There were casualties – the loss of the *Lancastria* amongst them – but the strength of the Royal Navy was sufficient to ensure that the Army survived to fight again.

Less successful were the parallel operations in the North Sea, where the German surface fleet was reinforced by U-boats formerly allocated to the Atlantic. Both fleets were to sustain heavy damage during the Norwegian campaign, the greatest prize being claimed by Germany with the sinking of the aircraft-carrier *Glorious,* then engaged on evacuating troops from Norway. Having previously taken RAF squadrons to Narvik as part of the doomed attempt to defend against the German invasion, the *Glorious* was returning in early June with a squadron each of Hurricanes and Gladiators; the 'planes and all but two of the pilots were lost, a heavy blow to take when the Battle of Britain was about to start.

The same period of activity, as the blitzkrieg re-drew the map of Europe, also saw two other maritime powers enter the lists against Britain. The first of these presented acute political questions, for the fall of France left the Vichy regime an ally of Germany and, though the armistace specifically stated that French warships under German control would not be used, Hitler's adherence to treaties was no longer trusted. With invasion threatened, Churchill had no option but to order an attack on the French navy. On 3 July 1940, British ships opened fire on the Atlantic fleet of its former ally. In the space of 16 minutes three capital ships were sunk at Mers-el-Kebir in Algeria; those French ships in British ports were seized at the same time by the Royal Navy.

The other enemy to take the field was Italy, whose navy had never enjoyed the same respect accorded to that of France, but which was inevitably a threat to British trading routes and to the forces in North Africa. On 11 October 1940 three destroyers were sunk by the *Ajax,* veteran of the *Graf Spee* encounter. A month later aircraft from the *Illustrious* attacked the Italian fleet at Taranto, putting half the ships out of action and inflicting major damage on the docks. In March 1941 a further attack on Italian ships off Cape Matapan proved successful; again aircraft launching bombs and torpedoes were involved in the action.

The use of aircraft against capital ships had been demonstrated earlier in both France and Norway, and of course the Battle of Britain had been fought by

Germany in an attempt to secure control of the Channel. However, it was a fact not yet fully appreciated that the days of stand-up fights between battleships were fast becoming obsolete in an era of airpower. The arrival of the Luftwaffe to bail out the Italians' floundering efforts in the Aegean was to drive home the effectiveness of control of the air.

The German victories in Greece and Crete in April-May 1941 were possible despite the Royal Navy's best endeavours simply because the Luftwaffe had such overwhelming air superiority. Three cruisers and six destroyers were sunk during the campaign and others, including two battleships, damaged. They were losses that could only have been reduced if the Navy had abandoned its obligations to evacuate the land forces from Crete, an option which Admiral Cunningham resolutely refused to consider: 'It takes the Navy three years to build a ship,' he insisted, 'it would take three hundred years to rebuild a tradition.' [2] Even so, the sheer strength of the enemy's air forces ensured that daytime operations were virtually impossible.

An even more devastating loss in terms of prestige came in May with the sinking off Greenland of the world's biggest battle cruiser *Hood,* a potent symbol of British naval pride. The victor that day was the *Bismarck,* Germany's most powerful vessel and, unlike *Hood* which dated from 1920, a fully modern ship. The subsequent hunting and sinking of *Bismarck* later in the month avenged the loss and set back once again German surface interventions in the Battle of the Atlantic.

The situation in the Mediterranean during the remainder of 1941 was undecided. The Luftwaffe continued to dominate the skies and lay siege to Malta, but the seas were very much the domain of the Royal Navy. Indeed the power of the Navy was the major reason for the prolonged assault on Malta; it was a critical outpost providing a base, particularly for aircraft carriers, from which the Navy's 'planes could strike at enemy supply lines. It was from Malta, for example, that five Axis ships bringing supplies to North Africa, together with their escort of three destroyers, were sunk in April. And in four months during the summer, three quarters of a million tons of Italian shipping were destroyed by British action, dealing a severe blow to Rommel's supply lines in North Africa.

In response a fleet of six U-boats arrived from the Atlantic in October, to be followed by four more the next month. On 14 November a torpedo from one of the U-boats struck the *Ark Royal,* then the only aircraft carrier in the Mediterranean Fleet. Less than two weeks later the battleship *Barham* was also sunk by U-boats.

1942 was again characterized by the unresolved question of who had command of the seas. For much of the year Malta remained besieged but defiant, with convoys somehow managing to break through the Axis blockade in sufficient strength to keep the island alive.

Further north, in February 1942, the battleships *Scharnhorst* and *Gneisenau* broke out of the docks at Brest and raced through the supposedly defended English

Channel to reach safety in Germany. The fact that British forces had failed to finish off the ships at Brest, despite over a hundred air-raids and the heroic endeavours of Coastal Command, and failed to prevent their escape, losing 42 aircraft in the process, did nothing to assert British control of its own water.

It was 1942, however, that also saw the first of the series of sea-borne invasions that were ultimately to bring an end to the war in the West. Operation Torch saw 800 British and American ships take a combined force into North-West Africa, seizing Algeria and Morocco. There was a price to be paid – the destroyer *Broke* was sunk at Algiers and two sloops *Walney* and *Hartland* lost at Oran – but that such an operation could have been staged at all, let alone with such immediate success, demonstrated a feeling that the enemy threat at sea was no longer an impediment to the prosecution of the war.

Torch was followed in 1943 by Operation Husky – the successful assault on Sicily and, at the time, the biggest sea-borne invasion ever – and by the landings in Italy. These in turn were effectively dress rehearsals for the greatest of all such operations: D-Day in North-West Europe when the largest fleet in history opened the long-awaited 'second front'. Over 6,000 ships were involved in Operation Overlord, mostly landing craft but also including six battleships, 23 cruisers and 104 destroyers; some 80% of them were British or Dominion vessels.

By this stage, an era of naval history had come to a close. The sinking of the *Scharnhorst* by the *Duke of York* in December 1943 off Norway had been the last time two battleships were to come into direct conflict in European waters. When the war ended the Royal Navy comprised nearly 10,000 vessels, of which only 14 were battleships, their role now virtually superceded by the new demands of modern warfare: 52 aircraft carriers (complete with 70 bomber and fighter squadrons), 250 destroyers and some 9,000 smaller craft were now the dominant elements in the new force. In addition there were 131 submarines, which though never prioritised in Britain as they were in Germany, played a full part in the Allied victory.

The War With Japan

In the far reaches of the Empire, the catalogue of catastrophes that was to characterize the initial phase of Britain's war with Japan began with a disaster for the Royal Navy.

As conflict became increasingly likely with the heightening tension of the trade war in the Pacific, a fleet was despatched to Singapore under Admiral Tom Phillips, supposedly to provide protection for Britain's colonies and Dominions. It arrived on 2 December 1941, less than a week before Pearl Harbour, and comprised the battleship *Prince of Wales* and the battle-cruiser *Renown*. There had also been plans to include an aircraft carrier, but it had scraped its bottom in Jamaica and was unable to participate. The ships were therefore dependent upon air cover from land, a far from comforting situation in a part of the world starved of resources for the RAF.

On 8 December, in response to intelligence that Japanese forces were landing in Thailand, the two ships sailed from Singapore in an attempt to intervene. The fact that no air cover was available was known, and presumably (in the light of the experience of the previous two years) the dangers inherent in proceeding without such cover were also known, but the argument for action was simple: the ships were there to defend against Japanese attack, it would be a denial of duty to do nothing. The consequence was terrible if predictable: on 10 December both ships were sunk by enemy aircraft – two capital ships lost at a cost to the Japanese of just three 'planes. 840 men died with their ships, 2,800 were subsequently rescued. Of the survivors, more than half were to serve again in the defence of Singapore and be taken into the nightmare of Japanese prisoner of war camps.

Further reversals were to come. In February 1942 two British destroyers were lost in the Battle of Java Sea, and in April there was an attempt to stage a second Pearl Harbour at Colombo in Ceylon. Fortunately in the latter case, advance information had led Admiral Sir James Somerville to take evasive action, and losses were comparatively light, though a few days later the aircraft carrier *Hermes* was sunk by enemy aircraft.

The entry of Japan into the war had, of course, brought the United States into the conflict, and from the Battle of Midway onwards the naval struggle in the Far East and the Pacific was largely between these two nations. There was, however, a British Pacific Fleet that was to grow to include an impressive array of vessels including four new battleships; in due course, this fleet came under the command of the US navy.

British ships were also active in the final phase of the war in their own right. The fleet based at Colombo and Trincomalee staged several attacks on Japanese shipping, including most notably perhaps a raid on the docks at Sabang in Sumatra in July 1944. In common with the exploits of their compatriots on land, the Royal Navy's actions in the Far East were eclipsed in the popular imagination by the war in Europe: the forgotten army was complemented by the forgotten navy.

Unorthodox Warfare

Paradoxically for a conflict waged on such a massive scale, and one that was ultimately resolved by sheer weight of forces, the Second World War precipitated the development of a wide range of unorthodox, often small-scale methods of operation: the creation within the Army, for example, of the SAS, Glider Pilot Regiment and Parachute Regiment. The Royal Navy too had its innovations, such as the X-Craft – midget submarines that were to score some notable successes. Arguably the most successful of all, however – certainly in terms of propaganda – were the Commandos.

The Commandos originated in Independent Companies formed in 1940 to serve as amphibious assault forces in Norway. Six such companies fought in that campaign, mostly comprising infantrymen from the Territorial Army. Such a function would have been fulfilled by the Marines, since it involved the Navy, but for a shortage of manpower: 'There were no Royal Marines available at that time,' commented Lieutenant-General Bourne, Adjutant-General of the Marines. 'The strength of the Corps at the outbreak of war was roughly 10,000, the sea commitments for the war roughly 11,000.' [3] Though individuals were to serve from the beginning, it was not until 1943 that amphibious operations officially became the responsibility of the Royal Marines.

In autumn 1940 the Independent Companies were subsumed into the new Commandos under the control of Combined Operations. Some 8,000 men were by now involved, and raids were staged across the Channel, small groups landing on unprotected parts of the French coast for purposes of sabotage, intelligence gathering and simple experimentation with the techniques. The most spectacular attempt at an amphibious landing of the period, however, came to nothing – the would-be invasion of Dakar by Marines and Commandos in conjunction with de Gaulle's Free French forces was driven off by Vichy ships and artillery.

Already the special nature of the Commandos was becoming apparent, the additional demands that such activity makes on the individual troops, and it is no coincidence that two of the most famous units of modern times – the SAS and SBS – evolved from within the new structure.

The SBS were particularly active in the Mediterranean, staging a number of effective attacks. Among their triumphs was the location by Lance-Corporal Bremmer of the London Scottish, of 200 Australian troops stranded on Crete; the men were rescued by submarine. More typical was a raid in May 1941 by a two-man canoe on Benghazi harbour in which a ship was sunk by a limpet mine.

This tactic of canoeing into enemy harbours to plant mines was to score some notable hits, such as the raid on Bordeaux in December 1942. Ten Marines set off to paddle some 80 miles down the Gironde estuary over a period of several nights. Only four men reached the end of the journey, and only two survived the operation, but the expedition resulted in four enemy merchantmen, a tanker and a naval auxiliary ship being blown up.

Nowhere was this procedure used to more impressive effect than in Singapore, where a canoe raid was staged from an old fishing-boat sailing some 2,000 miles from Australia. Like so many such actions, it brought together men from different service backgrounds, in this instance the leadership of Major Lyon of the Gordon Highlanders and Lieutenant Davidson of the Royal Naval Volunteer Reserve. Tragically both men were to die in a later, more ambitious but disastrous attack on Singapore.

Combined Operations, though still often regarded with some suspicion by the more established services, saw in 1942 a substantial increase in its size and scope. Partly this growth could be attributed to the acquisition of a new head in Lord Mountbatten, and partly to the ever more insistent demands from the Soviet Union for a second front in Europe and from the British people for more direct action against Germany.

In March that year an old American destroyer, the *Cambelltown,* was loaded with explosives and sailed into Bruneval harbour. The intention was to penetrate the huge gates protecting the German battleship *Tirpitz* and to destroy the dockyards. In the event, neither objective was fully realized, though damage was done and some 400 German troops killed in the explosion. The losses too were heavy – 169 Commandos killed, and all but four of the remainder captured. Five Victoria Crosses were won that day.

A later attack on the *Tirpitz* resulted in the awarding of two further VCs, when three midget submarines – each with a crew of four – broke through to the ship in Altenfjord in Norway in September 1943. Charges were successfully detonated and the battleship crippled; later German reports gloomily noted that 'as a result of the successful midget-submarine attack the battle-cruiser *Tirpitz* had been out of action for months.' [4]

Most of the landings staged were, of course, short-term operations with a specific objective, such as the destruction of factories and fuel stocks in Norway in March 1941. In May 1942, however, Royal Marines were amongst the troops invading Madagascar to secure the strategically important island for the Allies.

The biggest action undertaken by Combined Operations in 1942 was also the most costly. In the landing at Dieppe in August, the Royal Navy sustained 550 casualties, whilst amongst the Royal Marine dead was Lieutenant-Colonel J P Phillips, killed whilst signalling other landing craft to turn back – his sacrifice probably saved hundreds of his men. For the Canadian troops who made up the bulk of the force, the casualties were even more terrible, and the operation remains controversial, often having been regarded as misguided. It did, however, constitute the largest amphibious assault yet staged by the Allies, and from its failure lessons were learnt that were to be put to good effect in the landings in Africa, Sicily, Italy and Normandy.

Though no operation on the scale of Dieppe was attempted again, smaller raids on France and Norway continued throughout 1943, and were gradually scaled down only as the preparations for D-Day took centre stage.

The actions staged by Combined Operations and others may not have determined the course of the war, but there is no doubt that they were for the most part highly efficient and forced Germany into committing disproportionate resources to defending the territory it occupied. Even more importantly they were a major boost to morale at home, the deeds of the Commandos rapidly acquiring the status of modern myths; in itself, that was as vital a contribution as any other in a conflict when Britain sometimes had little but a spirit of determination with which to prolong the war.

[1]   Bassett *Battlecruisers* p.177
[2]   Tute *The True Glory* p.226
[3]   Macksey *Commando Strike* p.5
[4]   Warren & Benson *Above Us The Waves* p.138

THE ARMY

The Household Cavalry Regiment

comprising

THE LIFE GUARDS and THE ROYAL HORSE GUARDS (THE BLUES)

Principal Battle Honours 1939-45

Souleuvre – Brussels – Nederrijn
North-West Europe 1944-45 – Iraq 1941 – Palmyra
Syria 1941 – El Alamein – North Africa 1942-43
Italy, 1944

(These Battle Honours awarded to both The Life Guards and The Royal Horse Guards)

Horse Guards raised 1660; 1st Troop Horse Grenadier Guards raised 1678;
2nd Troop Horse Grenadier Guards raised 1702;
these regiments amalgamated to form The Life Guards 1788.

Royal Horse Guards raised 1661; amalgamated to form
The Blues And Royals 1969.

During The Great War the two regiments of the Household Cavalry – The Life Guards and The Blues – had joined forces to create a single combat regiment. On mobilization in 1939, this experience was drawn on to form three combined units: the Household Cavalry Regiment (to serve abroad), the Household Cavalry Reserve Regiment (on duty in London), and the Household Cavalry Training Regiment.

Not all the lessons from the Great War, however, were learnt. In 1918 the Household Cavalry had been operating as a motor machine-gun regiment, but it returned to the saddle on cessation of hostilities and, being seen in an essentially ceremonial role, was not considered a priority in the mechanization programme of the '30s. The consequence was that when the new regiment was posted to Palestine in February 1940 to join The Royals and The Greys already stationed there, it was still on horseback; together, these regiments comprised the last mounted division in the British Army.

While the Middle East was not a major theatre of war in 1940-41, there were many significant strategic concerns in the area, fraught with potential dangers; it was the Household Cavalry's task to police these interests.

In April 1941, for example, it was called upon to assist the suppression of the pro-German rebellion in Iraq, leading a task-force 500 miles across the desert.

By now the regiment was officially designated motorised cavalry, though the reality was less impressive than the title. An acute lack of equipment produced a patchwork outfit, with the CO travelling in a yellow taxi commandeered in Haifa, and supply transport provided by a collection of hired buses with local drivers. Of the latter, the regimental history notes drily: 'As they were paid by the day it was to their interest to make the journey last as long as possible. The drivers displayed remarkable skill in producing breakdowns.' [1]

Despite these logistical problems, and despite operating in the desert in the worst heat-wave for 25 years, the expedition was successful in securing Iraq for the Allies and restoring the pro-British Regent to power.

Similarly, a few months later it was discovered that the French colonial regime in Syria was allowing the country to be used by the Axis powers. The Household Cavalry Regiment played its part assisting Free French forces in defeating the Vichy troops.

And in September 1941, when it became essential for a link to be made with the Soviet Union (newly allied to Britain), the regiment marched to Tehran, entering the city at the same time as Soviet troops arrived from the other direction.

These campaigns earned the regiment the nickname of the Flying 55, in reference to the identification number on its vehicles and the amount of travelling undertaken. The vehicles were by now registering an average of 6,300 miles each, and the rigours of the terrain were exacting a price.

Such problems were soon to disappear; in February 1942 the Household Cavalry Regiment was converted to an armoured car regiment, a role it was to keep thereafter.

The transformation left a pool of surplus men, and a temporary outfit, officially entitled 101 Royal Tank Regiment but better known as Smithforce, was created. This unit, of some 120 all ranks, was equipped with dummy tanks – old lorries covered with painted canvas skins – and was to be used as a decoy in the Western Desert.

The regiment meanwhile, in its new capacity, was moved nearer to the action, serving briefly in Cyprus and then progressing on to North Africa. Although most of its work was as a support unit, it did fight at El Alamein, and in four days at the end of that battle advanced some 60 miles as the Germans retreated. Upwards of 1,000 enemy prisoners were taken.

The Household Cavalry also served briefly in Italy, landing at Naples in April 1944, but first there was a return to Syria for another tour of duty centred more on diplomatic than military issues. For four months, it patrolled the border with Turkey to lend support in the event of a German invasion. In October 1944 the regiment was withdrawn for home leave.

Whilst the senior regiment had been abroad, the Reserve Regiment had developed into a fighting unit in its own right. In September 1941 the 2nd Household Cavalry Regiment was created, soon also to be equipped with armoured cars.

This regiment landed in Normandy on 14 July 1944, its role being that of a highly mobile armoured unit, mostly employed for scouting purposes. It also distinguished itself in action; at the end of August 1944 it advanced some 60 miles in two days, seizing three crucial bridges across the Somme and holding them against German counter-attacks.

The rapidity of this advance was exceeded soon after with the sprint across country to liberate Brussels: armoured cars from 'A' Squadron were the first Allied vehicles to enter the Belgian capital. The regiment was also present at the liberation of Antwerp.

'C' Squadron was called forward in response to Germany's final offensive in the Ardennes, serving alongside the US Army during December 1944 and January 1945. According to Captain Clyde, it was the American rather than the German troops who made the greater impact:

'The immediate result was a new variety of rations: every third trooper started to chew gum, suddenly acquired an automatic rifle, rubber over-shoes and mackintosh jackets. There was a sudden and mysterious increase in the losses of complete ration boxes, bed-rolls and pistols.' [2]

The following February, as the Allies prepared for the final push, the senior regiment returned from the UK and the two Household Cavalry regiments fought alongside each other in the drive up through North Germany.

[1] Wyndham *The Household Cavalry At War: First Household Cavalry Regiment* p.22

[2] Orde *The Household Cavalry At War: Second Household Cavalry Regiment* p.418

The Royal Dragoons (1st Dragoons)

Principal Battle Honours 1939-45

Nederrijn – Rhine – North-West Europe 1944-45
Syria 1941 – Knightsbridge – El Alamein
Advance on Tripoli – North Africa 1941-43
Sicily 1943 – Italy 1943

Raised 1661; amalgamated to form The Blues and Royals
(Royal Horse Guards and 1st Dragoons) 1969.

On 4 August 1941 the *Daily Telegraph* announced the formal end of the age of the horse in the British Army:

'The 1st Royal Dragoon and The Royal Scots Greys (2nd Dragoons) have been mechanised and are now part of the Royal Armoured Corps.'

The Royal Dragoons were thus one of the last two cavalry regiments to be mechanized, though the process had actually begun some months earlier than the *Telegraph* report, the last mounted parade having been held the previous Christmas.

By this time too, the regiment had had its first taste of action in the War, as part of the force sent into Vichy-controlled Syria in June 1941. Though not one of the more celebrated operations of the era, the Syrian campaign was strategically significant in enforcing the neutrality of French colonies in the Middle East and thus protecting the flank of the Allies in the North African war.

Syria proved a more bloody and bitter encounter than many had anticipated, taking on something of the nature of a civil war as Vichy and Free French forces clashed in the territory. And, typically of such a situation, the experience was as chaotic as it was savage – on one occasion a troop of The Royals found itself ordered to rebuild a bridge it had been instructed to blow up just the previous day.

Having officially become part of the RAC, The Royals were posted to North Africa in November 1941 to join Crusader, the Allied operation then rolling back the Axis forces. On Christmas Eve the regiment's 'A' Squadron led a British contingent into Benghazi to accept the formal surrender of the city from the Mayor.

The following year, with Rommel's counter-offensive having recaptured all the ground gained during Crusader, the regiment was to re-enter the fray at Alamein. Its role in the early stages of that battle was to patrol the front in a reconnaissance capacity – a hazardous, if essential, undertaking in such a conflict.

Even more hazardous was its task in the immediate aftermath of the break-through at Tel el Aqqaqir. Advancing through the 51st Highland Division's forward position, the regiment infiltrated enemy lines on what was effectively a sabotage mission. The telephone wire connecting the southern front with Axis headquarters was cut, and damage inflicted on an estimated 181 vehicles, three tanks, one armoured troop-carrier, one medium gun, three field guns, 17 anti-tank guns, 20 Bren-guns and an aeroplane.

El Alamein was to become one of the regiment's major battle honours. Others from the same campaign – Advance to Tripoli, Sicily 1943, Italy 1943 – delineate the progress of The Royals across North Africa and the strike at what Churchill memorably called 'the soft underbelly of Europe'.

After only a short stay in Italy, the regiment was withdrawn just before Christmas 1943 to return home for the first time in many years.

The following year, with the battle for Normandy now the focus of the Western armies, The Royals landed near Arromanches on 27 July. Even at this stage, the situation in Northern France was still far from clear; the regimental diary tells of a Norman peasant employed by the Germans to erect misleading signposts in the area – in the confusion of battle, he arrived at The Royals' HQ demanding that the invoice for his disinformation activities be honoured by the British.

In September 1944 the regiment joined General Horrocks' famous XXX Corps in the advance across the Low Countries. By this time, Major Pepys – who had led 'A' Squadron in Africa and had lost a leg in the campaign – had convinced the authorities that he was ready to rejoin the regiment. He became the only commanding officer of an armoured regiment with such a disability.

Two days after the German surrender, The Royals entered Denmark as part of the peaceful liberation forces.

The Royal Scots Greys (2nd Dragoons)

Principal Battle Honours 1939-45

Hill 112 – Falaise – Hochwald – Aller – Bremen
Merjayun – Alam El Halfa – El Alamein
Nofilia – Salerno – Italy 1943

Raised 1661; amalgamated to form The Royal Scots Dragoon Guards
(Carabiniers and Greys) 1971.

The Scots Greys were in Palestine when war was declared in 1939, employed on internal policing duties. In this role and on this terrain, the horses still used by the regiment were appropriate, but in the context of the wider conflict, were clearly inadequate. Nonetheless, the remoteness of The Greys from the front-line meant that it was only in May 1941 that orders to mechanize were received.

Before that process could be completed, squadrons of the regiment were sent into action as part of the force despatched to Syria. Although the campaign was to prove successful in defeating the Vichy French and securing a significant sector of the Middle East for the Allies, it was a difficult experience for The Greys; one troop equipped only with small arms was outnumbered and surrounded at Merjayun, and was captured.

On 19 July 1941, the regiment officially became part of the Royal Armoured Corps, along with The Royals the last regiment to be mechanized in the British Army. Tanks were acquired and training began prior to a posting the following June to North Africa.

The delay in really getting to grips with the enemy was too much for some in the regiment, including Lieutenant Geoffrey Keyes – recipient of the Military Cross in the Syrian campaign – who left to form a Scots Greys commando unit. Promoted to Lieutenant-Colonel at the age of just 24, Keyes was to lead one of the most audacious operations of the war in November 1941. Landing by submarine some 250 miles behind enemy lines, his commando attacked Rommel's house in an assassination attempt. The raid cost Keyes his life, though he was posthumously awarded the VC.

Rommel, of course, escaped to mastermind the successful 1942 offensive in the Western Desert. His seemingly irresistible advance was not halted until the battle at Alam Halfa on 31 August, which marked not only Montgomery's first North African encounter, but also that of The Greys, who lost three of their tanks during combat.

The regiment was involved in the remainder of the campaign to drive the Germans from Africa, fighting at Alamein and pursuing the enemy to Tripoli, as part of the 2nd New Zealand Division. Despite the intensive desert training they had undergone with tanks, the men's cavalry habits did not entirely disappear; on the first day of the advance from Alamein, the light squadron came under fire from Italian guns and responded in time-honoured tradition with a full frontal charge. Taking the enemy by surprise, 11 guns, 30 vehicles and 300 prisoners were taken at the cost of just one tank and no casualties.

On 8 September 1943 the regiment landed at Salerno for the first stage of the Italian campaign. Though it was to leave before the horrors of Cassino, the regiment suffered a heavy toll in those first few months. Perhaps the greatest loss was that of the Commanding Officer, Lieutenant-Colonel Twisleton-Wykeham-Fiennes (known to his men as 'Lugs'), who had taken The Greys through the difficult process of mechanization; he died on 25 November 1943 from wounds inflicted by an enemy mine. [1]

28 January 1944 saw the regiment sail for a long-awaited period of home leave prior to the Normandy landings.

Arriving in France on 7 June, the regiment formed part of the 4th Armoured Brigade. Two of its greatest battle honours date from the early days in Northern Europe: Hill 112 at Caen, and Falaise, when the regiment, stationed on a hill overlooking the doomed German counter-offensive, destroyed hundreds of enemy tanks and other vehicles.

But the Germans were far from beaten, and the regiment's advance through the Low Countries and Germany was to prove a protracted series of minor but bitter struggles against determined opposition. There were, however, occasional moments of relief, as when a troop found a German ambulance stocked with what is reported as being very fine wine; the stores were successfully liberated.

By late April, with German collapse inevitable, the race between the Allied forces on the Western and Eastern fronts to occupy territory became critical. Alongside the 1st Canadian Parachute Regiment, The Greys raced to the Baltic to prevent the Red Army reaching Denmark. A frantic dash through retreating German soldiers and refugees got the regiment to Wismar eight hours before the Soviet forces arrived. In retrospect it can be seen as one of the first encounters of the Cold War.

[1] An anecdote in Miles Noonan's *Tales From The Mess* tells of the confusion that Lt-Col Twisleton-Wykeham-Fiennes' name caused amongst German intelligence personnel. Amongst the theories proposed to explain it was the distinctly un-British idea that 'the Scots Greys were commanded by a committee' (p.80).

1st King's Dragoon Guards

Principal Battle Honours 1939-45

Beda Fomm – Defence of Tobruk – Defence of Alamein Line
Advance on Tripoli – Tebaga Gap – Tunis
North Africa 1941-43 – Monte Camino – Gothic Line
Italy, 1943-44

Raised 1685; amalgamated to form 1st The Queen's Dragoon Guards 1959.

The senior regiment in the newly-formed Royal Armoured Corps, the 1st King's Dragoon Guards was converted to an armoured car regiment at the beginning of 1941. It was then in North Africa, having disembarked at Port Said just before Christmas the previous year.

At the time Wavell's offensive was driving the Italians back from the Egyptian frontier, and 'B' Squadron was sent forward at the end of January 1941. The first battle honour was won at Beda Fomm, the climactic conflict of the campaign. The KDG not only fired the first shots, but succeeded in taking large numbers of enemy prisoners whilst sustaining few casualties.

The defeat of the Italian forces, however, was but the prelude to the desert war; on 14 February, just a week after Beda Fomm, the regiment was attacked by Messerschmitts, the first evidence of the Luftwaffe's arrival in Africa. The following week, now the most advanced of the UK troops, it made its first contact with the Afrika Korps.

A major offensive was evidently in the offing, and on 1 April the regiment was ordered to withdraw in the face of an enemy advance. Reaching Tobruk three days later, it came under the command of the 9th Australian Division, then garrisoning the town. With the shortage of infantry, the regiment found itself a new role as it helped fight off a series of German assaults. By the beginning of May, it was clear that Tobruk was not going to collapse, leaving a thorn in the side of the advancing German army.

For seven and a half months, the garrison remained under siege, supplied from the sea (by which route the wounded were evacuated) and tying down enemy forces. An attempt at a counter-attack, Operation Battleaxe, failed in June, and it was not until the last week of November that a break-out from Tobruk linked up with troops of Operation Crusader pushing through from the east.

Withdrawn to Egypt for a period of recovery, the KDG returned for a short while to the battle-field in June 1942 at Gazala. There was not much direct involvement in the battle itself, although the men were repeatedly bombed by the Luftwaffe and, in the confusion of war, by the RAF too.

In the aftermath of Alamein the regiment advanced with New Zealand forces. The lengthy and heavily-contested march to Tripoli had begun, and the KDG were present throughout.

On one day in March 1943 'A' Squadron took prisoner 32 officers and 700 other ranks, a record for an armoured car unit. Two months later Corporal Darley and Trooper Embleton scored an even more impressive bag, bringing in 1,500 Germans from 21st Panzer Division. In fact the two men had themselves been captured, only to find the enemy so frightened about being caught by a Free French regiment of Morrocan troops fighting alongside, that they had chosen to surrender to the British.

On 21 June 1943, a month after the fall of Tunis and the ending of the war in Africa, the regiment was inspected by His Majesty The King. Also on parade that day were the Queen's Bays, with whom the KDG would later be amalgamated.

In September the regiment, leaving North Africa after nearly three years, landed at Salerno in Italy. The first half of 1944 was spent patrolling and skirmishing in the area of the river Garigliano as the Allies attempted to break through the Gustav Line. With the fall of Cassino, more rapid progress was made – the KDG advancing to Florence – only to be halted at the Gothic Line.

By December 1944, the regiment had been in action longer than any other British Army unit and had sustained more casualties than any other in the Royal Armoured Corps. Withdrawn from Italy, it departed for the Greek civil war.

Here too there were problems; after the clear-cut nature of the war with Germany, the Regimental War Diary attempted to understand this new conflict:

'The whole military set-up is very queer, and the politics even queerer. The opposite army is ELAS, who are in fact a fairly orderly Radical party, now being run and dictated to by KKE, which is allegedly a thoroughgoing anarchist party. As they do not wear any uniform, and rely chiefly on furtive sniping, one cannot tell who is who, or where they are.' [1]

[1] Mann *The Regimental History of 1st The Queen's Dragoon Guards* p.473

The Queen's Bays
(2nd Dragoon Guards)

Principal Battle Honours 1939-45

Somme 1940 – Gazala – El Alamein – El Hamma
Tunis – North Africa 1941-43 – Coriano
Lamone Crossing – Rimini Line – Argenta Gap

Raised 1685; amalgamated to form 1st The Queen's Dragoon Guards 1959.

The Queen's Bays were dispatched to Europe with the 1st Armoured Division in May 1940, more than a week after the German army had attacked the Low Countries. The last minute nature of the operation can be gauged by the fact that on the very morning of departure, some 50 new recruits joined the regiment.

The speed of the German advance was so unexpected that the Bays' orders to land at Le Havre were cancelled en route, it being discovered that the port was already behind the enemy front-line. Landing instead at Cherbourg, the regiment was soon in action around Amiens and the Somme. Casualties and tank losses were such that within ten days of arrival, the tanks were regrouped as a single squadron within a composite regiment that also contained vehicles from the 9th Lancers and the 10th Hussars. Other members of The Bays became motorised infantry as the regiment was split up. It was not to regroup until 14 June, just two days before it was evacuated from Brest.

15 months later The Bays sailed for North Africa, their Cruiser tanks now replaced by Crusaders and Honeys. They arrived on 25 November 1941 and were sent forward a few days before Christmas, joining the advanced units of the forces from Operation Crusader.

The regiment was thus in the front-line in January 1942 when Rommel launched a counter-attack. The Bays fought a retreat across the desert under conditions that were far from militarily ideal. Lieutenant Michael Halstead recorded the withdrawal in his diary:

'Horrible jumble of guns and transport streaming away with us. No orders so kept on trying to shoot whatever appeared. Some guns went down for a few minutes and then we saw the German tanks coming on and on at us. Horrible as their shells kept getting to us, and our little guns couldn't reach them at all.' [1]

In May, as the Afrika Korps continued to push forward, The Bays found themselves fighting through the desperate struggle to hold Gazala, a two and a half week battle centred on the British defensive boxes in the desert. It was a costly battle for the regiment, reduced from 46 tanks at the outset to just seven, with no victory to ameliorate the sacrifice.

Withdrawn to re-equip, The Bays were posted back to the front towards the end of June. The retreat continued, with more skirmishes and rearguard encounters, coming to a halt at Alam Halfa, where Rommel was shortly to encounter Montgomery for the first time.

The Bays played their part in the final counter-offensive of the North African campaign, advancing behind the infantry at the northern end of the Alamein battlefield.

At the end of 1942, a year of almost continual fighting, The Bays were withdrawn for a period, returning to the fray the following year to join the advance on El Hamma. The town fell on 29 March, by which time the Allied victory was inevitable.

Certainly the enemy's will to fight was evaporating. The regimental history records a chance encounter between Sergeant Smith and an Italian officer: 'Are you my prisoner, or am I yours?' the latter is reported to have said, at which the more resourceful Sgt Smith immediately claimed him. The Italian then proceeded to offer the surrender of his entire unit, some 12 other officers, 36 men and an 88mm gun. [2]

Landing at Naples on 27 May 1944 to join the Italian campaign, The Bays advanced northwards up the Adriatic Coast. In September that year they participated in the assault on the Gothic Line. The most memorable episode was the attempt to take Rimini. The Bays were beaten back, sustaining 64 casualties, but their efforts facilitated the taking of the town.

The regiment ended the war at Ferrara, just south of the river Po.

[1] Mann *The Regimental History of 1st The Queen's Dragoon Guards* p.409
[2] ibid. p.429

3rd Carabiniers
(Prince of Wales's Dragoon Guards)

Principal Battle Honours 1939-45

Imphal – Nunshigum – Bishenpur – Kangla Tongbi
Kennedy Peak – Shwebo – Sagaing – Mandalay
Ava – Irrawaddy

3rd (Prince of Wales's) Dragoon Guards raised 1685; 6th Dragoon Guards (Carabiniers) raised 1685; these two regiments amalgamated to form 3rd Carabiniers (Prince of Wales's Dragoon Guards) 1922; amalgamated to form The Royal Scots Dragoon Guards 1971.

Uniquely for a regular British cavalry regiment, the 3rd Carabiniers spent their entire war in the Far East. Stationed in India at the end of the '30s, the first contribution came with the despatch of 12 officers and 102 other ranks to form the nucleus of a new war-time regiment, the 25th Dragoons.

The Carabaniers were mobilized in October 1941, but even then the forgotten army was not high on the list of priorities, and training early the following year was conducted without tanks, other vehicles being pressed into service as stand-ins. Some tanks did appear later, but were subsequently taken away again to be replaced by other types. It was a process repeated often enough to make the troops confident there wasn't a tank in existence they couldn't handle.

It was not until more than four years of conflict had passed that the regiment was finally sent forward, arriving in Imphal in December 1943. One of the reasons for the delay was doubt in higher quarters about whether tanks were suitable for combat in the jungle at all – the bad conditions and difficult terrain added to their vulnerability to infantry attack – and in the event the 3rd Carabiniers had the only medium tanks in the theatre.

In February 1944 the Japanese U-Go offensive, touted by Tokyo radio as the march to Delhi, put intense pressure on Imphal. The regiment was split into squadrons, their task to assist infantry in whatever ways they could. Often this came down to rescuing the wounded, but tanks were also useful in breaking down the Japanese underground bunkers.

The first major action came at Nungshigum, an important hill position just north of Imphal, which had been taken by the enemy. An Indian battalion of Dogras was detailed to retake the hill, with 'B' Squadron in support. Progress was slow – the tanks unable to manage more than one mile per hour up the steep slopes – and visibility could only be achieved by tank commanders looking out the top of their turrets. The consequence was a high level of casualties. The position was taken and secured (to the extent that it was never recaptured), but in the process all the officers in both the Carabiniers and Dogras were killed or wounded, and the attack was led by NCOs. Squadron-Major Craddock was awarded the DCM for his contribution.

Fighting continued through May, principally around Bishenpur, but then the monsoon broke and the tanks were rendered useless in the mud.

By July the Japanese threat had been turned and the regiment was scheduled to return to India so that the tanks could be refitted. A lack of spare parts and equipment in India, however, defeated that intention and instead 'C' Squadron – and later the other squadrons – joined the pursuit of the enemy. Even with the tanks in such run-down condition, some managed to reach the top of Kennedy Peak, south of Tiddim, some 9,000 feet above sea level.

The last days of the year were spent by 'B' Squadron in the battle to take Shwebo – it finally fell on 8 January 1945 – and by the remainder of the regiment enjoying what was described as 'a remarkably festive and alcoholic Christmas' [1].

The major target for the Allies in the new year was the crossing of the Irrawaddy, where the enemy troops were concentrated, though pockets had yet to be cleared in the advance to the river. The crossing was successfully accomplished despite the primitive equipment available to ferry the tanks across, and despite the disappearance of more than a hundred of the more experienced campaigners, beneficiaries of a new repatriation policy.

The fall of Mandalay in March appeared to be yet another opportunity for the regiment to pull back for re-fitting, but the order came through that the Carabiniers were to press on to Rangoon. A song popular with the troops at the time gives an insight into the mood of wearied resignation: 'Divs may come and Divs may go, but the Carbs go on for ever.'

On 28 May 1945 the regiment finally entered Rangoon, driving tanks that had covered 1,100 miles and survived 15 months of hard fighting. When the Carabiniers sailed back to India in June, casualties stood at 25 officers and 204 other ranks dead or wounded.

[1] *I Serve* p.277

4th/7th Royal Dragoon Guards

Principal Battle Honours 1939-45

Dunkirk 1940 – Normandy Landing – Odon – Mont Pincon
Nederrijn – Geilenkirchen – Rhineland – Rhine

4th Royal Irish Dragoon Guards raised 1685; 7th Dragoon Guards raised 1688; these two regiments amalgamated to form 4th/7th Royal Dragoon Guards 1922; amalgamated to form the Royal Dragoon Guards 1993.

The first troops from the British Expeditionary Force landed in France on 11 September 1939; the 4th/7th Royal Dragoon Guards arrived one week later.

When the German army invaded Belgium in May 1940, the 4th/7th advanced with the BEF to Wavre, to a point where a bridge crossed the Dyle, and awaited the enemy. The first encounter came on 15 May. It was a reasonably successful skirmish, but elsewhere a French collapse was threatening the regiment's flank, and a withdrawal was ordered to Dendre.

On 19 May the heaviest fighting yet – on the Canal de Charleroi – saw one troop trapped as the regiment was ordered yet again to withdraw. There were 25 casualties that day. By now the whole position of the BEF was in jeopardy, with the Channel ports under threat. The regiment was turned around to form a line on the western front, but losses of men and equipment were taking their toll.

On 25 May a composite tank regiment was formed with the 5th Royal Inniskilling Dragoon Guards, and a dismounted regiment with the 15th/19th Hussars. It was a desperate measure and three days later the order for evacuation came. By 2 June all the survivors had escaped from Dunkirk.

There followed a frustrating four years in Britain. Once the immediate possibility of invasion had receded, a seemingly endless period of training was undertaken.

When the regiment was eventually informed of its forthcoming return to North West Europe, two squadrons were assigned a role operating DD (Duplex Drive) tanks – normal tanks (originally Valentines, later changed to Shermans) fitted with a canvas superstructure that enabled them to float in water as part of an amphibious landing force. Landing on D-Day, the vehicles proved mostly successful, though some did get stuck.

On the first day, six miles of ground were made, but this was no indication of what was to come. The Normandy countryside was not conducive to tank attack:

the narrow country lanes and the proliferation of hedgerows hindered the vision and operation of the tanks. For a month, progress was slow, with the enemy having to be patiently weeded out from each position.

A record of the ammunition expended during the first week after D-Day gives some indication of the level of activity: 2,900 rounds of 75mm high explosive, 850 rounds of 75mm armour piercing shot (for use against other tanks), 130 rounds of 17 pdr shot, and 200,000 machine gun rounds.

Even more debilitating than the French countryside was the assault on Mont Pinchon. This heavily defended, densely wooded, steep hill commanded a strategic view of the area and took two weeks of bloody fighting to take.

After two months of this morale-sapping conflict, the men were not entirely convinced when told by Lieutenant-General Horrocks of the plan to trap the enemy at Falaise and break-out from the position in Normandy, as the regimental history of the war records:

'This was a very cheering thing to hear, and it was very pleasantly told, but there were not many . . . who could really believe it was true . . . . We had grown so used to the idea that any tank which advanced 500 yards beyond the front line was likely to be knocked out that it did not seem credible that this would ever cease to be the case, or that the war would ever change from its present form . . . one slogging attempt after another to push the line further forward.' [1]

When the break-out did come, it was as rapid and secure as Horrocks had promised. The 4th/7th were the first British armoured unit to cross the Seine on 27 August 1944 and they entered Belgium early the next month.

The speed of the drive was not entirely uninterrupted. In the attempt to break through to Arnhem, the 4th/7th followed behind the Guards Armoured Division, and found themselves trapped between the Rhine and the Lower Rhine when the Germans counter-attacked. Despite these problems, the regiment fought through into Germany itself. Its first battle on German soil was around Geilenkirchen in November 1944, where the main problem was not so much the Germans as the mud: by 5pm on the first day, 23 tanks were bogged down in soft ground, with enemy fire making retrieval difficult.

In February the regiment was involved in Operation Pepper Pot, the massive combined shoot into the Reichswald Forest prior to an infantry assault. The 4th/7th shot 10,000 rounds into the German positions in one afternoon. The following month, the DD tanks were again called upon in the crossing of the Rhine.

After the mixed exertions of the previous nine months, the remainder of the war is described by the regimental history as 'rather an anti-climax', with the Germans now certain of defeat.

The regiment, fighting exclusively in North-west Europe, sustained 400 casualties, 150 of them fatal.

[1] Stirling *The First and The Last* p.92

5th Royal Inniskilling Dragoon Guards

Principal Battle Honours 1939-45

Withdrawal to Escaut – St Omer-La Bassée – Dunkirk 1940
Mont Pincon – Lower Maas

5th Dragoon Guards raised 1685; 6th (Inniskilling) Dragoons raised 1690; these two regiments amalgamated to form 5th Royal Inniskilling Dragoon Guards 1922; amalgamated to form The Royal Dragoon Guards 1993.

The 5th Inniskilling Dragoon Guards received the news of mechanization in 1935, though it was not to be until 1938 that the last mounted parade was held and the horses finally pensioned off.

The period leading to the declaration of war was difficult. The drive to build up to war strength demanded the recall of reservists, but – in an experience common to many cavalry units – they soon found that the new equipment had completely changed the nature of the regiment. 50 former Royal Tank Regiment reservists were subsequently drafted in to boost the numbers, but even with this complement, there was still a shortage of officers, and in due course a new rank of Troop Sergeant Major had to be created; in battle these NCOs were often called upon to command troops.

When war did finally come, the 5th Dragoon Guards were amongst the first to depart for France, arriving in late September 1939. For the first seven and a half months, there was no war to fight. The endless training, false alarms and lack of action, combined with the severity of the weather, did nothing for morale, and some were beginning to doubt that conflict would ever come when, on 10 May 1940, the German war machine swung into the Low Countries.

Following the pre-ordained plan, the 5th Dragoon Guards, as part of II Corps, advanced with their Mark 6B tanks and Bren carriers to the river Dyle.

Even before contact was made with the enemy, the signs were far from auspicious, with a steady stream of refugees swelling within just a few days to a near flood, and with retreating Belgian forces much in evidence. Even more disturbing was the realization that whilst the Dyle was being held, the main thrust of the German advance was to the south, sweeping through the supposedly impregnable Ardennes. The French army, anticipating a repeat of the static conflict of the Great War, was effortlessly thrown back, and the BEF threatened with isolation.

A retreat was ordered and a new challenge was presented – to stage an orderly, fighting withdrawal whilst all around was confusion and panic. Under the circumstances, it can be counted a successful operation, though the loss of equipment meant that the regiment was obliged to form composite units – both cavalry and infantry – with the 15th/19th Hussars and the 4th/7th Lancers.

On 28 May instructions were received to make for Dunkirk for evacuation, and by 2 June the regiment was back in Britain. Casualties, by the standards of the time, were relatively light: 60 men were reported killed, wounded or missing.

A return to the battlefield did not come for more than four years. On 10 July 1944 – with the battle for Normandy over a month old – the regiment was sent to France with orders immediately to relieve the 4th County of London Yeomanry. The urgency was somewhat misplaced when, on arrival, it was discovered that the Yeomanry were actually moving forward into the front-line. A curious situation arose in which the 5th Dragoon Guards had to conceal their assignment in case it affected the morale of the men they were supposed to replace.

By the end of the month, however, the regiment was cleared for action, and the first week of August saw it back in action. 50 enemy prisoners were taken on 2 August, and three days later the Odon was crossed and high ground seized at Butte-Le-Bouquet and Hamars. When the 7th Armoured Division was withdrawn soon after, the regiment remained and pursued the now retreating enemy.

In a drive to Ghent, 250 miles were covered in six days, with pockets of enemy resistance causing problems throughout. In one incident, Corporal Cooper left his tank and in a display of solo courage took a machine-gun post and 11 prisoners; he was subsequently awarded the Military Medal for his action.

The next six months saw a series of isolated and often very hard encounters, with the German forces now defending the approaches to their homeland. By March 1945, with both the Rhine and Roer successfully crossed, the end was finally in sight, and the remaining months were often more like a rout than a battle. On 1 April the regiment advanced 25 miles in just four hours, taking more than 200 prisoners and reaching the river Ems. When the enemy surrender was announced, the 5th Dragoon Guards were at the Kiel Canal.

3rd The King's Own Hussars

Principal Battle Honours 1939-45

Sidi Burrani – Buq Buq – Beda Fomm – Sidi Suleiman
El Alamein – North Africa 1940-1942 – Citta del Pieve – Citta di Castello
Italy 1944 – Crete

Raised 1658; amalgamated to form The Queen's Own Hussars 1958;
amalgamated to form The Queen's Royal Hussars 1993.

Stationed in England at the outbreak of war, the 3rd Hussars saw their first action early on when a detachment of men participated in the unsuccessful attempt to free Norway in April-May 1940.

In September of that year, following the Italian invasion of Egypt, the regiment was posted to North Africa, where it formed part of the 7th Armoured Division. A two-month campaign culminated in the interception of the Italian army's retreat at Beda Fomm on 8 February 1941, the first major British victory of the war. It was a battle that saw the tally of enemy troops taken prisoner rise to 130,000 – and this by a British force of just 30,000. Amongst the other regiments fighting that day were the 7th Hussars, later to be amalgamated with the 3rd to form The Queen's Own Hussars. Beda Fomm was the first battle honour to be awarded to both regiments since the days of the Peninsula War, nearly a century and a half earlier.

The success of the first North Africa campaign, however, was short-lived, for in April 1941 the regiment was posted to Crete to defend it against an expected German invasion. Stationed alongside troops from New Zealand at Maleme airport in the west of the island, the 3rd Hussars were – in common with the rest of the British forces in Crete – ill-equipped and battle-weary. Unable to hold off a massive air and parachute assault, a costly withdrawal was forced.

Returning to North Africa, the regiment rejoined the struggle against the remnants of the Italian army, now greatly strengthened by the arrival of Rommel's Afrika Korps.

At the ensuing battle of El Alamein, the 3rd Hussars fought with the courage and commitment expected of a great cavalry regiment. Receiving his orders at the climax of the battle, the commanding officer Lieutenant-Colonel Sir Peter Farquhar commented that the task allotted to the regiment was a suicide mission, to which General Montgomery is reported to have replied, 'It's got to be done and, if necessary, I am prepared to accept 100% casualties in both personnel and tanks.' Sir Peter later wrote: 'I have always admired Montgomery for this frank reply – tough but typical of him.' [1]

It was indeed a costly encounter: at the end of the 12 days of conflict, 21 officers and 98 men of the 3rd Hussars were reported killed, wounded or missing, while of 51 tanks sent into action, only four survived.

This heavy toll was such that the regiment was withdrawn from the front line for a period of rebuilding and retraining. The leadership of Sir Peter Farquhar was critical at this time. Writing much later, Colonel A H N Reade – who was then the 3rd Hussars Recce Troop leader – was generous in his praise: 'No words of mine can possibly do justice to the debt the regiment owed him. After El Alamein he reformed and retrained us to the highest standard of efficiency.' [2]

In April 1944 the regiment returned to the fray, serving in Italy with distinction. It was subsequently posted to Egypt in January 1945, and remained in the Middle East for the remainder of the War, being stationed in Lebanon and Syria.

[1] *The Queen's Own Hussars* p.43

[2] ibid. p.45

4th Queen's Own Hussars

Principal Battle Honours 1939-45

Ruweisat – Alam el Halfa – El Alamein
Coriano – Senio Pocket – Rimini Line – Argenta Gap
Proasteion – Corinth Canal – Greece 1941

Raised 1685; amalgamated to form Queen's Royal Irish Hussars 1958;
amalgamated to form The Queen's Royal Hussars 1993.

On 18 November 1940 the 4th Queen's Own Hussars set sail from Liverpool for North Africa at the start of their war service. Even before this, however, the regiment could claim to have made a decisive contribution to the outcome of the conflict with the most famous former 4th Hussar of all: Winston Churchill had enlisted in 1895, and earlier in 1940 had taken over the premiership from Neville Chamberlain. The association between the Prime Minister and his old regiment was to continue through the war years.

Arriving in Egypt as part of the 1st Light Armoured Brigade, the 4th Hussars spent some months in their light tanks engaged in desert training. When the order into battle came, however, it was not to be in North Africa, but in Greece.

Strategically valuable, Greece had always been regarded as vulnerable to Axis attack, despite its neutrality. Italy had invaded the country in November 1940, and been swiftly repulsed, but the possibility of a German campaign was a more serious threat. Extended negotiations between Britain – seeking an anti-Axis Balkan coalition – and Greece led to the promise of troops to defend the country.

That force – 80% of it from Australia and New Zealand – landed in March 1941. The 4th Hussars immediately moved to take up a position on the key defensive line centred at Aliakmon in the north-east of the country. On 6 April the German army marched into both Yugoslavia and Greece; the following day the regiment blew up bridges in advance of the line and waited for the enemy.

It was not a long wait; the typical rapidity of the German advance threw back the forward infantry and on 13 April – Easter Sunday – the 4th Hussars took a stand at Proasteion. Six hours of fighting successfully brought the enemy to a halt and gave the infantry a chance to withdraw. Elsewhere, however, all was disaster – the swarming German assault splintered the Allies, and a general withdrawal was ordered.

For eight days, the 4th Hussars formed a rearguard for a retreat down the whole length of the country. By the end only ten tanks were left, most of those lost being damaged by the arduous conditions rather than by enemy strikes. On 24 April the Greek army finally surrendered, and an Allied evacuation was ordered. The 4th Hussars made one last contribution, holding a key bridge at Corinth linking the Peloponese to the mainland, until an assault by 1,000 German airborne troops overwhelmed them. The bridge was successfully blown, but many Hussars were captured.

Those who escaped fared little better: attacked before they could be evacuated, the troops dispersed in search of boats to escape. Some did so, but others – including a group of 200 – spent months hiding out in the hills, protected by courageous civilians. By the end of August, almost all had been taken. The Greek campaign had cost the regiment over 400 prisoners, including all its senior officers.

The survivors returned to Egypt for a slow process of rebuilding. Battered morale was somewhat restored by the appointment of Churchill as Colonel of the regiment in October 1941, and by the issuing of new tanks (Honeys and Grants) the following April.

In June 1942, the 4th Hussars were sent forward to the battlefield of Gazala. The men, however, saw no concerted action, for their tanks were assigned to other troops and they were dispersed to a variety of tasks, including the guarding of prisoners of war. 'B' Squadron was issued with tanks and sent into battle, but was ambushed and escaped with just one of eleven tanks surviving.

Though it was not for the most part involved in front-line fighting, the regiment sustained serious casualties, returning at the end of June with just 12 officers and 152 other ranks. Even so, 'A' and 'C' Squadrons saw service at Ruweisat on 4 July. Later that month, the remnants of the regiment joined with the 8th Hussars to form the 4th/8th Hussars, a temporary composite regiment. It was in this form that the men fought at Alam el Halfa and El Alamein. In the aftermath of the latter it chased the enemy some 400 miles in ten days. By the end only 17 tanks were still operational – they were handed over and the regiment returned to Egypt.

1943 was a year of regrouping – for six months in Cyprus (where a half-expected German invasion never materialised) and then in Egypt. There were inspections in both places by the Prime Minister.

On 4 May 1944 the 4th Hussars landed in Italy in its new role as an armoured reconnaissance regiment. Equipped with 88 tanks (including 46 Shermans), the strength now stood at 39 officers and 666 other ranks. The next couple of months took their toll. The struggle against the Germans' Gothic Line was a bitter, ridge-by-ridge progress. Particularly intense was the ten-day battle to take Coriano.

The regiment, with the exception of 'B' Squadron, ended the war in a 'kangaroo' capacity – driving converted, turret-less Shermans through battle-fields with a cargo of infantry.

17 officers and 140 other ranks were killed in action during the war.

7th Queen's Own Hussars

Principal Battle Honours 1939-45

Egyptian Frontier 1940 – Beda Fomm – Sidi Rezegh 1941
North Africa 1940-41 – Ancona – Rimini Line
Italy 1944-45 – Pegu – Paungde – Burma 1942

Raised 1690; amalgamated to form The Queen's Own Hussars 1958;
amalgamated to form The Queen's Royal Hussars 1993.

Mechanized in early 1937, the 7th Hussars were stationed in Egypt at the start of the war, and thus had the advantage of having trained in desert conditions before the conflict, which was to stand them in good stead in the opening struggles against the Italians in North Africa. One of the first successes in North Africa came on 14 June 1940 – just four days after Italy had declared war on Britain – when the 7th Hussars captured Fort Capuzzo, taking more than 200 prisoners of war.

In Wavell's great campaign at the end of the year, the 7th Hussars played a central role, particularly at the climatic battle of Beda Fomm. In that conflict the regiment was reduced to just a single tank, and even that required running repairs to its tracks.

The early victories were soon reversed, of course, with the arrival of the German Afrika Korps, to bolster the fading Italian forces. At the battle of Sidi Rezegh in November 1941, the 7th found themselves in tanks armed only with two-pounders up against more than a hundred Panzers fitted out with much heavier armour and access to anti-aircraft 75mm guns. It was perhaps the biggest con-frontation the regiment was to experience during the War, and certainly one of the most costly: Colonel Freddie Byass, the commanding officer, was killed in action, whilst one of the three squadrons was completely overrun and taken prisoner.

Soon after, in January 1942, the regiment was sent as part of the 7th Armoured Brigade to Malaya to defend it against the Japanese invasion. The mission, however, was soon aborted, for the fall of Singapore was already inevitable before the reinforcements had a chance to arrive. Instead the troops were diverted to Burma, where they landed to find the Rangoon docks deserted in anticipation of the arrival of the Japanese, and had to unload the tanks and equipment themselves.

The first Burma campaign – the withdrawal from that country – presented new challenges to a regiment coming from North Africa. The terrain of jungle and paddy fields was unsuited to tank warfare and the difficulties were exacerbated by the Japanese tactics of continual harrying from all sides, with enemy troops out-flanking the retreating forces and setting up road-blocks and ambushes to hinder their progress.

It was in one such skirmish that the lead tank of the 7th Hussars was hit and its commander, Lieutenant Patteson, captured. Subjected to violent interrogation, Lt Patteson refused to co-operate with his captors, and in frustration at their failure, they tied him to the next road-block, leaving him to be killed by his own men as they cleared a path through. The advancing tanks opened fire to smash the road-block, but miraculously did not hit Lt Patteson. Even more amazingly, a fragment of shell cut his bonds and enabled him to escape and return to his regiment, taking with him information on Japanese positions.

The regiment made a fighting withdrawal in tanks some 480 miles to the banks of the river Chindwin. Unable to progress further, all but one tank were destroyed and the remainder of the retreat – another 140 miles – was covered on foot, under the torrential onslaught of the monsoon. The tank that did manage to cross the Chindwin lasted long enough to return to Rangoon in 1945 as the command vehicle of the 7th Indian Light Cavalry.

In his autobiography, Field-Marshal Viscount Slim was to write of 7th Armoured Brigade's work in the retreat: 'what we should have done without that brigade I do not know.' [1]

In 1944 the 7th Hussars returned to Europe, joining the Allied forces advancing through Italy. They were in Trieste as the War ended.

[1] Slim *Defeat Into Victory* p.61

8th King's Royal Irish Hussars

Principal Battle Honours 1939-45

Villers Bocage – Lower Maas – Roer – Rhine
North-West Europe 1944-45 – Buq Buq – Sidi Rezegh 1941 Gazala – El
Alamein – North Africa 1940-42

Raised 1693; amalgamated to form The Queen's Royal Irish Hussars 1958;
amalgamated to form The Queen's Royal Hussars.

Equipped with light tanks, the 8th Hussars were part of the 7th Armoured Division, the justly famous Desert Rats, stationed in North Africa at the beginning of the war.

In the early skirmishing on the Egyptian border, the Hussars, together with the 2nd Cameron Highlanders, made their first real contact with the enemy at Maktila, where there was believed to be an Italian battalion or possibly a brigade. When the opposition turned out to be an entire division, a strategic withdrawal was ordered. It was in its way indicative of the setbacks that the regiment was to face through the Western Desert campaign and that were to demand the utmost resilience of the men.

During the great series of victories over the Italians in Wavell's offensive, the rate of vehicle failure was such that the 8th Hussars had their tanks taken away for distribution amongst other units. By the time the regiment was re-equipped, the German arrival in Africa had transformed the nature of the conflict, and much of 1941 was spent in the desert as part of 7th Armoured Brigade, waiting for action. The Brigade War Diary recorded this uneasy period:

'The presence of German armoured troops, active patrols and superiority in the air made us constantly alert, and the men stood this severe strain in a spirit that is beyond praise. Our drinking water was at times undrinkable. NAAFI stores were non-existent and flies were very persistent.' [1]

When the British struck back against the Afrika Korps in Operation Crusader, the 8th Hussars were caught by a German counter that saw the Hussars' Honey tanks comprehensively out-gunned. In a single day's fighting, on 19 November 1941, 20 tanks were lost, despite heroic attempts to use the greater speed of the Honeys to get close to the enemy's more powerful vehicles.

The following year, even greater damage was inflicted in the assault on the Allies' defences on the Gazala Line. A German attack on the night of 26/27 May

1942 fell heavily upon the 8th's position at Bir Hakeim. Major Huth later described the speed of the onslaught of some 100 enemy tanks:

'We all opened up at once . . . . Fighting lasted about 15 minutes by which time all out tanks except two had been hit and put out of action.' [2]

By the end of the day, the 8th Hussars were effectively finished as a fighting unit. New tanks were, however, acquired for the survivors (who included some Hussars who had been taken prisoner and subsequently escaped) and a composite squadron formed with the remnants of the 3rd Royal Tank Regiment. Later a composite 4th/8th Hussars unit was formed that was to fight at Alam el Halfa and El Alamein.

With the ending of the African campaign, the regiment returned home to Norfolk to prepare for the return to Northern Europe. Officially now in a new role as an Armoured Reconnaissance Regiment, with a consequent emphasis on light armour, the 8th Hussars actually continued to serve in the same capacity as before, effectively no different to the fully armoured regiments.

The regiment was involved in the stab into enemy territory that reached Villers Bocage before being forced back, fighting in the rearguard of the withdrawal.

The progress of the regiment towards Germany was disrupted by the new system of repatriation introduced in November 1944, that affected the 8th Hussars particularly, since so many had been abroad for very considerable periods of time. Even so the regiment continued and reached perhaps its most joyful moment in North-West Europe at Fallingbostel, where 22,000 Allied prisoners of war in Stalag XIB were liberated. By the time the Hussars arrived, the camp was being run by the prisoners, under the command of Regimental Sergeant-Major Lord of the Grenadier Guards, who had been captured at Arnhem.

In the last days of the war, the 8th Hussars crossed the Elbe alongside the 1st Rifle Brigade to become the first Allied troops into the ruins of Hamburg.

[1] Verney *The Desert Rats* p.59

[2] Macksey *A History of the Royal Armoured Corps and its Predecessors 1914 to 1975* p.123

9th Queen's Royal Lancers

Principal Battle Honours 1939-45

Somme 1940 – North-West Europe 1940 – Gazala
Ruweisat – El Alamein – El Hamma – North Africa 1942-43
Lamone Bridgehead – Argenta Gap – Italy 1944-45

Raised 1715; amalgamated to form 9th/12th Royal Lancers (Prince of
Wales's) 1960; amalgamated to form The Queen's Royal Lancers 1993.

The 9th Lancers were latecomers to the British Expeditionary Force, not sailing
to France until May 1940. When they did arrive, they suffered the usual
problems of the time, the Regimental History commenting that the men 'were then
in a very high state of training and efficiency and it was a great disappointment
that they were equipped with such an inferior and mixed bag of tanks.' [1] Tanks
were sent on the expedition without guns in the hope that they could be picked up
from a damaged vehicle at some point along the way, whilst one tank is reported to
have had a plywood turret.

Failures of political leadership having thus ensured that the regiment was too
late and too ill-equipped to make a significant contribution, the men spent a single
frustrating month in France before being evacuated to Britain.

When the widely anticipated invasion of Britain was forestalled by the RAF, the
9th Lancers – as part of the 2nd Armoured Brigade within the 1st Armoured
Division – were posted to Egypt in November 1941.

The first encounter with the enemy was not long in coming, with the German
offensive of January 1942. Forced back to the Gazala Line, the regiment continued
its desert training, now using a few General Grant tanks that been supplied to
augment the existing Crusaders. In May the German advance broke through the
Gazala Line and, despite fierce resistance, pushed onwards. It was not until the
struggle around Ruweisat Ridge that the offensive was to be halted; a squadron of
the 9th Lancers served in that encounter.

One of the ever-present concerns of the armoured regiments during the first half
of the War was the inadequacy of the equipment compared to that of the enemy.
For the 9th Lancers, this was a problem now resolved by the arrival of Sherman
tanks for 'B' and 'C' Squadrons ('A' Squadron continued to use Crusaders).

The new vehicles were soon to prove invaluable at El Alamein, being
responsible for inflicting heavy casualties on the enemy. Corporal Nicholls of 'B'

Squadron, in particular, was personally congratulated by the Army Commander for his work in destroying nine panzers. The 9th Lancers were in the forefront of the forces that took Tel el Aqqaquir in the battle, later pursuing the retreating Germans and chasing them out of Egypt.

In the subsequent advance across North Africa, the regiment was repeatedly in the thick of the fighting, serving in battles at El Hamma, Gousellat and Kournine. The confusion of the times, as the Allied advance pushed the Germans back across the desert, is illustrated by the experience of the regiment's padre on the day before El Hamma. Approaching an 88mm battery that he believed to be British, he found himself confronted by an enemy unit; fortunately it promptly surrendered to him.

By the time of the break-through to Tunis, however, the long months of conflict had taken their toll; the regiment had been reduced to just 18 tanks and had suffered casualties of 13 officers and 60 other ranks. It was pulled back from the front to mop up the remaining pockets of opposition.

The remainder of 1943 was spent re-grouping and re-equipping. Spending the winter in Algiers (billeted in buildings for the first time in two years), the men somehow acquired some horses and managed to stage some race meetings to bolster morale.

In May 1944 the regiment landed at Naples. Originally intended to be held in reserve during the assault on the Gothic Line, the struggle became so protracted that the 9th were called upon to lead the ultimately successful attack on San Savino.

During the Italian campaign, the 9th Lancers expanded their role to act on occasion as infantry and to become adept at the technique of kangaroo-borne infantry.

Some of the most intense fighting the regiment was to face came during the battle around the river Lamone. A rifle company had been surrounded by the enemy in the village of Pideura, and a troop of the 9th Lancers fought its way through to relieve them. Several days of heavy counter-attacks ensued, but the village was held. The contribution of 'C' Squadron was such it was awarded three Military Crosses, a Distinguished Conduct Medal and two Military Crosses.

The final battle of the war came on the banks of the Po in an encounter that saw ten enemy tanks destroyed at the cost of just one. The regiment had suffered the deaths of 19 officers and 100 other ranks during the course of the conflict.

[1] Hanwell *A Short History of the 9th Queen's Royal Lancers* p.55

10th Royal Hussars
(Prince of Wales's Own)

Principal Battle Honours 1939-45

Somme 1940 – Saunnu – Gazala – El Alamein
El Hamma – Tunis – Coriano – Santarcangelo
Valli di Comacchio – Argenta Gap

Raised 1715; amalgamated to form The Royal Hussars 1969;
amalgamated to form the King's Royal Hussars 1993.

Like the Queen's Bays and the 9th Lancers, with whom they were brigaded in 1937, the 10th Hussars were modernised relatively early. The units of the 2nd Armoured Brigade – as it was later named – were g0ranted what was for the era a reasonable period to adjust from horses to tanks, before being thrown into the front-line.

Even so, the impact they could make was strictly limited; sailing for France on 21 May 1940, the regiment was to be evacuated from Brest less than a month later. During that time, the first battle honour was won in the vain assault on the Somme bridgehead. Ten of the regiment's 30 tanks were lost in the battle, the remainder having to be destroyed prior to evacuation.

The frustrating start to the war, common to much of the cavalry, was followed by a year at home, stationed in Wiltshire.

October 1941 saw the regiment embarking for North Africa, landing at Suez the following month. Equipped there with Crusader and US-supplied Honey light tanks, they advanced to Cyrencia – recently taken by the Allies – at the end of the year.

There the 10th were to meet the Germans again. Rommel's offensive, launched on 21 January 1942, was met by the regiment at the Saunnu depression in a series of tough encounters over the next few days. Heavy losses were sustained – 45 casualties and the loss of 27 tanks to 'B' Squadron alone – and the men were forced back. Their delaying action had nonetheless been invaluable.

The following month, the regiment again faced Rommel's forces, this time in the shape of some 160 tanks. After 12 hours of combat, with no shells left to fire, and – in the case of 'B' Squadron – no tanks to fire them even had they existed, a retreat was ordered.

These defeats, of course, were soon avenged at Alamein. The 10th Hussars featured prominently in that battle, fighting to the left of the 51st Highland Division, and advancing along the coastal road in support of the assault on Kidney Ridge. It was a slow, painstaking advance that cost the regiment many lives and tanks, but cost the enemy even more dear. On 2 November, the 10th were amongst those making the decisive break-through at Tel el Aqqaqir.

Two days later, in the confused aftermath of battle, Captain Grant Singer, out on a reconnaissance patrol, captured the famous General Ludwig von Thoma.

With only a short period of recuperation, the regiment returned to the pursuit of the enemy, attacking and taking El Hamma and fighting through to the final surrender in Tunisia.

For most cavalry units in North Africa, the vanquishing of the Axis forces was followed by several months spent recovering. The invasion of Sicily was not an operation in which the cavalry could fully participate, and for a year the 10th Hussars rebuilt their ranks and equipment and trained in Libya and Algeria, in preparation for the call to Italy.

That call came in May 1944, though the 10th were to spend the first months away from battle in Rome. Rejoining the 2nd Armoured Brigade on the Adriatic Coast, the regiment participated in the British offensive that punched through the Gothic Line that August.

It was an offensive that, despite the early successes, was to last through the rest of the war, whilst never achieving its objective of breaking out of Italy toward Vienna. This was due partly to the determined resistance of the Germans – many of them survivors of the epic struggles at Cassino – and partly to the relentless running down of the British forces. With the war in France taking priority, the ranks were depleted and the equipment worn out; many of the tanks had long since exceeded their track mileage and stocks were so low that the 1st Armoured Division – of which the 10th Hussars were part – was eventually withdrawn and disbanded.

In mid-January 1945 the regiment was converted to an infantry role and returned in that capacity to the front-line, where it served for two months.

11th Hussars (Prince Albert's Own)

Principle Battle Honours 1939-45

Villers Bocage – Roer – Rhine – Egyptian Frontier 1940
Sidi Barrani – Beda Fomm – Sidi Rezegh 1941
El Alamein – Tunis – Italy 1943

Raised 1715; amalgamated to form Royal Hussars 1969; amalgamated to
form the King's Royal Hussars 1993.

Stationed in the Middle East since 1934, the 11th Hussars were in Egypt at the beginning of the war and were destined to serve through the entirety of the North African campaigns. On being mechanized, they became an armoured car regiment within the 7th Armoured Division.

A week after the Dunkirk evacuation and believing the fighting to be effectively over, Italy declared war on Britain on 10 June 1940. The next day the 11th Hussars ventured over the border into Libya, reportedly surprising enemy forces unaware that they were actually at war: two armoured cars captured four lorries and 70 prisoners. The next few months were spent in a series of minor skirmishes, harrying the enemy's rear forces when the Italian army advanced into Egypt.

On 9 December the British counter-offensive began, with the 7th in the vanguard. The enemy's lack of will to fight was apparent from the outset. 'C' Squadron picked up 300 prisoners as the Italians vacated Buq Buq on 11 December, whilst on the same day 'B' Squadron took an astonishing 7,000 prisoners, including four colonels.

Pushing forward in a reconnaissance capacity, the regiment were part of the force that cut off the retreat of the Benghazi garrison at Beda Fomm. That battle, in February 1941, marked the end of the offensive, and the 11th Hussars returned to Egypt to regroup.

By April, they were back in the fray, this time with the Germans as the major enemy. That summer was to prove a trying time, a prolonged tussle with the Afrika Korps in the desert heat, with more failures – particularly Operation Battleaxe intended to liberate the besieged Tobruk garrison – than successes to show for it.

Another two-month break in Cairo was followed by Operation Crusader in November 1941. This time the offensive was to meet with success, but there was a heavy price to pay: on one day at the battle of Sidi Rezegh, the 11th Hussars lost more men than on any previous day of fighting. Lieutenant P F Stewart recorded some of the confusion of that battle:

'I do not know what happened that day. I don't think anyone does . . . . Not only was one very wrapped up in one's own personal little battles, but one had no information of what was going on elsewhere. We fought privately and bitterly.' [1]

The chaos was such that one regimental lorry is reported to have mistakenly joined a German convoy in an attempt to escape pursuing British troops.

By this stage the 11th Hussars' knowledge of the realities of desert campaigning had led them to introduce a system whereby new officers arriving from England were started off in a lowly job such as driving or operating a wireless. They then had to work through the ranks before it could be assumed that they had enough practical experience to take over command of a troop. A similar system was later adopted by other regiments.

In January 1942 Rommel advanced yet again and for a short period the 11th were again in the front-line. In February, however, they were withdrawn for a period of rest and were then sent to the Middle East. Whilst they were away, Rommel made much progress, and German intelligence papers reported that '[n]ow the 11th Hussars have left we can afford to take more risks.' [2]

The back-handed compliment was given new life when the 11th returned to Egypt in July 1942, just before the German campaign was halted at Alam el Halfa and then turned back at El Alamein. The regiment, now at a strength of 30 officers and 471 other ranks with 32 armoured cars, fought at the latter.

In the ensuing advance, the 11th distinguished themselves, being the first British troops into Tripoli and fighting in the assault on the Mareth Line. In Tripoli they provided a personal escort for the Prime Minister on his visit there, and in June 1943 were inspected in Tunisia by the Colonel-in-Chief, King George VI.

The 7th Armoured Division was to serve briefly in Italy and later in North-West Europe, with the 11th Hussars still serving as its reconnaissance regiment, but it was the North African wars that proved to be the major contribution. The 11th Hussars achieved the double distinction of winning more battle honours in the Western Desert than any other regiment, and of being mentioned more often in the official history of the Afrika Korps than any other British regiment.

[1] Brett-Smith *The 11th Hussars* p.262
[2] ibid. p.270

12th Royal Lancers (Prince of Wales's)

Battle Honours 1939-45

Dyle – Dunkirk 1940 – North-West Europe 1940
Chor es Sufan – Gazala – Tunis
North Africa 1941-43 – Bologna – Italy 1944-45

Raised 1715; amalgamated to form 9th/12th Royal Lancers (Prince of Wales's); amalgamated to form the Queen's Royal Lancers 1993.

One of the first mechanized regiments in the British Army, the 12th Lancers had trained with armoured cars – albeit vehicles of poor quality – for 11 years prior to the outbreak of war. This did not, however, mean a great deal in the confusion of 1939, and initial orders were that the men were to re-train with tanks, before wiser counsel prevailed and the original role was confirmed – the 12th Lancers were to serve as an armoured car unit throughout the war.

Sent to France in October 1939, the regiment was in the vanguard of the advance the following May to take up a position on the river Ghette. Even at this early stage, the signs were not favourable: the Belgian troops alongside 'already gave the impression of a defeated army' [1] according to one troop-leader, and an initial skirmish was sufficient to cause a major collapse of the line. The remainder of May was spent in retreat to Dunkirk, where the cars were destroyed (though the guns were saved) and the men evacuated.

In November the following year the regiment returned to the attack, this time in North Africa. Before that, however, a small detachment under Lieutenant Morris had another duty to perform in providing a mobile guard for the King and Queen, a function later expanded to cover the Prime Minister and other members of the government.

The situation in Africa was far from clear in late 1941. The Allies were advancing, but Rommel was so expert at disengaging that the Afrika Korps remained intact, ready to strike again. The 12th Lancers spent more than a month in pursuit of the enemy, with supply lines so stretched that essentials ran desperately short: water was rationed to half a gallon per man a day, though this was augmented by draining the water from the radiators of abandoned vehicles found along the way.

When the German counter-thrust came, it caught the regiment in the front-line, 'C' Squadron being in the Knightsbridge box at the time. A month of fighting saw the Allies driven back to the Alamein line, where they dug in for the battle to come.

The role of armoured cars at the two Alamein encounters was mostly limited to reconnaissance and patrolling, but this was dangerous enough. 'At one point,' recorded the regimental journal shortly after the war, 'visibility was down to 400 yards owing to a sandstorm; locating and reporting Panzers under such conditions is never easy but always exciting.' [2]

With the breakthrough at Alamein, the speed of the armoured cars came into its own; in the first four days of pursuit, 1,000 prisoners were taken, whilst soon after 200 miles were covered in just two days as the regiment struck out from Buq Buq to take the Matruba airfields.

Later on, No. 5 Troop became the first unit of the 8th Army to make contact with the Americans advancing from the west.

Sitting out the Sicilian campaign, the Lancers proceeded to Italy in April 1944, landing at Naples. For most of the first year, its task was that of patrolling, which in that mountainous terrain often entailed a return to horseback. 'Our chief memories of those times,' reported an officer of the regiment, 'were the cold, the hunger and those awful steep walks.' [3]

A more active part was to be played in the battle to take Bologna in April 1945. Joining the famous 2nd New Zealand Division, the men forced a path through to the city against a desperate last stand by German paratroopers. With that success, the war in Italy was effectively over, and rapid progress was made to the Po, and thereafter by 'C' Squadron to Venice, where Major Speke was the first Allied soldier to enter the city.

The remainder of the regiment meanwhile, was pressing on to Trieste. Foreshadowing the Cold War, there was some pressure to reach the city before Tito's partisans could do so. In the event, both sides arrived almost simultaneously, though the Germans chose to surrender to the Lancers rather than take their chances with the communists. The City Fathers likewise handed the city over to Major Abraham and Captain Monroe-Smith.

[1] Stewart *The History of the XII Lancers* p.352

[2] ibid. p.399

[3] ibid. p.425

13th/18th Royal Hussars
(Queen Mary's Own)

Principal Battle Honours 1939-45

Ypres-Comines Canal – Normandy Landing – Caen
Mont Pincon – Geilenkirchen – Roer – Rhineland
Goch – North-West Europe 1940, 44-45

13th Hussars raised 1715; 18th Hussars first raised 1759; these two
regiments amalgamated to form 13th/18th Royal Hussars (Queen Mary's
Own) 1922; amalgamated to form The Light Dragoons 1993.

The 13th/18th Royal Hussars returned to Britain from India in late October 1938, and began the process of mechanization the following January. Light tanks and Bren-gun carriers were eventually provided, but there was a woeful lack of resources available for instruction and maintenance; the result was that when the regiment was inspected by Queen Mary in July 1939, only one of the three squadrons was at fighting strength.

The demands of war could not, however, be ignored, and in September the 13th/18th were on their way to France as divisional cavalry in the 1st Division. From then until 30 May 1940, when the last of the troops were evacuated from Dunkirk, the story was essentially that of the British Expeditionary Force in general: an advance into Belgium, followed by a retreat a few days later when Holland capitulated and it became apparent that the German thrust was cutting through the French defences to the south. Casualties were comparatively light, though the regiment did serve in a rearguard capacity for the division.

A lengthy period of training and preparation for the re-opening of the European front followed. Initially equipped with Covenanters, the 13th/18th were assigned a new role in autumn 1943 using double duplex (DD) tanks. These were Valentines converted into amphibious vehicles by means of inflatable superstructures and twin propellers, intended for use in the Normandy landings.

On D-Day 'A' and 'B' Squadrons led the assault on France, with the tanks covering the last two miles under their own power. DD tanks were never the most stable of sea-going vessels, and the journey resulted in many cases of sea-sickness, but the extensive training and exercises paid off: the venture went according to plan and made a major contribution to the success of the whole operation.

The first month on the continent, when the invading forces were fighting to maintain the toe-hold that had been achieved, saw the regiment score notable successes at St Honorine – in support of the Cameronians – and at the river Orne, where it destroyed 21 enemy tanks.

July saw the final capture of Caen, but for the 13th/18th Hussars the greatest battle in Normandy was to come on 6 August at Mont Pincon. Repeated attempts that day to take the steep, heavily defended hill by the Somerset Light Infantry and The Wiltshire Regiment had been beaten back, and it was not until six o'clock in the evening that an unguarded track was discovered. Two troops of Hussars raced up the narrow path in an assault that took the Germans by surprise, and held their ground until the remainder of the regiment and the infantry could join them to clear the enemy from the position.

Returning to the conflict after a few days of recovery, the 13th/18th participated in the remainder of the campaign in Europe, advancing across the Seine and the Somme and arriving in Brussels on 7 September. The last time the regiment had been here was in May 1940 during the retreat to Dunkirk; on that occasion they had been warned by the citizens that the Germans were entering the city behind them and that the Burgomaster was negotiating with the enemy in an attempt to minimise destruction.

Further action was seen at Arnhem, Geilenkirchen and Reichswald before the crossing of the Rhine on 24 March 1945. The last battle was at Bremen on 26 April.

By the end of the war, the regiment had lost 11 officers and 131 men.

14th/20th King's Hussars

Principal Battle Honours 1939-45

Bologna – Medicina – Italy 1945

14th Hussars raised 1715; 20th Hussars originally raised 1759; these two regiments amalgamated to form 14th/20th King's Hussars; amalgamated to form the King's Royal Hussars 1993.

The 14th/20th Hussars were destined to spend most of the war years in the Middle East, engaged in unspectacular though necessary work that can perhaps best be seen as preventative action. Stationed in India at the outbreak of war, the regiment was still in the process of mechanization, and it was not until May 1941 that the conversion was completed, with the issuing of Mark VIB light tanks and Bren-gun carriers.

The following month, the 14th/20th embarked at Bombay with the 2nd Indian Armoured Brigade, bound for Basra in Iraq.

The pro-Axis rebellion in Iraq had just been suppressed and the regiment arrived in a country seemingly far removed from the war. Setting up camp at Shaiba, 'C' Squadron were impressed by what they took to be a swimming pool and made full use of the facilities – the rest of the regiment was less impressed when it was discovered that this was actually the only supply of drinking water available.

The situation in the Middle East at the time was far from stable. The region was of immense significance both as an oil producer and as the gateway to Asia, but while it came under the British sphere of influence, it did not form part of the Empire and was theoretically neutral. In 1941 this neutrality was looking increasingly fragile in the context of a three-pronged German encroachment: through Greece and Crete to the west, from Africa in the south, and through the Soviet Union from the north. One of the many tasks of the British Middle East Command – in addition to prosecuting the war in Africa and the Mediterranean – was to counter the threat.

In mid-July 1941 the 14th/20th left for Baghdad, where they remained for six weeks preparing for a move into Persia. A Soviet-British ultimatum to that country in August demanded access to Gulf ports and the expulsion of German nationals, and the troops were intended to give force to that ultimatum.

Some resistance to the invasion was expected from the Persian army, but in the event the greatest danger to the 14th/20th came from a detachment of the Warwickshire Yeomanry, who fired upon the Hussars by mistake. When the Persians were engaged and passage into the country gained, it was at minimal cost on both sides – though 'C' squadron were reported to have picked up 'four dead Persians, one prisoner and one dirty picture'. And when the main defending force was met, the Shah ordered a cease-fire and effectively surrendered to the Allied forces under General Slim.

The 14th/20th were stationed in Persia for just over a year, the country now being under the dual control of Britain and the USSR. In November 1942 they proceeded to Shaika and were issued with Grant tanks.

For the next two years, the regiment remained on internal policing duties in the region on a series of postings. When mountain training was deemed essential, the 14th/20th went to Syria to train. When the Greek Brigade mutinied at Burg-El-Arab, they covered 800 miles in three days to produce a show of strength that forced the Greeks to back down. And when there was some concern about the status of Turkey, they proceeded to the borders to carry out manoeuvres.

In December 1944, however, a new posting was ordered: to Italy to relieve the 3rd Hussars. The following month, they arrived and for the first time came into conflict with the major enemy. For the final few months of the war, the regiment fought with XIII Corps in the continuing assault on German fortifications in North Italy. Although for the most part it operated as an armoured regiment, one squadron was trained as a kangaroo unit, carrying infantry into battle.

15th/19th The King's Royal Hussars

Principal Battle Honours 1939-45

Withdrawal to Escaut – Seine 1944 – Nederrijn
Rhineland – Hochwald – Rhine – Ibbenburen – Aller
North West Europe 1940, 1944-45

15th Hussars raised 1749; 19th Hussars first raised 1759; these two
regiments amalgamated to form 15th/19th The King's Royal Hussars 1922;
amalgamated to form The Light Dragoons 1993.

The 15th/19th Hussars was one of the last cavalry regiments in the British Army to be mechanized, the process not being completed until August 1939, just a month before the declaration of war. The establishment at that time stood at 21 officers and 434 other ranks, equipped with light tanks and carriers. (They did train with amphibious tanks later in the war, but were not called upon to use them in battle.)

The regiment was posted to France in October 1939 as Divisional Cavalry for the 3rd Armoured Division, commanded by Major-General B L Montgomery. Its duties were essentially those of a reconnaissance unit, a task that 'A' Squadron had performed for the same division during the Great War.

In response to Germany's strike against the Low Countries, the regiment advanced to Louvain in Belgium, but the position was to prove unsustainable, as the Dutch and Belgian armies alongside the BEF collapsed under the assault of the German blitzkrieg.

Stationed at Assche, eight miles northwest of Brussels, and struggling valiantly to hold the town, the regiment fought one of its hardest battles of the war on 18 May. By the time the order came to abandon the position, many had lost their lives and many more were captured, including the commanding officer, Colonel D S Frazer. The survivors – some of them by now in a composite regiment with the 4th/7th Royal Dragoon Guards – joined the retreat of the BEF. The nightmare emotions of that withdrawal, and the British soldiers' response, was summed up in the regimental history:

'During the past week we had seen a constant stream of refugees moving west, they knew not whither, apparently without plan. When we halted anywhere, peasant women, tears streaming down their faces, would come to ask us whether we were staying to fight there and whether they should stay or go. It was so difficult to answer . . . . But we tried to present a cheerful face to them all.' [1]

166 members of the regiment were killed, wounded or taken prisoner in the campaign; the remainder were evacuated from Dunkirk. Amongst them was the next commanding officer, Lieutenant-Colonel W R N Hinde, who had been wounded at Assche. His replacement in August 1942 was Lieutenant-Colonel A D Taylor, who had been taken prisoner at the same battle, but had escaped early on, returning home on 7 June 1940.

These two colonels commanded the regiment during a four year period of rebuilding and retraining in the UK, in preparation for the resumption of the West European war.

On the night of 14/15 August 1944, the regiment landed at Arromanches in their capacity as the Armoured Reconnaissance Regiment of the 11th Armoured Division. The long battle to take Caen was by now over, and in the first six weeks an advance of some 350 miles was made, against resistance so dogged that the troops were afforded not a single day's respite.

The scale of the fighting in those early days in France made for much chaos and confusion. On one occasion the commanding officer, on a reconnaissance patrol, found his vehicle in the midst of 200 German soldiers. Fortunately, they failed to notice his presence and, although he came under fire as he beat a hasty retreat, he escaped unscathed.

The regiment's experience of the campaign was typical of the times. The regimental history reports that the five months to 16 February 1945 had cost 110 men dead or wounded, and comments:

'It is interesting to note that the casualties during this period, in which no major battle took place, account for 45% of the total casualties sustained by the Regiment in the campaign in North-West Europe.' [2]

On 2 April a synthetic oil plant, previously unidentified as such, was captured, dealing another body blow to the German war machine. Barely a week later, the imminent collapse of the enemy was apparent when the Burgomaster of Eilvese came out to meet the Hussars, bearing a white flag. Uncertain whether to trust such a novel gesture, the men sat the official on the first tank as they entered the village, just to be on the safe side. When Eilvese was taken without a fight, and when the experience was repeated elsewhere, it became clear that the end was finally in sight.

Fighting through Germany, the regiment came to rest in the little Baltic town of Keppeln in May 1945, where they remained during the summer.

[1]   Courage *The History of 15th/19th The King's Royal Hussars 1939-1945* p.36

[2]   ibid. p.165

16th/5th The Queen's Royal Lancers

Principal Battle Honours 1939-45

Fondouk – Bordj – Djebel Kournine – Tunis
North Africa 1942-43 – Cassino II – Liri Valley
Advance to Florence – Argenta Gap – Italy 1944-45

5th Lancers first raised 1689; 16th Lancers raised 1759; these two
regiments amalgamated to form the 16th/5th The Queen's Royal Lancers
1922; amalgamated to form The Queen's Lancers 1993.

Although the 16th/5th Lancers did not themselves serve in the British
Expeditionary Force, there was still some regimental interest in its fate, for
Brigadier C Nicholson – the CO in the immediate pre-war period – commanded the
three battalions of riflemen who fought such an heroic rearguard defence at
Dunkirk. He was captured and died in a prisoner-of-war camp in 1943.

In mid-1940 the 16th/5th were redesignated a Motor Machine-Gun Regiment
and, together with the 17th/21st Lancers and the 2nd Lothian and Border Horse,
formed the 1st Motor Machine-Gun Brigade. The strength of the regiment at that
stage stood at some 20 officers and 400 men.

November 1942 saw the launch of Operation Torch, the first joint British-
American campaign, designed to neutralise the potential threat from Vichy forces
in France's North-East African colonies and to open a second front against the
Afrika Korps. Landing in Tunisia, the regiment soon dealt with the Vichy
opposition, confronting it and spending the first few months watching and waiting
for orders.

Equipped at the time with Valentine and Crusader tanks, the men took
possession of 61 Shermans in February 1943. They had, however, no chance to
train in the new vehicles before being sent into the fighting around the Kasserine
Pass and were obliged to use the old equipment one last time.

Two months later, the advance of the 8th Army, sweeping the German forces
before it, threw the 16th/5th into heavy fighting at and around Fondouk. The
intention was to cut off the enemy's retreat, an operation that just failed, due to the
greater than expected resistance of the enemy and the errors of generalship that
cost the 17th/21st Lancers so dear at the same battle. Nonetheless, the regiment
successfully destroyed a large number of tanks and anti-tank guns and took many
prisoners, as well as tying up enemy divisions at a crucial time.

Amongst the engagements around Fondouk was a battle at Bordj on 11 April 1943 that was as close as a modern armoured unit could come to the old cavalry encounters of the past, with the whole regiment charging directly at the enemy under heavy fire.

Despite this echo of former days, the nature of tank warfare in the desert was unlike anything in the experience of the regiment. It also threw up some peculiarities – during the three days of fighting at Kournine, a scout car arrived at the forward tanks to deliver mail.

In the final assault on Tunis, the regiment was amongst those diverted to take Hamman Lif, one of the last strongholds of the Germans, and one which was taken with surprising ease. The officer commanding the 10th Panzer Division was later to comment: 'I was amazed at the break through of a complete armoured division through the defile at Hamman Lif. I did not think it was possible.' [1]

The remainder of 1943 was spent regrouping in North Africa. When the call to ship over to Italy did come in January the following year, it took the regiment by such surprise that the CO had to be hurriedly recalled from leave.

The regiment landed in Naples to find the advance through Italy, initially so rapid, reduced to a painfully slow pace. For ten days the men fought in the consolidating battle at Minturno, before being sent further up the line to assist in the lengthy assaults on Monte Cassino. Re-united with the 17th/21st Lancers and the 2nd Lothian and Border Horse, the 16th/5th crossed the Rapido river in the final offensive at Cassino and advanced up the Liri valley. The fighting was intense, but fortunately casualties were light, though the Commanding Officer, Lieutenant-Colonel J N R Loveday, was killed by an enemy shell.

Once past Cassino, progress was more rapid until the German defences at the Appennines were reached in autumn 1944.

Much of that winter was spent by the regiment fighting in the vicinity of Florence. A brief pause came with a move to the east coast in expectation of an assault on Greece, but the operation never happened and the regiment returned to Florence. It served for a short period in an infantry capacity. The Allied troops in Italy were at the time much reduced as units were transferred to North-West Europe and to the Riveria.

The final battle was at Argenta in April 1945, and the 16th/5th ended the War in the appropriately named Finale.

[1]   Barclay *History of The 16th/5th The Queen's Royal Lancers* p.105

17th/21st Lancers

Principal Battle Honours 1939-45

Terborba Gap – Kasserine – Fondouk – El Kourzia
Tunis – North Africa 1942-43 – Cassino II
Capture of Perugia – Italy 1944-45

17th Lancers raised 1759; 21st Lancers first raised 1759; these two
regiments amalgamated to form 17th/21st Lancers 1922; amalgamated to
form the Queen's Royal Lancers.

The 17th/21st Lancers were mechanized in 1938 whilst stationed in India. Though they were to return to Britain the following year, their entry into the war was delayed by the lack of organisation so characteristic of the British Army at the time. The officers and men returning from India had trained with tanks in preparation for their new mechanized role, but their ranks were augmented by reservists who had had no such experience and were offered no immediate opportunity to gain any, for the regiment was not fully equipped with vehicles until late 1940.

In September of that year, it became part of 26th Armoured Brigade within the 6th Armoured Division, and commenced a long period of intensive training under General Crocker. 18 months in Southern England culminated in a massive exercise in Ayrshire, and produced one of the best trained divisions in the Army.

In November 1942 the regiment embarked at Glasgow and set sail for North Africa. Landing at Algiers, its immediate task was to participate in the advance upon Tunis. Rapid deployment of better-equipped German forces, however, and superior enemy air cover soon ended hopes of an early capture of Tunis and stalled the British advance.

The following January saw a German counter-offensive. Initially overwhelmed by the assault, the Allied line was forced back, with the 17th/21st in the midst of the struggle. In February 1943, they fought a desperate rearguard action as the enemy seized the Kasserine Pass, their Valentine and Crusader tanks hopelessly inadequate when confronted by the German weaponry. Falling back to a defensive position at Thala, they prepared to dig in for the night, only to find enemy tanks infiltrating the position. A further night of heavy fighting was required before the German attack could be repulsed.

Thala was the last engagement in which the regiment was expected to fight with inferior tools. They were now issued with Sherman tanks, newly arrived from America and equipped with much more powerful armaments.

Their first major encounter in the new vehicles, however, gave the regiment no real chance to exploit their virtues. With the Germans retreating in the face of the Eighth Army, orders were given to cut them off, a task that required the immediate capture of the Fondouk Pass. The enemy held the two ridges that overlooked the 1,000-yard wide pass and, following uncoordinated and unsuccessful attempts to dislodge them, the 17th/21st were ordered to advance straight through, regardless of the consequences.

In an action reminiscent of the Charge of the Light Brigade (in which the 17th Lancers had also served), the tanks of the regiment advanced across a mine-field under heavy fire from both sides. The lack of strategic planning was matched only by the courage and determination of the men: '[one] squadron then another, rapidly reduced by 80 per cent of their number, tried with incredible persistence to flounder through the mines until hardly a tank could move.' [1] Though the pass was eventually taken, the objective of clearing up the German troops was not achieved.

It was only a stay of execution for the Axis forces. In May the long-awaited assault on Tunis finally succeeded in taking the city, while the 6th Armoured Division struck out to the south, breaking through a German defensive position at Hamman Lif and isolating the last enemy troops, stranded on the Cap Bon peninsula. It was to be the last action of the war in North Africa.

With this success came a break from the fighting for the 17th/21st. Tanks were clearly going to be of little value in Sicily, and the regiment spent the next nine months re-grouping and re-training in Tunisia.

Disembarking at Naples in March 1944, the regiment found itself in the midst of a wholly new environment, in which the hilly, broken terrain offered little opportunity for the free-ranging tank warfare seen in North Africa. There is no doubt that the 17th/21st found their new role in support to the infantry difficult; Major Sam Buxton commented, 'This is real war, and makes Africa seem a picnic.' [2]

Nonetheless the regiment distinguished itself in the Italian campaign, playing its part in the massive effort to break down the German line concentrated on Monte Cassino, and subsequently in the assault on the Gothic Line.

In November 1944 it was ordered to re-train in anticipation for a landing in Yugoslavia, later amended to be an invasion of Greece. In the event, the whole operation was abandoned, and the regiment remained in Italy until the end of the War.

[1] Macksey *Crucible of Power: The Fight for Tunisia 1942-43* p.253
[2] Blake *The 17th/21st Lancers* p.143

The Royal Tank Regiment

Principal Battle Honours 1939-45

Rhine – North-West Europe 1940, 44-45 – Abyssinia 1940
Tobruk 1941 – El Alamein – North Africa 1940-43
Sicily 1943 – Italy 1943-45 – Greece 1941 – Burma 1942

Formed as Heavy Branch, Machine Gun Corps 1916; named The Tank
Corps 1917; redesignated Royal Tank Regiment 1939.

As the country lurched toward war, the Royal Tank Corps came within the compass of the newly-created Royal Armoured Corps and was re-named the Royal Tank Regiment. It comprised at that time some eight battalions; by the end of 1940 a further four battalions had been raised.

Even this, however, was insufficient to meet the needs of the new demands, and large numbers of infantry territorial battalions were converted to battalions of the RTR during the course of the war, though often these conversions were initially little more than nominal, with the necessary vehicles simply not available.

Nonetheless some of these battalions were to make spectacular contributions in their brief periods of existence. The 6th Glosters, for example, became the 44th Royal Tank Regiment and served in Egypt, Libya, Sicily, Italy, France, Belgium, Holland and Germany before being disbanded at the end of the war. Such were the demands made on tank-crews of the time.

The ubiquity of the regiment can also be judged from the battle honours awarded to it. Of the ten major honours, only three are single battles, the remainder being whole campaigns; so much action was seen that only the most significant could be recognized.

In the chaos of the BEF, the tanks created the one moment of success, when 4RTR and 7RTR staged a counter-attack at Arras on 21 May 1940. 70 Matilda tanks broke through German infantry lines, using machine-gun fire to penetrate and counting on the heavy armour of the Infantry Tanks to resist enemy attack. The offensive was halted by an ominous development – the use of 88mm anti-aircraft guns, against which the Matilda's armour was useless. The 88mm gun was to be one of the key factors in Rommel's victories.

There were other notable encounters in North-West Europe – all the light tanks of 3RTR were sacrificed at Calais to defend the evacuations, and 4/7RTR delayed the Germans at La Bassée – but it was not to be until the war with Italy that the RAC really came into its own.

The initial conflict in the Western Desert was deceptively straightforward: the Italians had no weaponry to match the armour of the Matildas and were tactically inept. The only real problem was the sheer numbers of captured enemy; one tank commander commented: 'So far as I can see there are twenty acres of officers and a hundred acres of men.' [1] At Beda Fomm alone, where units including 2RTR were joined belatedly by 1RTR who had got lost in a sandstorm, 3,000 British troops took 20,000 prisoners. By this stage, confidence was running so high that 7RTR even felt able to send two tanks into battle with jammed turrets.

Elsewhere, progress was not so easy. 3RTR escaped from the disaster of Greece but without its tanks, whilst six tanks of 7RTR could do little to help in Crete.

The arrival of the Germans in Africa also seemed to spell disaster. The success of 88mm fire soon led to a belief that the Afrika Korps was vastly better equipped, though in reality the British approach to armoured warfare was as much to blame for Rommel's successes. An excessive reliance on tanks produced full-frontal attacks that often played directly into the hands of the 88mm gunners – it was a more balanced appraisal of the tank in relation to the field-gun and the infantryman that won victory at Alamein.

Two Victoria Crosses were won in the ebb and flow of desert war: one by Captain P Gardner of 4RTR for rescuing crewmen of the KDG during Operation Crusader, and one by Lieutenant-Colonel H R B Foote of 7RTR during the battle of the Cauldron. Perhaps the most heroic battalion action came at Mareth in March 1943, when 50RTR lost 27 tanks and its Commanding Officer, Lieutenant-Colonel J E Cairns, in an attempt to force an anti-tank ditch. The diversion of enemy resources allowed a break-through further down the line.

The scale of the Royal Tank Regiment's commitment to the desert war can be seen by the fact that ten battalions were involved in Crusader; ten also were at Alamein, together with detachments of three others. Though Sicily and Italy were not such easy terrain for tanks, the Mediterranean theatre remained the heart of the regiment's war; even at the height of the second North-West Europe campaign, more battalions were serving in the south.

There was obviously less involvement in the Far East, though 2RTR was sent to Rangoon in February 1942, and participated in the retreat from Burma. Restricted to roads, the men were able to contribute little in a jungle-based conflict.

The last great battle of the war with Germany, the crossing of the Rhine, gave the regiment a major battle honour. During the crossing 44RTR employed DD tanks whilst 4RTR used Buffalos, just two of the types of adapted vehicles that, together with the new models of tanks, gave the RTR such a range of options. Perhaps most spectacular of all were the Crocodiles equipped with flame-throwers and used by, amongst others, 7RTR.

[1] *To The Green Fields Beyond* p.4

Royal Regiment of Artillery

Royal Artillery established 1716; renamed
Royal Regiment of Artillery 1722.

Despite its name, the Royal Regiment of Artillery is in its scale and diversity more akin to a corps than a regiment. Its ubiquity is such that there was scarcely a single campaign, operation or encounter during the war that did not involve the Gunners to some degree.

The RA entered the war in perhaps a better state of preparedness than many other wings of the Army. New techniques and bigger, more effective weapons were to be developed during the six years of conflict, but even at the outset there was quality equipment available, albeit sometimes in short supply. Many of the gun types employed during the Great War could still profitably be used (including, later on, some of the actual weapons themselves, ordered to be put in storage by Churchill when he was at the War Office in 1919), and there were some new innovations, such as the 25-pounder gun-howitzer, with its range of seven miles.

The speed of the German victory in North-West Europe soon denuded the Artillery of much of this initial arsenal. The evacuation from Dunkirk, however impressive an operation in personnel transport, could not hope to bring back all the heavy equipment of the British Expeditionary Force, and somewhere around 2,000 guns had to be abandoned in France, destroyed to prevent their re-use. As Britain entered a state of siege, expecting a German invasion at any moment, the strength of the field artillery stood at just 500 pieces, with a particularly desperate lack of anti-tank guns.

Fortunately, of course, the invasion never came, and the defensive gun emplacements were never called upon, though those at Dover did engage in exchanges of fire with the enemy across the Channel.

Meanwhile, new guns were arriving, some newly manufactured, some acquired from the Royal Navy and others bought from America to replenish the arsenals. Many of the newly-mobilised territorial army battalions were being converted to anti-tank and anti-aircraft duties to supplement the regulars of the Royal Regiment. (It is worth noting, however, that even as early as 1939, almost 75% of gunners were TA.)

The first great British offensive of the war was in the deserts of North Africa, and the Artillery was naturally there to play its part. When Tobruk was isolated by the German advance of 1941 and besieged for eight months, the garrison was mostly comprised of Australian troops, but also included three units of the Royal Horse Artillery and the 51st Field Regiment, RA. At the battle of Sidi Rezegh in

November 1941, Lieutenant G Gunn and Brigadier J C Campbell both won VCs – the former awarded posthumously, the latter just a fortnight before his unfortunate death in a car accident. And at Alam el Halfa, where the German advance was finally halted in August 1942, Rommel himself cited the British artillery as having played a decisive part in his defeat.

During the same period of offensive and counter-offensive in the desert, new techniques and weapons were being introduced and improvised. The 25 pdr gun, intended for anti-infantry bombardment, was adopted as an anti-tank gun, the 2 pdr having proved an insufficient weapon in combat with the Panzers. Radio was used for the first time to control large numbers of guns, the facility of rapid communication allowing whole regiments (of 24 guns) or divisions (72 guns) to be trained upon a single target with the emphasis now on the density of attack rather than pinpoint accuracy. The self-propelled gun (mounted on a Grant tank) was introduced, as were Air Observation Posts. These latter were light, unarmed Auster aircraft piloted by RA officers, whose task was observation and identifi-cation of targets; during the Italian campaign, more than 8,000 flights were undertaken.

In the invasion of Normandy, even more radical departures were made, with some artillery being flown into battle even before the sea-borne landings. The 53rd Airlanding Light Regiment, for example, arrived by glider at the river Orne complete with a light battery to support the infantry.

The later air assault on Arnhem built on this experience, with a combination of 75mm howitzers and 6- and 17-pounders being flown in with the 1st Airlanding Light Regiment. The operation may have been unsuccessful, but these guns, together with the long-range support that came from the artillery of the 1st Army, helped sustain the isolated troops beyond all expectation.

The scale of the artillery at the Allies' command can be seen at the crossing of the Rhine in 1945. Some 3,000 guns – British and American – concentrated their fire on the remnants of the German army in the last massive battle of North-West Europe.

It should also be noted that the Royal Artillery had visited Europe between Dunkirk and D-Day. On 19 August 1942 some 6,000 men had landed at Dieppe in a tragically mistimed and unsupported landing. The force was mostly comprised of Canadian troops, but the Gunners were also present, and Major Patrick Porteous was awarded a VC for his part in the operation.

Meanwhile, in Burma, the men of the Regiment were facing enormous logistical challenges, Field Marshal Slim later commenting that 'for artillery, it was the most difficult theatre of all.' [1] The British gunners, together with their Indian and African colleagues, were called upon constantly to improvise new modes of transport in their attempt to take heavy guns through jungle, across swamps and in the mud of the monsoon. There were lessons here that were learnt the hard way: in the initial retreat from Burma in 1942, only 25 of the 150 British guns were saved.

One other wing of the Artillery has yet to be mentioned: the Anti-Aircraft Command, working alongside the RAF to defeat the Luftwaffe's bombing campaign. The critical early days were not characterised by major success in actually hitting enemy 'planes, but the ability to fragment large formations of the Luftwaffe went a long way to making the task of Fighter Command easier.

By May 1941 over 300,000 men and some 3,500 women were staffing nearly 2,500 anti-aircraft guns. It was a role that sometimes seemed to lack the prestige of the front-line forces, but was nonetheless a vital part of the war effort.

[1] Brookes *Battle Thunder* p.199

Corps of Royal Engineers

Engineer Officers established 1757; Royal Military Artificers established 1772; these two units amalgamated to form The Royal Engineers 1855.

Like the Artillery, the motto of the Corps of Royal Engineers is 'Ubique', and they too served in every theatre during the Second World War, finding themselves confronted by new challenges and required to perform new tasks. The essential function of the Corps, however, did not change: its twin duties were, as they have always been, to facilitate the operations of the British Army and to hinder as much as possible those of the enemy.

Both these roles were crucial to the survival of the ill-fated British Expeditionary Force. The 'Phoney War' had seen massive preparations made along the French-Belgian border, but when the German campaign opened, its rapidity and mobility rendered much of this work irrelevant. Instead the Engineers were called upon to improvise in the face of a blitzkrieg assault that no-one had expected. In the retreat from the Low Countries, there was a repeated and urgent need for fortifications to be built on every river and every canal where the line halted. When each position was abandoned, there was the corresponding need to destroy everything that could prove of value to the enemy. More than 600 bridges were destroyed during that retreat.

Even more important was the work done at Dunkirk and on the other beaches, when piers and bridges were built to enable the evacuation to take place.

The return to Britain was to provide an urgent and diverse range of tasks. 330,000 troops from the BEF, together with the rapidly expanding army at home, had to be accommodated, requiring the building of a vast new military infrastructure. At the same time, the potential arrival of German troops demanded fortifications and defences. And when the Battle of Britain commenced, there were airfields to be built and repaired.

Closer to the hearts of the civilian population was the work carried out by RE bomb disposal experts. During the course of the Luftwaffe's protracted assault on Britain, a total of 35,000 unexploded bombs were made safe, whilst teams of Engineers were employed on rebuilding roads and railways in areas that had been hit.

Meanwhile, in the to and fro of the desert campaigns, minefields were laid and cleared, wells were sunk and contaminated, lines of communication were built and destroyed. The struggle in North Africa often depended as much on resources as on more direct military action, and the RE's contribution to the tightening of the grip on the Afrika Korps was considerable.

When the turning-point finally came at Alamein, the RE expanded their role to include the creation of an elaborate series of dummy equipment – tanks, 'planes and guns – designed to convince the Germans that the main thrust of the attack was to come from the southern end of the line, whilst the real forces gathered in the north.

Similar tasks were undertaken in East Africa, and the Middle and Far East. In the latter campaign, working closely with Indian engineers, the RE desperately struggled to hold the Japanese advance through Malaya. It was a vain attempt and the Allied engineers suffered 3,500 casualties from just 6,000 men; many of the remainder were taken prisoner.

The long struggle to retake Burma, of course, produced even more difficult problems to be solved, with the jungle conditions making the tasks harder than ever. It was in Burma too that the Sappers were called upon to build two warships for the Royal Navy; launched by Field-Marshal Slim, these vessels were to see active and useful service in the war against Japan.

The campaigns in the Middle East were to prove more immediately successful. With the concern that the Soviet Union might not be able to withstand the German onslaught, and the consequent vulnerability of Britain's Arabic interests, the oil pipeline from Kirkup, in northern Iraq, to the Lebanon was removed, and Syria prepared for a potential attack. Projects were also undertaken in Turkey, though with this country being neutral, the Sappers had to work in the unconvincing guise of civilian engineers.

The key need in an undeveloped region was communication, and several roads and railways were built or expanded. The most impressive was possibly the railway between the Persian Gulf and the Caspian Sea, an important link to the USSR. A track that could carry only 200 tons per day in 1941 was improved by British, and later American, engineers to take 10,000 tons a day.

Perhaps the most celebrated performance of the Royal Engineers was to come in the Normandy landings with the construction in Britain of the artificial harbours code-named Mulberries that were to be towed over to France. Despite the heavy mid-June storm that damaged the second such structure, the main Mulberry Harbour was assembled and was ultimately to see 2′ million troops, half a million vehicles and four million tons of supplies pass through to mainland Europe.

This key role in an amphibious landing was one which the RE had prepared in Operations Torch and Husky – in North-West Africa and Sicily respectively. It was in these actions that the concept of bulldozers and engineers being in the first line of troops was established within the military hierarchy.

Amongst the other contributions of the Royal Engineers was the development of airborne forces, in which the RE had a critical part. Similarly, in the often unrecognized but vital duty of providing a postal service for troops overseas, the Sappers were the key players. And finally due acknowledgement must be made of one of the most celebrated inventions of the war years, the Bailey bridge. This structure, which worked equally in both a fixed and a floating capacity, was to become a standard part of the equipment carried by all RE units.

In 1939 the Corps of Royal Engineers had contained 90,000 men; by 1945 – though never up to the record levels achieved in 1918 – there were 280,000 men in its ranks. 25,000 casualties were sustained.

Royal Corps of Signals

Originated 1908 as Royal Engineers Signal Service; Corps formed 1920.

The experience of the British Expeditionary Force was not a happy one for the Royal Corps of Signals. The anticipated re-run of the static conflict of the Great War meant that the emphasis during the winter of 1939/40 was placed upon building line communications, rather than on wireless work; indeed, use of the wireless was heavily restricted for security reasons. When the blitzkrieg struck North-West Europe therefore, the Signals were ill-prepared for the fluidity of action. It was not an entire disaster, but it was certainly a hard lesson in modern warfare.

Rapid and mobile combat was of course the dominant feature of North Africa. The speed with which advances could be made – 1,100 miles in four months during the East African campaign, 1,800 miles in six months after Alamein – meant that the wireless came to be an essential piece of equipment for all army units. The major problems came with maintenance and with recharging of batteries, problems that became ever more acute as the supply lines stretched further and further out into the difficult conditions of the desert.

Despite the reliance on the wireless, a decision was made early on to undertake a long-term programme of building a military network. Existing tele-communications, which were inevitably somewhat primitive and inadequate for the Army's needs, were gradually linked up to form a single military system centred on Cairo.

The entry of the United States brought new challenges to the Corps. American signallers soon out-numbered the British on joint operations where communication and co-operation was absolutely crucial, and signalling techniques had rapidly to be harmonized. The presence of the Americans also brought more unexpected consequences: British journalists began to realize that their American counter-parts were provided with better facilities than they, and it became the Signals' responsibility to pass copy on to the nearest civilian cable office for despatch.

In common with many of the Corps, the Signals found that much of the experience they gained in Sicily and Italy was to stand them in good stead in the battle for Northern Europe. In the invasion of Sicily, for example, underwater cables were laid to connect the island to Malta and to North Africa to facilitate safe lines of communication; a similar project in Normandy saw one speech and three telegraph cables connecting Britain to France, laid within four days of D-Day.

Similarly the exploitation of the existing system of underground telephone lines in Italy as the basis for a military network was repeated in Northern Europe. There were, however some new challenges: telecommunications in France and Germany were better developed than in the Mediterranean countries, but were also subject to more widespread sabotage.

And the experience of taking cables across rivers where the bridges had been blown by the retreating enemy was a problem common in both campaigns. In the case of narrower waterways, wires were suspended bank-to-bank, at other times they were strung out on whatever remained of the bridges, or were laid across the river bed; one cable across the Po spanned some 1,100 feet.

The use and expansion of an existing civilian network was also a feature of the Signals' work in Britain, where new line was added to the Post Office's system to bring the more outlying posts into contact with the chain of command. The one place where such a technique was not appropriate was in the Far East, where existing telecommunications were hopelessly inadequate for a jungle war that covered enormous areas; here communication by air became almost as important as the wireless.

At the outset, the Royal Corps of Signals could call upon 34,000 men, including territorials and reservists; by the end it had grown to 150,000 men and some 15,000 women of the ATS.

Grenadier Guards

Principal Battle Honours 1939-45

Dunkirk 1940 – Mont Pincon – Nijmegen – Rhine
Mareth – Medjez Plain – Salerno – Monte Camino
Anzio – Gothic Line

Raised 1660.

Comprising three regular battalions in 1939, the Grenadier Guards raised a further three during the course of the war, all of whom were to see active service. Of these, the 1st, 2nd and 3rd all served in the British Expeditionary Force and were evacuated from Dunkirk.

Whilst in Flanders, the 3rd fought a courageous defence of their position on the river Escaut, in which Lance-Corporal H Nicholls won the first Victoria Cross to be awarded in the conflict; firing a Bren-gun from the hip, he charged and destroyed three enemy machine-gun posts, before falling wounded. Early reports listed him as dead, but he later turned up as a prisoner-of-war.

The 3rd, 5th and 6th Battalions fought in North Africa, arriving separately between November 1942 and March 1943. The first to see action were the 3rd at the battle around Djebel Mansour in February 1943. As part of the 1st Guards Brigade, they constituted the most mobile section of the 1st Army and consequently fought across a wide range of the front. They were later to assist in the taking of Hammam Lif and Hammamet in the final stages of driving the enemy from North Africa.

The other battalions were also involved in key battles – the 5th at Djebel Bou Aoukaz, and the 6th at The Horseshoe, one of the key elements of the Mareth Line.

These same three battalions all subsequently moved on to Italy, the 6th arriving first, landing at Salerno in September 1943. Two months later they found themselves ordered to take and hold Monte Camino, a 2,500 foot peak occupied by the enemy. Against heavy opposition and in terrible weather conditions, the hill was duly taken and held, despite the problems of counter-attacks, dwindling ammunition and rations and even an earthquake. Of 483 men at the outset of the battle, only 263 were still there to withdraw five days later.

The 5th Battalion landed at Anzio in January 1944, where the resistance was much more intense than had been anticipated. In the first six weeks of fighting, the Battalion sustained 606 casualties and had to be reinforced by two companies from the 6th Battalion, recently disbanded. It returned to England in March 1945.

The 3rd Battalion, however, served out the rest of the war in Italy. Perhaps the most difficult of all its tasks was the siege of Monte Cassino. Sent in to relieve troops from New Zealand, the men found themselves amidst some of the most bitter and protracted warfare any British unit was to experience. The eventual break-through did not come until May 1944, some two months after the Grenadiers had taken possession of the network of cellars and bomb-shelters that constituted the Allied position.

Advancing up through Italy, the 3rd became the first battalion to cross the Po in April 1945.

By this stage, the 1st and 2nd Battalions had re-joined the fray. As the Grenadier Group, they had landed on D-Day, later being engaged in the battle to take Drouet Hill in August 1944. Some indication of the chaos of the times can be gained from the experience of the 4th Grenadiers, also in the Normandy landings, who were prevented from joining their comrades by the traffic jamming the roads of Northern France. (They did, however, arrive in time to help repulse the German counter-attack.)

The following month, the Grenadier Group was amongst the units advancing up to 100 miles in one day to liberate Brussels; its progress was delayed only by a bitter encounter with the SS at Pont à Marcq.

Soon after, they were in the forefront of the desperate struggle to break through Nijmegen to the troops stranded at Arnhem. Lieutenant-Colonel Horrocks was later to write that 'of the many battle honours which the Grenadier Guards can claim none can have been more richly deserved than Nijmegen.' [1]

Both the Grenadier Group and the 4th Battalion advanced into Germany. The last action of the Grenadier Group was a battle against the SS to liberate Sandbostel concentration camp.

[1] B Horrocks et al *Corps Commander* p.116

Coldstream Guards

Principal Battle Honours 1939-45

Dunkirk 1940 – Mont Pincon – Rhineland
North-West Europe 1940, 44-45 – Sidi Barrani
Tobruk 1941, 1942 – Tunis – Salerno
Monte Ornito – Italy 1943-45

Raised 1660.

Both the 1st and 2nd Battalions Coldstream Guards arrived in France in October 1939 as part of the British Expeditionary Force, and spent the next seven months on the Franco-Belgian border before advancing the following May.

Despite long planning, the situation they found was one of total confusion. The 1st Battalion took up three separate positions around Louvain on consecutive days, unable either to establish stability or to rest, and often finding its instructions disputed by the host nation's army. When the German attack came on 14 May, the Belgian forces were immediately pulled back, and an order came for the Coldstream to do the same. The following day the order was countermanded and the position was retaken from the enemy, only to be abandoned again with the general withdrawal on the 16th.

From there on, the experience was one of seemingly endless retreat, most of it undertaken on foot, across Belgium and Northern France. Captain Pilkington of the 2nd Coldstream later wrote of that nightmare:

'Weariness came down like a board on our heads. As I marched my eyes kept closing, and I knew that I was walking about like a drunkard. After a little, nausea overcame me, and I fell out for a few minutes. When we halted for a ten minutes' rest I lay flat on the cold wet road and found a few minutes' relief.' [1]

For the last six miles into Dunkirk, the 2nd Battalion was provided with lorries, offering at last a chance for some rest since the roads were so jammed that it took four hours to cover the distance.

Both battalions fought on the Bergue-Furnes Canal, protecting the perimeter of Dunkirk, before being evacuated.

The 1st Coldstream, now converted to an armoured battalion, were to return to North Europe in 1944, as part of the Guards Armoured Division. Also in that division was the 5th Battalion, a newly-raised lorried infantry unit. For nearly two months, the two battalions fought through the struggle in Normandy over the hazardous bocage terrain that proved so difficult for armoured combat.

On 30 August the division began the drive north from the Seine to Brussels, an advance where the major problem was not so much the enemy as the large numbers of civilian well-wishers. Thereafter the fighting began again, with the German army defending the fatherland in depth.

Another new battalion, the 4th, had been formed as an armoured battalion, equipped with Churchill infantry tanks, and it too served in the North European campaign.

The 3rd Battalion had been stationed in Alexandria at the outset of the war, and fought through the various North African campaigns. Stationed at Mersa Matruh, it was involved in the initial skirmishing around the border country and then, in September 1940, in trying to repulse the Italian invasion. By now the battalion had taken under its command a motor company containing the first Free French troops to fight in the war.

For the 3rd Coldstream, the ebb and flow of the desert war came to a climax in May 1941, with the establishment of the famous Knightsbridge box outside Tobruk. Nine days of preparation – constructing trenches and wire fences, laying mine-fields and digging in guns – were followed by a 17 day assault by the Afrika Korps, fiercely resisted until the position became untenable. The battle, conducted in intense heat amidst dust storms that could completely obscure an enemy attack, was celebrated in a song written by Sergeant G Burton:

'Twas in the Box at Knightsbridge
Where the Guardsmen made their stand,
Where shot and shell were firing
And Death walked hand in hand.
The Germans were around them,
With their Stukas in the sky;
And as the Bosche drew nearer
They prepared to do or die.' [2]

In the ensuing collapse of Tobruk, the Commanding Officer was captured early on, and Major Santhill took over command. Refusing to accept that surrender was the only option, he instructed the battalion to break out: 'Head roughly due south, drive hard, shoot hard and go right through in a confusion of dust and bullets.' [3] Of some 600 men who entered Tobruk, there were nine casualties and 388 taken prisoner, whilst 200 escaped. Maj Santhill was awarded the DSO for his actions.

On the other side of the theatre, the 2nd Battalion arrived with Operation Torch in November 1942. Perhaps its most distinguished contribution came in the first assault on Longstop Hill, one of the key features in Tunisia. Taking the higher of the two peaks on 22 December, the Coldstream were relieved by American troops. Unfortunately a German counter necessitated a return to the hill and further bloody fighting before the whole operation was called off. The battalion had sustained

178 casualties in three days, including the Commanding Officer and four other senior officers.

Both the 2nd and 3rd Coldstream went on to fight in the final stages of the African war and then to move to Italy.

[1] Howard & Sparrow *The Coldstream Guards* 1920-1946 p.47

[2] Quilter *'No Dishonourable Name'* p.151

[3] Howard & Sparrow op. cit. p.102

Scots Guards

Principal Battle Honours 1939-45

Quarry Hill – Rhineland – North West Europe 1944-45
Gazala – Medenine – Djebel Bou Aoukaz 1943, I
North Africa 1941-43 – Monte Camino – Anzio
Italy 1943-45

Raised 1660.

Comprising two regular battalions in peace-time, the Scots Guards raised a further three battalions during the Second World War, though not all were to see action.

The 1st Battalion, Scots Guards served in the first British action of the war, the doomed campaign to protect Norway from German occupation. With a landing on 16 April 1940, the expedition lasted for less than three weeks before the men were evacuated.

Even before this, however, a 5th Battalion was raised in early 1940 as a ski unit, intended for Finland in response to the Soviet invasion of that country the previous November. Fortunately – given the general level of British preparedness – the attempted salvation of Finland was put firmly off the agenda by its capitulation, thus ensuring that the Soviet Union was not added to the ranks of Britain's enemies. The battalion, which had recruited experienced skiers not only from the Scots Guards but also from the whole army and even from civilians, was disbanded after a period of training in France.

The 2nd Battalion had more direct early involvement in the war, serving in North Africa from April 1941 onwards. Its participation, however, was temporarily halted at Gazala the following year; the power of the 21st Panzer Division proved too great and the anti-tank batteries were over-run. When the advance in the wake of El Alamein brought Allied forces back to the battlefield, the bodies of the men were discovered still at their posts. A witness to this ghostly spectacle later wrote:

'A position which impressed me greatly was the 6 pounder anti-tank positions manned by the Scots Guards. They must have fired their guns until the German tanks were right on top of them. Almost every gun had the body of a Scots Guardsman drooped across the shoulder piece or slumped over the breech.' [1]

Following a period of re-building, the battalion was to return and on 6 March

1943 met the 21st Panzer Division again at Medenine. This time the result was very different, with 15 enemy tanks being destroyed.

Whilst in North Africa, the 2nd Scots Guards contributed some of the first men to join the newly-formed SAS, whose leader, David Stirling, was himself from the regiment.

The 1st Battalion also fought in North Africa, landing in Tunisia as part of the campaign to open a second front. At the battle of Djebel Bou Aoukaz on 27 April 1943, Lieutenant (temporary Captain) The Lord Lyall was posthumously awarded the Victoria Cross for his single-handed attack on an enemy position, taking out a heavy machine gun and an 88mm gun, and facilitating the further advance of his company.

Both the 1st and 2nd Battalions went on to Italy, landing at Anzio and Salerno respectively. The 2nd were involved in the taking of Monte Camino and in the battle at Cassino, perhaps the most desperate struggle of Western Europe.

Nonetheless there was still time for recreation, and it is reported that some officers succeeded in organising a duck shoot for the New Year. Tales also survive of the battalion's Intelligence Officer, whose excursions into enemy territory yielded some curious booty, including on one occasion a full bridal dress which, with traditional British humour, he later wore to dinner.

With the shift of focus to North-West Europe, the battalion was withdrawn from Italy to serve in France.

Already in that campaign was the newly-raised 3rd Battalion, who landed at Normandy in Churchill tanks. By the time the Germans surrendered, it had fought its way through to the Elbe. Officers serving in the campaign included such later luminaries as Robert Runcie and William Whitelaw.

Also newly-raised was the 4th Battalion, formed in 1941. It was disbanded before it could be posted, though two companies did survive: 'S' Company served with the 2nd Battalion, Coldstream Guards in Italy, whilst 'X' Company served with the 3rd Battalion, Irish Guards and then with 1st Battalion, Welsh Guards in North West Europe.

The hostilities cost the Regiment the lives of 98 officers and 943 other ranks.

[1] Goodinge *The Scots Guards* p.102

Irish Guards

Principal Battle Honours 1939-45

Norway 1940 – Boulogne 1940 – Mont Pinchon – Neerpelt
Nijmegen – Rhineland – North-West Europe 1944-45
Djebel Bou Aoukaz 1943 – North Africa 1943 – Anzio

Raised 1900.

The 1st and 2nd Battalions, Irish Guards were involved in the two disastrous campaigns of 1940, in Norway and France.

The 1st landed at Harstad, in the north of Norway, on 15 April 1940 and spent the next six weeks awaiting orders to engage the enemy, before being evacuated in June with only the briefest of contacts having been made. In fact the major incident of the guardsmen's stay was one over which they had no control: the bombing of the Polish motor ship *Chobry* on which they were embarked. Casualties were relatively few in number but devastating in effect: the Commanding Officer, Second-in-Command, Adjutant and three Company Commanders were all killed, with the remaining two Company Commanders wounded.

Around the same time, the 2nd Battalion made two expeditions to the European mainland. Early on 13 May the battalion, its numbers augmented by 200 men from the 2nd Welsh Guards to cover those on leave in Ireland, landed at Hook of Holland with instructions to proceed to the Hague as reinforcements. On arrival, however, it became apparent that such an operation was not feasible, and the men were evacuated the next day, their role reduced to escorting the Dutch Royal Family and members of the British Embassy from the continent.

A week later, this time in the company of the entire 2nd Welsh Guards, they sailed for Boulogne to cover the withdrawal of Allied personnel. The odds were stacked against the guardsmen, with just four 2-pdr guns in the battalion to hold off a German armoured division, and casualties were high: some 200 reported killed, wounded or missing. But the resistance offered was significant, and the German High Command described the battle for Boulogne as 'a grim fight'.

Posted to Tunisia in March 1943, the 1st Battalion made its presence felt immediately with typically boisterous celebrations of St Patrick's Day, before settling in for the real business at hand. Though the North African war was entering its final phase, the Germans were not inclined to relinquish the field without a fight, and the men were plunged into the struggle centred on the Medjez Valley, the key approach route to Tunis.

On 27 March an attack by No. 2 Company was ordered on a German-held position known as Recce Ridge. That day illustrated how dangerous a lack of secure communication could be; the attack was expected by the Germans and of 103 men, only seven returned.

Less than a month later, there was an even more hazardous assault. In the attempt to wrest control of the peak Djebel Bou Auokaz from the enemy, the battalion's task was to advance across a plain well-covered by German guns to take two key foothills. Under fire so intense that one guardsman remarked 'they threw everything but their cap-badges at us' [1], the men succeeded in taking one of the objectives, but at a terrible cost; only 173 all ranks were left. Despite reinforcements, two days of enemy counter-attack reduced that number to just 80. But the fighting was by no means one-sided, and when the Germans finally abandoned the position, they left behind more than 700 dead.

It was during this action that Lance-Corporal (later Sergeant) John Kenneally won his Victoria Cross, the citation stating: 'His extraordinary gallantry in attacking single-handed a massed body of the enemy and breaking up an attack on two occasions was an achievement that can seldom have been equalled.' [2]

Such desperate experiences of war are, of course, the traditional lot of the infantry, and the 1st Battalion, reduced to a single company by the Bou, soon rebuilt and made its return to the front-line, this time in Italy. A total of 1,080 guardsmen, including reinforcements, landed at Anzio in January 1944; by the time the battalion was pulled out in late February, there were just 267 left fighting fit.

Soon after St Patrick's Day 1944, the 1st Battalion was withdrawn to England. Its overseas tour had lasted barely more than a year, but in that time it had faced potential annihilation on two separate occasions and had survived.

Ensuring that the Irish Guards remained in the forefront of the war against Nazism, the 2nd and 3rd Battalions formed part of the famous Guards Armoured Division that fought with such distinction in the second North-West European campaign of 1944-45. By September 1944 the two battalions had come together to form The Irish Group.

[1] Verney *The Micks* p.112

[2] Fitzgerald *History of the Irish Guards in the Second World War* p.183

Welsh Guards

Principal Battle Honours 1939-45

Defence of Arras – Boulogne 1940 – Mont Pincon
Brussels – Hechtel – Fondouk – Hamman Lif
Monte Ornito – Monte Piccolo

Raised 1915.

The 1st and 2nd Battalions of the Welsh Guards fought in both North-West European campaigns. The 1st saw its initial battle at Arras in Belgium to where it had advanced on 17 May 1940. The arrival of the enemy on 20 May heralded three days of spirited defence, despite the usual problems of the time, which meant on occasion that GHQ could only be contacted via the War Office in London. When the signal came to withdraw, the battalion covered the retreat from the town, an action for which Lieutenant the Hon Christopher Furness was awarded a posthumous Victoria Cross.

Around the same time, the 2nd Battalion was just arriving in France, landing at Boulogne on 22 May alongside the 2nd Irish Guards. Their task was to hold the perimeter of the town during the evacuations. Having been assured that heavy guns, transport and equipment were awaiting them, the men were rushed across the Channel with just their personal weapons, only to find on arrival that there wasn't even an accurate map that could be used. Nonetheless the position was held until evacuation was ordered.

Unfortunately Major J C Windsor Lewis did not receive the command in time and turned up at the quay to discover that the last boat had gone. Gathering together what troops he could find, he staged a final defence until his force was overwhelmed. He was wounded but later escaped to England. Others were not so fortunate – 453 men from the two battalions were captured.

Newly promoted, Lieutenant-Colonel Windsor Lewis led the 2nd Welsh Guards back to France in June 1944. Its role was now that of an armoured battalion within the Guards Armoured Division, equipped with Cromwell and Honey tanks. In the same division was the 1st Battalion, serving as lorried infantry.

The two battalions were both in the 100-mile advance to reach Brussels on 3 September, fighting three actions along the way and capturing hundreds of prisoners in that astonishing day. Prior to that, the 2nd Battalion had completed another lightning strike, driving 135 miles in 48 hours to the Seine, where the change in terrain from the bocage country of Normandy and the disarray of the enemy made for easy pickings: in a single day No. 1 Squadron took 500 prisoners and accounted for 100 German dead.

Both battalions were also involved in the battle to take the village of Hechtel which was strongly defended by crack enemy troops and took four days to overcome.

Further heavy fighting followed in Holland and Germany, particularly in the treacherous conditions of the Reichswald Forest, but there were easier times as well. On 1 March 1945, the 1st Battalion War Diary recorded:

'St David's Day but nothing much to show for it. Companies have been feeding so well lately that it was difficult to make dinners any better than they would have been in any case.' [1]

For the 3rd Battalion, then fighting its way through the solid German lines in Italy, things were not so comfortable.

Formed in October 1941, the 3rd Welsh Guards had been sent to Algeria in February 1943 and won battle honours at Fondouk and Hamman Lif. At the former the Adjutant, Captain G D Rhys-Williams, rallied the demoralised troops and led a victorious charge to take Djebel el Rhorab, losing his life in the process.

A long period of inactivity followed the fall of Tunis, a period mostly devoted to training, though some light relief was obtained in the form of the occasional race meeting and even an Eisteddfod.

When the battalion was eventually sent to join the Italian campaign in February 1944, it was plunged immediately into the fighting around Ornito on the Gustav Line. In a typical action, a position was taken on Monte Cerasola and held for two weeks against German counters, until the men were relieved. The key problem, as elsewhere in Italy, was one of supply lines up the mountain. This was especially acute for the wounded, whose journey back down to base could take up to 36 hours under enemy fire.

A similar encounter followed at Monte Piccolo, where Lance-Sergeant Frank Goodwin displayed immense personal courage in charging an enemy machine-gun post. He eventually silenced it, thus enabling his comrades to advance, by throwing himself on top of the gun.

During the siege of Cassino, the proximity of the enemy lines demanded confidential communications, a situation to which the guardsmen responded by sending all radio messages in Welsh. The Germans, however, had linguistics experts available and within 24 hours propaganda leaflets were being dropped. The leaflets were written in flawless Urdu. [2]

The 3rd Welsh Guards remained with the advancing Allies through to the end of the war, reaching Austria by May 1945.

[1] L F Ellis *Welsh Guards At War* p.273

[2] J Ellis *Cassino: The Hollow Victory* p.276

The Royal Scots (The Royal Regiment)

Principal Battle Honours 1939-45

Defence of Escaut – Odon – Aart – Flushing – Rhine
North-West Europe 1940, 1944-45 – Gothic Line
Italy 1944-45 – Kohima – Burma 1943-45

Raised 1633 (early years spent mostly in French service);
renamed The Royal Scots 1881.

The senior regiment in the Army, in common with so many Scottish infantry regiments, suffered heavily in the first years of the war, with both regular battalions taking the full brunt of enemy assault.

The 1st Battalion was sent to France in September 1939, and spent the long cold winter of the 'Phoney War' preparing to advance into Belgium when the German attack came. In the event, of course, the advance was rapidly turned into retreat, and the 1st Royal Scots found themselves fighting a series of rearguard actions. Ordered to defend the evacuations that followed, they were surrounded and the survivors taken prisoner.

The speed and success of the German advance had not been anticipated and the retreat across unsuitable terrain was chaotic in the extreme, with major traffic congestion adding to the Army's problems. Symbolic, at times, of the almost surreal confusion was the hitting of a passing circus, recorded by the Adjutant, Captain Bruce in his diary:

'We have vivid recollections of three wounded elephants charging in terror through the fields. They were followed hotly by four white Liberty horses dragging the unconscious figure of a girl rider.' [1]

The 2nd Battalion was also captured by the enemy. Stationed in Hong Kong, the men of the battalion were the first British troops to face the Japanese. The siege of the colony lasted for two and a half weeks before the garrison finally surrendered on Christmas Day 1941. The difficulties of defending Hong Kong made defeat inevitable, but it was nonetheless a desperate and hard-fought battle; the 2nd Royal Scots were reduced by the end to just four officers and 98 other ranks.

Both battalions were re-formed at home – the new 2nd from the 12th Battalion – and saw further action. The 1st were posted to India in 1942 and joined the campaign in the Arakan region in March the following year. That campaign proved unsuccessful and the battalion suffered heavy casualties; of an original complement of 700 men, subsequently reinforced by a further 500, just 400 returned unwounded.

When the struggle was resumed in the 1944 fighting season, the story was different. The 1st Royal Scots assisted in the lifting of the siege of Kohima in the middle of the year, and spent the next months in pursuit of the retreating Japanese forces.

By the time the battalion crossed the Irrawaddy in February 1945, the enemy was effectively beaten in Burma, with just 20,000 Japanese troops remaining. With their part played, and with battalion pride restored, the 1st Royal Scots returned to India.

The 2nd Battalion, meanwhile, was fighting in Europe. Posted to Gibralta in 1943, it was sent into the Italian campaign the following year. The struggle around the Gothic Line was entering a critical phase, and in September the 2nd Royal Scots were thrown into a major assault on the German lines. Attacks on Monte Pratone and Monte Pagiano were rewarded with the taking of the latter, though the offensive failed to yield the decisive result that had been sought.

With the regular battalions engaged in Burma and Italy, it fell to the territorials to contribute to the liberation of North-West Europe. The 8th Battalion fought with the 15th Scottish Division from June 1944 onwards, being awarded a battle honour at the River Odon, where they helped open what was known as the Scottish Corridor.

A further battle honour was won at the crossing of the Rhine in 1945, in which both the 8th and the 7th/9th Royal Scots served.

[1] Brander *The Royal Scots (The Royal Regiment)* p.83

The Queen's Royal Regiment (West Surrey)

Principal Battle Honours 1939-45

Villers Bocage – Tobruk 1941 – El Alamein – Medenine
Monte Camino – Anzio – Gemmano Ridge
North Arakan – Kohima

Raised 1661; amalgamated to form Queen's Royal Surrey Regiment 1959;
amalgamated to form The Queen's Regiment 1966; amalgamated to form
The Princess of Wales's Royal Regiment 1993.

With the mobilization and expansion of the territorial army in anticipation of the coming conflict, the Queen's Royal Regiment brought six territorial battalions into what was soon to be the front-line. Unusually these six – organized into 131 Queen's Brigade and 35 Queen's Brigade – were to see more action than the regular battalions.

Both new brigades were posted to France in April 1940. Despite its late arrival, the 131 Brigade fought at Escaut and Dendre during the retreat to Dunkirk. The men of the 35 Brigade, on the other hand, were never intended as combat troops, serving instead in the Lines of Communication far back from what was expected to be the front-line. With the German drive through the Ardennes, they were sent forward to Abbeyville; with a desperate lack of training, equipment and support, however, they were clearly no match for the triumphant Germans, and were soon evacuated.

The 2nd Battalion, meanwhile, was in the Western Desert awaiting the commencement of hostilities with Italy. It played its part in the first British offensive of the North African war, fighting at Sidi Barrani and Bardia, before being withdrawn to assist the defence of Crete. In fact, the battalion never made it to the island, the Luftwaffe successfully preventing the troop carriers making the journey.

The 2nd West Surreys returned to the desert long enough to win a battle honour in the struggle to relieve Tobruk, and were then posted to the Far East in 1942.

The same year, 131 Queen's Brigade arrived to join the 8th Army. As a lorried infantry unit, it fought at El Alamein and in the pursuit across the desert, leading the advance from Tripoli to the Mareth Line. It was there, at Medenine, that the brigade faced its strongest test. Two Panzer divisions turned from the withdrawal to face the pursuers, but without much success; 131 Brigade knocked out 27 enemy tanks.

Also with the 8th Army by now was 135 Queen's Brigade – the old 35th Brigade renamed and posted overseas in late 1942. Initially stationed in Iraq, it advanced more than 3,300 miles in just 31 days to join the front-line, fighting at Enfidaville.

Both brigades served in the invasion of Italy, landing at Salerno, though 131 Brigade was withdrawn in December 1943 to return to England. 135 Queen's Brigade remained to prosecute the war in Italy. It was involved in some of the toughest battles of the conflict, at Monte Camino and the crossing of the Garigliano, and was in Venice when the Germans surrendered.

131 Queen's Brigade landed in Normandy two days after D-Day, winning yet another battle honour for the regiment at Villers Bocage. Two of the constituent battalions were finally withdrawn from action in December 1944, but the other – the 1/5th Battalion – fought right through the North-West European campaign, ending the war in Hamburg, where it proudly raised the regimental flag over the captured Town Hall.

Elsewhere the 1st Battalion was in Waziristan, engaged in policing the North-West Frontier: a thankless task but one which – in the light of reports that the Fakir of Ipi was under the influence of German advisers – was clearly necessary.

More spectacular was the Arakan campaign that commenced in late 1943. The 1st West Surreys established Braganza Box, a defensive position that withstood the Japanese offensive of 1944. That year also, the battalion helped relieve the siege of Kohima, before returning for a period of recovery to India. In March 1945 it was back in Burma for the final stages of the campaign, crossing the Irrawaddy and fighting around the Sittang river.

The 2nd Battalion also served in Burma in the 1944 Chindits campaign.

The Buffs (Royal East Kent Regiment)

Principal Battle Honours 1939-45

North-West Europe 1940 – Alam Hamza – El Alamein
Robaa Valley – Sicily 1943 – Trigno – Anzio
Argenta Gap – Shweli

Raised 1572 for Dutch service; taken into King's service 1685;
amalgamated to form The Queen's Own Buffs 1961; amalgamated
to form The Queen's Regiment 1966; amalgamated to form
The Princess of Wales's Royal Regiment 1993.

In 1939 The Buffs could lay claim to being the oldest regiment in the British Army, and their service in the war added several chapters to their distinguished history. The 1st Battalion, stationed in the Middle East, first saw action in June 1941 in the failed effort to relieve Tobruk. Advancing some 60 miles, Fort Capuzzo was taken and held for two days until a withdrawal was ordered.

The most notable encounter was to come in December of that year. During the battle of Alam Hamza, The Buffs successfully seized a hill known as Point 204, but were isolated when the nearby Point 208 was held by the enemy. The following day the Germans counter-attacked in force. For more than 24 hours the position was held. The Buffs inflicted heavy damage on the enemy who succeeded in wiping out almost the whole of the 105th Lorried Infantry Regiment. With dwindling ammunition, however, there was no way for a weakened infantry battalion to resist the advance of a Panzer Regiment. The position was over-run; of 550 men who had started the battle, casualties and prisoners accounted for all but 39.

A period of rebuilding followed – so successful that the battalion earned the nickname The Resurrectionists, and was ready to fight again at El Alamein. Alongside New Zealand troops, it fought too at El Hamma.

In February 1944 the 1st Buffs were sent to Anzio to reinforce the bridgehead that had been so hard fought for. The remainder of the war was to be spent in Italy.

The tag The Resurrectionists was appropriate to much of the regiment, particularly to the three battalions in the BEF, all of whom suffered high losses. The order to withdraw did not reach the 2nd Battalion, who were holding a position at Meteren, and many of the men, including the Commanding Officer, were taken prisoner. The 4th and 5th Battalions, stationed well back from the frontline, were also caught in the German sweep through the south. The former lost most of two companies and only just escaped from Cherbourg, whilst the latter were over-run with less than 80 men returning. All three were to rebuild and return.

The 2nd Buffs spent some time in North Africa, fighting at El Alamein and providing the British guard of honour at the Tehran Conference in November 1943, the first of the historic meetings between the three Great Powers.

The following year the battalion transferred to the third great theatre of war, the Far East, where a battle honour was won at the crossing of the river Shweli in 1945. It was intended to be an unopposed crossing, but turned into a major struggle, in which a bridgehead was established but proved to be unsustainable.

The 4th Battalion served on Malta during the siege of that island. The campaign was conducted by air and sea, but the support provided by infantry – rebuilding air-strips etc. – was invaluable.

In September 1943, with the agreement of the new Italian government, British troops were sent in to take the Dodecanese islands. The 4th Buffs sailed for Leros, though a ship carrying one company was sunk before it could arrive. For those who did arrive, the future too was bleak. A German assault succeeded in forcing the islands' surrender, and virtually the whole battalion was taken prisoner.

The 5th Battalion also saw active service in the Mediterranean. It landed as part of Operation Torch in North-West Africa, and fought at the battle to take Longstop Hill in April 1943. Nearly 100 casualties were sustained, but at the expense of many more of the enemy and with 300 prisoners taken.

The battalion later contributed to the Sicilian invasion and the Italian campaign.

The King's Own Royal Regiment (Lancaster)

Principal Battle Honours 1939-1945:

Dunkirk 1940 – North-West Europe 1940
Defence of Habbaniya – Merjayun – Tobruk Sortie
North Africa 1940-42 – Montone – Lamone Bridgehead
Malta 1941-42 – Chindits 1944

Raised 1680; amalgamated to form
The King's Own Border Regiment 1959.

Most of the fighting undertaken by The King's Own Royal Regiment was in the Mediterranean and North Africa, but the 5th Battalion did serve in the British Expeditionary Force. Helping in the defence of the Dunkirk perimeter, it was amongst the last units to be evacuated.

For one of the men, Private Roberts, the return from France was not so easily accomplished. Captured by the Germans, he managed to escape only to find that the retreat had passed him by, and he was unable to find the British forces. Taken prisoner again, he once more escaped, and spent some months wandering across France alone, reaching Spain in April 1941. He finally got a passage back to Britain as a stowaway.

Also in the BEF were four territorial battalions of the regiment in a Pioneers capacity. One of these, the 8th Battalion, was later stationed in Malta during the siege of that island, winning a battle honour for its work there.

Of the regular battalions, the 1st King's Own were flown into Habbaniya air-base in Iraq in April 1941. Soon after their arrival, the rebel forces of Raschid Ali laid siege to the base, but were repulsed and the rebellion effectively broken.

The following year saw the 1st Battalion in North Africa, fighting at Halfaya Pass and later at Tobruk. Disaster, however, was soon to strike. Travelling via Cyprus, the men were sent in to take the tiny Aegean island of Leros, believed to be under threat from German forces in Italy. The Germans did in fact arrive shortly afterwards and took the island in three days of conflict. 75 men of the battalion were killed, with many more taken prisoner; just one officer and 57 other ranks escaped. They were later augmented by veterans of the 8th Battalion, and the 1st was re-born.

Early in 1944 the new 1st Battalion joined the war in Italy, where the first major battle was fought at Montone. This hill town had resisted previous attempts to dislodge the German occupiers, but the 1st King's Own, advancing 12 miles in a single-file night-march, staged a dawn attack that took the defenders by complete surprise. Six hours of close fighting resulted in the taking of the town, and the awarding of the battle-honour 'Montone', The King's Own Royal Regiment being the only unit to carry the honour.

The 1st fought on in Italy until the close of the war, ending up at Gorizia, before being moved to the Tyrol to supervise enemy prisoners.

The 2nd Battalion had also served in North Africa, this time in the early tussles around the Egyptian-Libyan border against the Italians. The men fought at Sidi Barrani and were later sent in by sea to reinforce the besieged garrison of Tobruk, and then to assist the break-out from that town.

The following year, the battalion was posted to Ceylon to commence a process of jungle training that culminated in the 1944 Chindits operation. Flying in by glider some 150 miles behind the Japanese front-line, the men subsequently covered over 1,000 miles in its harrying of the enemy's supply lines. By the time the battalion was pulled out at the end of July, it was severely weakened by casualties and by disease and spent the remainder of the war in India in an internal security role.

The regiment's only involvement in the campaign to liberate North-West Europe came with the 5th Battalion, now re-named the 107th Regiment, Royal Armoured Corps (King's Own). Landing on 1 July 1944, equipped with the lumbering Churchill infantry tanks, the battalion fought in the lengthy battle to take Caen, and later at Falaise and the Reichswald Forest.

The Royal Northumberland Fusiliers

Principal Battle Honours 1939-45

Dunkirk 1940 – Caen – Rhineland – Sidi Barrani
Defence of Tobruk – Tobruk 1941 – Cauldron
El Alamein – Salerno – Cassino II

Raised 1674; amalgamated to form The Royal Regiment of Fusiliers 1968.

Though the bulk of The Royal Northumberland Fusiliers' fighting was in the Mediterranean theatre, there were four battalions in the British Expeditionary Force in France, including the 7th Battalion in the 51st (Highland) Division and the 2nd who fought as a machine-gun unit at Dunkirk.

The regiment's first success came with the 1st Battalion, also a machine-gun unit, in Wavell's offensive in the Western Desert in 1940/41. Its progress was such that when German troops landed in Africa, the men of 'Y' Company were amongst the most advanced of the Allied forces, with No. 12 Platoon – over-run by the tanks of the Afrika Korps – being the first casualties of Rommel's counter-attack. The battalion was forced back, and on 9 April 1941 entered Tobruk, where it was to remain for the duration of the eight month siege.

With the first flurry of action failing to break the defence of the town, the men settled down to a routine where the main enemies were the heat, the ubiquitous flies and the sheer tedium, aggravated by a lack of recreation and fresh food. An early water shortage, however, was solved by the distillation of sea water.

When the orders came to fight their way out of the town and link up with the advancing armies of Operation Crusader, the men were plunged into some of the heaviest fighting they were to encounter. At El Duda Ridge their determination was such that a total of 12 awards for gallantry were won, including a Victoria Cross awarded posthumously to Captain Jackman.

1941 ended on a high note for the Allies, but Rommel was far from beaten. The following May an Axis offensive broke through the Gazala Line, where the 4th Northumberland Fusiliers were amongst the defending troops. In the fire of the Cauldron, the battalion's Commanding Officer was killed; an eye-witness account describes the incident:

'Lieut-Colonel des Graz appeared over the ridge, standing in a carrier, and drove straight up to a gun. He jumped out and brought the gun into action . . . . The [enemy] tank stopped and opened fire, scoring two hits on the gun shield from a range of about one hundred yards . . . . Colonel des Graz was standing immediately behind the 2-pr. and he and two of the crew were hit.' [1]

The level of casualties across the whole battalion was such that, by the time it had been pushed back to the Alamein Line, it was effectively finished as a fighting unit and was withdrawn, to be re-built later at home and to serve in North-West Europe.

It was thus left to the 1st Battalion to take up the struggle again at El Alamein and in the ensuing advance to Tunisia. After a year touring some of the quieter parts of the Middle East, the battalion returned to the front-line in Italy in March 1944.

Already involved in that campaign was the 2nd Battalion which, equipped with heavy mortars and anti-aircraft guns, had won a battle honour in the heavily opposed landing at Salerno. Further fighting, particularly at the crossing of the Volturno, was followed by an involvement in the Greek civil war.

In the war with Japan, the regiment had only a minor though traumatic role. Arriving in Singapore too late to make any serious contribution, it lost 22 men in action; a further 151 were to die in captivity after the surrender of the island. A few, however, evaded capture: Major B J Leech and six others were dispatched to keep the battalion's name alive, escaping in a dinghy on an 80 mile journey to Sumatra.

When the survivors of the Japanese prison-camps paraded in Rangoon immediately after their release, Major-General Thomas paid tribute to their spirit and dignity:

'I have heard how simply marvellous they were in captivity – they even won the admiration of the Japanese . . . . When they came through here every man had his cap badge polished as for ceremonial parades. I don't think I have met a finer battalion before or since.' [2]

[1] Barclay *History of The Royal Northumberland Fusiliers in the Second World War* p.82

[2] Peacock *The Royal Northumberland Fusiliers* p.97

The Royal Warwickshire Regiment

Principal Battle Honours 1939-45

Defence of Escaut – Wormhoudt – Ypres-Comines Canal
Normandy Landing – Caen – Mont Pincon – Venraij
Bremen – North-West Europe 1940, 44-45 – Burma 1945

Raised 1673; amalgamated to form The Royal Regiment of Fusiliers 1968.

The 2nd Battalion of The Royal Warwickshire Regiment was joined in the BEF by two territorial battalions, the 1/7th and the 8th; all three were to suffer heavy losses.

Initially, however, the usual problems were the familiar ones of cold, boredom and inactivity. When the German offensive did commence, the regiment's early role was largely confined to dealing with the huge number of refugees fleeing back from the Low Countries and the concomitant confusion. In one incident, three priests were picked up by the 1/7th Battalion and, suspected of being 5th Columnists, were interrogated at length by the Padre, before being declared to be genuine.

By the time the battalions were sent forward, their task was essentially that of covering the retreat. The dangers of that work were emphasised on 19 May 1940, when German dive-bombers attacked a jammed road at Tournai, killing large numbers of refugees and troops. The next two days saw all three battalions engaged in a bitter and costly fight at Hollain on the river Escaut. The German advance was halted, but the 2nd Battalion emerged with half its number killed or wounded. The loss of so many experienced officers and men was compounded by the departure of the Commanding Officer, who had been suffering with a stomach ulcer that burst during the battle.

Worse was yet to come. The 1/7th and 8th Battalions fought valiantly around the Ypres-Comines Canal on 27 May, incurring yet more casualties, whilst the 2nd was halted at Wormhoudt, 12 miles south of Dunkirk, to cover the evacuation. The order read: 'Hold your present positions at all costs, to the last man and the last round.' [1] It was an order fulfilled almost to the letter.

On 28 May a Waffen-SS assault on the town was fiercely resisted, but proved unstoppable. The positions were soon surrounded and many men were taken prisoner. A number of them – together with a few prisoners from the Royal Artillery and the Cheshire Regiment, a total of about 90 men – were taken by the

105

Germans to a barn, and there murdered. Grenades were thrown into the barn, men were dragged out and shot, and the few survivors left for dead. Perhaps a dozen or so survived, but unlike the survivors of the similar massacre of the 2nd Norfolks, were unable to convince the authorities to prosecute those responsible.

When the 2nd Battalion reorganized at Dunkirk to be evacuated, just 141 all ranks remained. The 1/7th Battalion was reduced to 235, and the 8th to 142.

Despite these losses, both the 2nd and 1/7th Battalions were to return to Europe for the Normandy campaign.

On 7 June 1944 the 2nd was sent in to clear Lebisey Wood, on the way to Caen. Unfortunately a battalion of Panzer Grenadiers had dug into positions in the wood the night before and, lacking proper support and communication, the 2nd Warwicks took casualties of ten officers and 144 men, including the death of the Commanding Officer. Much of the next month was spent in the same area, in the slow process of weeding out the opposition.

Both battalions were to join the successful Operation Charnwood that finally took Caen. Colonel Jerram of the 1/7th has left an account of the battle that gives some indication of the weight of the firing involved:

'The roar . . . was terrific. It was quite impossible to hear any one gun or shell or another man speak; there was just a surging roar and the whole landscape was blotted out in smoke and dust.' [2]

The 1/7th was disbanded in August 1944, but many of the men went on to serve with the 2nd Battalion, who fought all the way through the campaign to reach Bremen by the end of the war. The men's actions there earned them the congratulations of perhaps the most famous former member of the regiment, Field Marshal Montgomery.

An equally distinguished general who had also served with the Warwicks in the Great War was Field Marshal Slim. During the Second World War he commanded the forces in Burma, the major contribution of the regiment to the Far Eastern campaign. The 1st Battalion was stationed in India, but was mostly kept on internal policing duties. When it was finally sent forward, it was on Operation Dracula, a river assault on Rangoon that proved unnecessary – the landing was made without a single shot being fired.

[1] Aitken *Massacre on the Road to Dunkirk* p.52

[2] Cunliffe *History of The Royal Warwickshire Regiment* 1919-1955 p.92

The Royal Fusiliers
(City of London Regiment)

Principal Battle Honours 1939-45

Dunkirk 1940 – North Africa 1940, 43 – Mozzagrogna
Salerno – Garigliano Crossing – Anzio – Cassino II
Gothic Line – Coriano

Raised 1685; amalgamated to form The Royal Regiment of Fusiliers 1968.

The Royal Fusiliers' first battle honour of the war was won by the 2nd Battalion in the defence of Dunkirk. Having marched over 30 miles in a single night, carrying heavy equipment and their weapons, the men were ordered to stop and defend the perimeter. By the end of the encounter, there were just 150 men left to be evacuated.

The 1st Royal Fusiliers had been posted from India to North Africa in 1939 and were to fight at Sidi Barrani. Then, in early 1941, came a move to East Africa, where they saw action in the battle to take Keren. The conditions on that bleak mountainside were described by Major Searight:

'Rations of water had to be carried up by the men of the reserve company from the dump over a thousand feet below. Both food and water were therefore extremely short. By day it was very hot and there was no shade; by night it could be bitterly cold. The smell of the old battlefield and the flies made life almost unbearable . . . . Whatever lay in store, the relief of leaving that insanitary, fly-ridden, battle-scarred hillside cannot be described.' [1]

What lay in store, however, was a catastrophic involvement in the Syrian war. The battalion took the town of Kuneitra and, under Lieutenant-Colonel A D G Orr, an Arabic speaker, established a de facto military governorship.

When the Vichy forces attacked on 16 June 1941 with nearly 40 tanks, 12 armoured cars and artillery, the Fusiliers had just two armoured cars of the Royal Dragoons at their disposal. A desperate defence ended in surrender to avoid an otherwise inevitable bloodbath. A Free French officer attached to the regiment commented:

'I have seen German and French infantry in action, but I have never seen a finer lot of men. Surrounded on all sides, they maintained their fire and handled their grenades with the greatest efficiency throughout the day, inflicting terrible losses on the enemy.' [2]

A total of 332 prisoners were taken at Kuneitra, though the battalion had been re-formed from 'C' Company who were not present that day. Some time later they met again the officer who took the surrender, he was one of the few Vichy officers in Syria who came over to the Allied cause.

Elsewhere the 8th and 9th Battalions were part of the 56th (London) Division, and were posted forward from guard duties at Kirkup in 1943 to join the final stages of the African war, advancing some 3,000 miles in less than a month. Already in that campaign was the 2nd Battalion who had landed with the 1st Army in January 1943.

These three battalions, together with the re-constituted 1st Royal Fusiliers, were to fight in Italy.

Amongst the toughest of the battles faced in that country was to come at Monte Camino. It took the men of the 9th Battalion eight hours to reach even the start-line, before an assault on a 3,000 foot high position, which was attacked in driving rain. One of the most difficult aspects of the struggle was extracting the wounded from the mountain when the stretcher bearers themselves were under fire. It was a problem not helped by the killing of the medical officer, Captain Munn.

The 1st Battalion won a battle honour at Mozzagrogna, The Royal Fusiliers being the only regiment to carry the honour on their colours. The town was supposed to have been secured, but in the event required house-to-house fighting before it could be cleared.

An even more characteristic example of the spirit of the regiment was seen at an audience given by the Pope to the Catholic members of the 56th Division, when the Vatican hierarchy was taken aback by the enthusiasm of the three cheers given to His Holiness.

[1] Foss *The Royal Fusiliers* p.129
[2] Parkinson *Always A Fusilier* p.88

The King's Regiment (Liverpool)

Principal Battle Honours 1939-45

Normandy Landing – Cassino II – Trasimene Line – Tuori
Capture of Forli – Rimini Line – Athens
Chindits 1943 – Chindits 1944

Raised 1685; amalgamated to form The King's Regiment 1958.

Without question, the greatest of the battle honours won by The King's Regiment was Chindits 1943, awarded to no other regiment in the British Army.

The battalion involved in that campaign was the 13th, which had arrived in India in January 1942 and was chosen a few months later to join the 77th (Indian) Infantry Brigade then being formed by the legendary Orde Wingate. A veteran of unorthodox warfare (most spectacularly in the restoration of HIM Haile Sellaisse to the throne of Ethiopia), Wingate had conceived the notion of small groups of soldiers penetrating deep behind enemy lines on sabotage missions. It was a concept that was not received with unqualified support, but in the dark days of 1942, with the Japanese army seemingly unstoppable and the Allies clearly not yet ready for full-scale combat, it was one of the few suggestions that offered any chance of gaining an initiative.

Six months of heavy jungle training reached their culmination on 18 February 1943 when the men of the 77th Brigade crossed the river Chindwin. 13th King's were split into three columns, their major objectives being two railway lines some 100 and 150 miles respectively inside enemy territory. The 1943 Chindits (the name came from a misspelling of the mythological Burmese creature the Chinthes) covered these distances on foot, over terrain that consisted of jungle, rivers, mountains and forests. Each man had a pack comprising over 60 pounds of equipment, with mules carrying heavier loads.

Typical of the actions of the campaign was No. 5 Column's first encounter with the enemy on 6 March. 15 Japanese were killed at the cost of five men from the Column; perhaps even worse was the prospect facing the wounded, four of whom were too badly injured to walk any further – they had to be left behind whilst the men moved on. The same day, a bridge was wrecked and a railway blocked by the rubble from a blown hillside.

By the end of the month, the Chindits had reached the Irrawaddy, where the intention was to cross and push onwards to the next railway. It was discovered, however, that the enemy was holding the river in force, and Wingate, deciding that progress was impossible, ordered the columns to disperse and make their own way back to India. The withdrawal was even more difficult than the advance. The pre-arranged supply drops were proving hazardous now that the Japanese were aware of what was happening, and the groups of men were too small and too numerous to be kept fully supplied.

Effectively asked to fend for themselves whilst within hostile territory, where the local population could not be relied upon, the men resorted to hunting water buffalo, killing the mules carrying the heavy equipment, and even eating grass to survive.

The first survivors emerged from the jungle towards the end of April, and over the next ten weeks small groups returned, including No. 7 Column who had driven north from the Irrawaddy and ended up in China as the guests of Chiang Kai-Shek's army, before being flown back to India by the US Air Force.

It was an impressive operation that shattered the myth of Japanese invincibility. Field-Marshal Wavell was to say of the 13th King's:

'These men were not specially picked dare-devils who had volunteered for a hazardous enterprise in the love of fighting or in the hope of glory, but mostly men of an ordinary line battalion sent originally to India for Garrison duty. Yet as a tale of toughness and good comradeship their story would be hard to beat.' [1]

The following year the 1st Battalion was to repeat the expedition as part of the second Chindits campaign, a larger, better-organized affair that drew on the experience of the earlier operation.

Back in Europe, the 2nd Battalion had spent much of the war in the tense safety of Gibralta, suffering the occasional bombing raid by the Italians and French, but playing no direct part in the war. In March 1944 it joined the fighting in Italy, seeing its major actions at the Rapido river and at Forli before being sent to Greece.

The 5th and 8th King's served as Beach Group Battalions on D-Day, securing the landings, establishing perimeters and clearing mine-fields, and then remaining to assist the off-loading of equipment. The Commanding Officer of the 5th, Lieutenant-Colonel Board, was killed on the first day, but otherwise casualties were thankfully not too high. Within a month, both battalions had begun to disintegrate, being used to provide replacements for other units.

[1] Burke-Gaffney *The Story of The King's Regiment 1914-1948* p.117

The Royal Norfolk Regiment

Principal Battle Honours 1939-45

St Omer-La-Bassée – Normandy Landing – Brieux Bridgehead
Venraij – Rhineland – North-West Europe 1940, 44-45
Singapore Island – Kohima – Aradura – Burma 1944-45

Raised 1685; amalgamated to form 1st East Anglian Regiment 1959;
redesignated 1st Battalion, The Royal Anglian Regiment 1964.

Called back from its posting in India in 1940, the 1st Battalion, The Royal Norfolk Regiment arrived too late to serve in the BEF. For four years, despite repeated indications that an overseas posting was imminent, the battalion remained in the UK training, as it transpired, for the Normandy landings.

On D-Day the 1st Norfolks were in 181 Brigade, who formed the follow-up units of 3rd British Division, securing the bridgehead stormed by the assault brigade. The battalion was involved in the interminable series of assaults on Caen, and then the advance across France, in which periods of rapid progress alternated with bitter struggles against pockets of the enemy.

Throughout, the 1st Norfolks distinguished themselves in battle. A single day's fighting in August 1944 at Sourdevalle brought the award of a Distinguished Conduct Medal and three Military Medals, as well as a Victoria Cross awarded to Corporal S Bates for his continuing resistance to an enemy counter-attack despite being wounded three times, the last time fatally.

Two months later the battalion was in Holland. During the advance on Venraij, two companies actually passed through an enemy minefield, entirely unaware and unscathed. Such fortune was not, however, always forthcoming in the subsequent four days of fighting, 211 casualties were sustained.

Having entered Germany in February 1945, the battalion engaged in the battle to take Kervenheim, and was subsequently involved in the capture of Bremen. It was during this latter incident that Lieutenant A R Gill, the Pioneer Officer, went on a solo reconnaissance patrol, returning with a column of 100 enemy troops who had surrendered to him. The spirit had clearly left the German Army and the taking of Bremen on 26 April 1945 was the battalion's last major engagement of the war.

The 2nd Battalion's experience was in stark contrast to that of the 1st. Arriving in France in September 1939, it made its mark early during the so-called 'Phoney

War', being awarded the first decorations for courage of the war, as well as sending the first patrol onto German soil since the commencement of hostilities.

When the German offensive came, the battalion moved to forward positions in Belgium and was soon in the thick of the fighting. There it remained, and during the evacuation from Dunkirk fought a desperate and ultimately doomed rearguard action at La Bassée canal. That stand saved the lives of thousands, but the casualties were terrible. On 27 May, with the battalion down to less than a hundred, and surrounded by vastly greater enemy forces, a surrender was ordered.

The prisoners of war were paraded in triumph before being taken to a field and shot in cold blood by the SS. Only two men survived the massacre, and it was their evidence after the war – particularly that of Private Albert Pooley – that ensured the trial and execution of the German officer who had ordered the slaughter.

The battalion was re-formed back home by men who had been successfully evacuated, by men from the headquarters and by detachments from the Royal Berkshire and Essex Regiments. An essential period of training and of home defence duties was followed in 1942 by a posting to India.

The Japanese offensive of 1944 saw the battalion sent forward to relieve Kohima. During the ferocious fighting that ensued, Captain Randle – armed only with a rifle – charged a machine-gun post and, despite being hit several times, successfully blew it up, his last act being to cover the slit of the bunker with his body to seal it. He was posthumously awarded a Victoria Cross.

He was not the only casualty – Kohima cost the battalion 86 lives.

There was little time for recovery, however, for the stemming of the Japanese offensive was succeeded by the sustained British push through Burma. The battalion advanced through Imphal and Mandalay and on to Rangoon to complete more than a year's fighting, much of it under monsoon conditions.

The territorial battalions of the regiment also saw action. Both the 4th and the 5th were posted to Singapore, arriving on 29 and 13 January 1942 respectively. Despite courageous service, the lack of time for training and the rapid surrender of the island left little opportunity to make a decisive contribution.

Also present in Singapore were the survivors of the 6th Battalion who had arrived in Malaya in January 1942, only to be forced back by the relentless Japanese advance. Thus three battalions of the Norfolks were taken prisoner in the Far East; many of the men were later to die on the infamous Burma railway.

The 7th Battalion was scarcely more fortunate. Newly raised, and with inadequate training and equipment, it was sent to France with the BEF, and was fighting alongside the 51st Highland Division at St Valery when that division was taken prisoner. Just 31 men returned.

Re-formed at home, the 7th subsequently returned to North-West Europe in the aftermath of D-Day. In the fighting around the Orne bridgehead in August 1944, Captain Jamieson was awarded the Victoria Cross.

The Royal Lincolnshire Regiment

Principal Battle Honours 1939-45

Dunkirk 1940 – Normandy Landing – Fontenay le Pesnil
Antwerp-Turhout Canal – Rhineland – North Africa 1943
Salerno – Gothic Line – Ngakyedauk Pass – Burma 1943-45

Raised 1685; amalgamated to form 2nd Battalion,
the Royal Anglian Regiment 1960.

Though the British war with Japan in the years following the fall of Singapore has been referred to as the forgotten war, there were episodes that did spark the public imagination – the retreat from Burma, the Chindits operations, the heroic resistance of Kohima and Imphal. Perhaps the real forgotten army comprised those units that were not involved in these events but served in the more routine operations of the campaign.

One such was the 1st Battalion, The Lincolnshire Regiment. Sent in to reinforce the Allied troops in South Arakan in early 1943, the Lincolns' first experience of war was holding the front-line that stretched across the Mayu Peninsula, facing the Japanese on the southernmost tip. It was not full-scale fighting, but under sniper and mortar fire, and with patrols encountering the enemy in the jungle, it was a nerve-wracking situation.

The action intensified in March, when the battalion joined 6 Independent Brigade (alongside battalions from the Royal Scots, Royal Berkshires, Royal Welch and Durham Light Infantry) for an assault on the Japanese-held town of Donbaik. The 1st Lincolns fought for eight hours, taking all their objectives, before being informed that the attack was not progressing so well elsewhere and being ordered to withdraw to their original positions under cover of night. The withdrawal was, if anything, even more difficult: it took six hours to cut a path through the jungle and pass single-file through the enemy lines, carrying the wounded on stretchers.

A similar operation followed at Point 201, a hill to the south of Taungmaw, where it was discovered that estimates of the Japanese forces had been woefully short of the mark, and a retreat ordered.

Actions such as these were typical of the times – minor but frequent encounters that inexorably took their toll. By the time the battalion was pulled back, it was reduced to 350 men from its original complement of 830.

The struggle for Arakan continued, reaching a climax in February 1944 with a major Japanese offensive. Though mostly directed to the north of the region, the Lincolns found themselves heavily engaged in the south. At the battle for Point 315, Major Charles Hoey was awarded a posthumous Victoria Cross, the citation stating:

'Although wounded at least twice in the leg and head he seized a Bren gun from one of his men and firing from the hip, led his Company on the objective . . . where he killed all the occupants before being mortally wounded.' [1]

Two other significant battles had yet to be fought: the taking of the twin hills known as 'Spit and Polish', in which it is claimed more Japanese were killed than in any other single action in the Arakan, and the landing on Ramree Island. The latter required nearly six weeks of fighting to clear all opposition from a terrain dominated by mangrove swamps. The battalion went on to serve in the liberation of Rangoon.

By this stage, the 2nd Battalion was also facing the enemy. Having trained for the Sicily invasion, only to learn at the last moment that they weren't going to go, the men landed instead in Normandy on D-Day. The battalion history records the sense of frustration during the first tense weeks on French soil:

'There followed . . . what must have been one of the most trying periods in this, or any, war. Still eager to press forward and still confident that we could do so, we were compelled to sit and hold . . . . It was a wearying business.' [2]

When called upon to fight, the 2nd Lincolns often found themselves in stiff encounters away from the spotlight. The battle to take Le Bisey Wood, one of the keys to Caen, resulted in two days at Herouvillette with 30 dead and 140 wounded.

Worse was to come in July 1944 in the assault on Troarn. The battalion was instructed to create a diversion, but found itself engaged in a desperate struggle in what was to become known as 'Black Orchard'. More than 200 casualties were sustained, including the Commanding Officer, Lieutenant-Colonel Welby-Everard. His successor fared little better, being wounded the next month in securing a bridgehead on the river Vire.

Depleted by these battles, the ranks were re-built with the assistance of the Bermuda Volunteer Rifles, a regiment affiliated to the Lincolns.

In early 1945 the battalion crossed into Germany to begin the final stage of the campaign with the clearing of the Rhineland.

[1] *History of The First Battalion, The Lincolnshire Regiment 1939-1946* p.36

[2] *The History of The Second Battalion, The Lincolnshire Regiment* p.18

The Devonshire Regiment

Principal Battle Honours 1939-45

Normandy Landing – Caen – Rhine
North-West Europe 1944-45 – Landing in Sicily
Regalbuto – Malta 1940-42 – Imphal
Myinmu Bridgehead – Burma 1943-45

Raised 1685; amalgamated to form The Devonshire and
Dorset Regiment 1958.

Britain's declaration of war against Germany in 1939 did not, of course, mean that the problems of empire ceased to exist and, even with the spread of conflict beyond Europe, there were still obligations to be met. The 1st Battalion of The Devonshire Regiment, stationed in Rawalpindi in the latter part of the '30s, thus spent the first 18 months of the war engaged in the perpetual skirmishes common to the North-West Frontier.

The battalion was subsequently called upon to assist the war effort, but circumstances conspired against an early entry. The men were in the process of training for the North African desert when the Japanese invasion of Malaya changed the plan. By the time they were trained for jungle warfare, Burma had been abandoned, and the battalion was again put on hold.

In October 1943 the 1st Devons were sent forward to positions on the Tamu Road. Though not the scene of full combat, conditions were dangerous. Patrols made occasional contact with the enemy, whilst a typhus epidemic further reduced the ranks. Nevertheless, there were also periods of calm, with visits from ENSA, and the Commanding Officer even managed to get in a spot of fly-fishing.

The following March the Japanese launched the U-Go offensive and the hills of the Tamu Road, already more than familiar to the battalion, became the front-line. A counter-offensive produced a bitter and bloody battle around Nippon Hill that eventually saw the Japanese pushed back. It was a struggle characterised by what the regimental history would later describe as 'the extreme tenaciousness of the enemy, who generally had to be stamped to death like a snake.' [1]

With the liberation of Kohima, the 1st Dorsets finally left the Tamu Road behind them and pursued the enemy back into the jungle. With just a three month break in late 1944, they were back into the fray, seeing particularly heavy fighting around Kyaukse.

The men of the 2nd Battalion were also stationed abroad in 1939, in their case in Malta. As the 'Phoney War' in Europe gave way to blitzkrieg, the vulnerable position of Malta became ever more apparent, and preparations for its defence were the priority of the battalion. The sense of tension and anticipation is revealed in a laconic diary entry by the Intelligence Officer on 10 June 1940: 'Mussolini has had quite a bit to say this evening in a speech and decided to declare war on the Allies. Everyone is very relieved, but at the same rather annoyed about it.' [2]

With the Italian declaration, Malta entered a state of siege that was not to be lifted until the defeat of the Axis at El Alamein signalled the final reversal of fortune in the Mediterranean.

The task for the infantry on the island was essentially that of assisting the RAF in its battle with the Luftwaffe. The 2nd Devons were responsible for maintaining (and rebuilding, after raids) Halfar airfield and the seaplane base at Kalafrana. The scale of their task, and the unpredictability of the onslaught, can be gauged by the figures for tonnage of bombs dropped: 174 tons in February 1942 on Halfar alone, rising to 374 tons in March and 750 tons in April. The fact that the island remained defiant in the face of such attacks is tribute to their work.

During the same period, at the other end of the Mediterranean, the 4th Battalion was garrisoning Gibralta, though conditions here were not as hazardous – the worst air raid came in September 1940 at the hands of the French.

With the lifting of the siege, the 2nd Devons, as part of the Malta Brigade, proceeded to Sicily, landing on 10 July 1943 – the first time the regiment had come directly into contact with the enemy. Rapid progress was made against demoralised Italian troops, though the advance slowed somewhat when German opposition was met.

The major action for the battalion came at Regalbuto Ridge, where the 1st Hampshire Regiment had been unable to make a break-through; the Devons were successful in taking and holding the position, but the encounter cost them more than a hundred casualties.

A short spell in Italy was followed by a return to Britain in late 1943. On D-Day the 2nd Devons were again in the vanguard of a sea-borne invasion force, fighting with distinction through the whole of the subsequent campaign.

[1] Taylor *The Devons: A History of The Devonshire Regiment 1685-1945* p.182

[2] ibid. p.100

The Suffolk Regiment

Principal Battle Honours 1939-45

Dunkirk 1940 – Normandy Landing – Odon – Falaise
Venraij – Brinkum – Singapore Island – North Arakan
Imphal – Burma 1943-45

Raised 1685; amalgamated to form 1st East Anglian Regiment 1959;
amalgamated to form The Royal Anglian Regiment 1964.

The 1st Battalion The Suffolk Regiment shared the experience of many infantry battalions. Posted to France early on, it waited through the freezing winter of 1939/40 for the anticipated German attack. On 12 May 1940 it advanced forward to a position near Louvain, and spent most of the next three weeks retreating back to Dunkirk. Orders were received to establish and then abandon a series of positions on the familiar roll-call of rivers: the Dyle, the Dendre, Escaut, Lys.

It was on the Dendre that direct contact was first made with the enemy, with firing from opposite sides of the river. One of the casualties was Lieutenant-Colonel E G Fraser, the Commanding Officer, fatally wounded on 20 May. At Watrelos, on the French-Belgian border, a counter-attack was attempted but beaten back with 75 casualties sustained. With withdrawal now inevitable, much of the regiment's equipment was left behind.

The battalion was evacuated on 1 June 1940. Almost exactly four years later, on D-Day, it returned to France, landing on 'Queen' Beach. Casualties that first day were thankfully light, but enemy attack was a permanent feature of life; the regimental history records that it was not until 10 July that a day passed without German shells landing on the battalion area.

By that stage, the 1st Suffolks had engaged the enemy in heavy fighting around Château de La Londe. Two days of battle resulted in victory, but at a high cost; on one day alone, there were 161 casualties.

Smaller struggles ensued, as well as time for rest and recreation. The regiment's traditional commemoration of Minden Day on 1 August 1944 proceeded as normal, with the customary roses worn in head-dresses, with beer-fuelled celebrations and with a visit to the cinema.

The autumn saw the 1st Suffolks regroup, with the battalion strength reported in September 1944 to be 925. A week-long struggle the following month to capture the towns of Overloon and Ventura, however, resulted in 173 casualties.

The advance through France, Belgium and Holland into Germany included a stop at Roubaix in December, where three regimental side-drums, abandoned during the retreat of 1940, were returned by townsfolk.

Beyond Europe, the regiment served mainly in the Far East. The 4th and 5th Battalions sailed in October 1941 in a belated attempt to forestall Japanese attacks on British colonies.

Arriving in Singapore in time to assist the defence of the island, they were denied the opportunity to make any major contribution. During the fighting, instructions were received to cease-fire as a surrender party was soon to come through their ranks. The disbelief at this collapse is recorded by Captain R M Oliver, a company officer who stopped a car carrying Union Jacks and white flags:

'[My] only retort was 'What the b——y hell are you doing with those flags?' I was then thinking of Fifth Column, as rumours of Fifth Column activities had been very rife.' [1]

In fact, the car contained senior military and diplomatic figures bearing surrender terms, and reluctantly Capt Oliver was obliged to let them pass.

Both battalions were taken prisoner, and were subsequently put to work on the notorious Burma railway. 286 men of the 4th Battalion and 271 of the 5th were to die in captivity; a further 58 men were tragically killed in transport at sea in an Allied air attack.

It was left to the 2nd Battalion to avenge the capture of their comrades. The first years of the war, however, were spent in the more mundane tasks of policing the Empire, for the advent of world war did not guarantee the security of the colonies. Frontier activity kept the battalion busy at Razmak in 1940 and Tochi Valley the following year, whilst Gandhi's 'Quit India' campaign necessitated policing duties in 1942.

In October 1943 the men were finally posted forward to the Arakan province, where they helped repulse the Japanese offensive. They spent most of the next year in the fighting around Kohima and Imphal.

One of their actions was an attack on Japanese positions on the road between these two cities in May 1944. The lack of preparation and reconnaissance left the CO, Lieutenant-Colonel H R Hopking convinced that his men's lives were being unreasonably jeopardized, and he insisted on being relieved of his position. In the event, the attack was unsuccessful, defeated by shortages of ammunition and supplies and the battalion, stranded in advance of friendly lines, was withdrawn.

Further campaigning was undertaken, but the monsoon was bringing new problems of disease and sickness. In the nine months of action, 78 men were killed and 149 wounded; during the same period, there were a total of 1,599 cases evacuated to hospital, from which 437 men did not return to the regiment. At the end of July 1944, the battalion was withdrawn from the front-line.

[1] Nicholson *The Suffolk Regiment 1928 to 1946* p.206

The Somerset Light Infantry (Prince Albert's)

Principal Battle Honours 1939-45

Hill 112 – Mont Pincon – Rhineland
North-West Europe 1944-45 – Cassino II
Cosina Canal Crossing – Italy 1944-45
North Arakan – Ngakyedauk Pass

Raised 1685; amalgamated to form The Somerset and Cornwall Light Infantry 1959; redesignated 1st Battalion, The Light Infantry 1968.

Initially stationed on the North-West Frontier, it was not to be until May 1943 that the 1st Battalion of The Somerset Light Infantry was sent into action in the Arakan.

In common with many other units in the theatre, the battalion was under-strength and was to face personnel problems throughout its campaigning; on a single day, 120 promotions were enacted in an attempt to clear a backlog, but it was still not enough – soon after, a further 60 promotions were necessitated by sickness and casualties. The scale of the problem is evidenced by the fact that in the 12 months spent in Arakan before being pulled back to India, there was a 300% turnover of NCOs.

The last quarter of 1943 saw a series of patrols encountering the Japanese for the first time, encounters in which the enemy generally came out on top. The major contribution, however, was to come in January 1944 with a major offensive in the Kalapanzin Valley.

As the 1st Battalion was getting to grips with one enemy, the 30th was landing in Algeria to assist the struggle against another. Serving in North Africa, Sicily and Italy, the 30th was for the most part deployed in a support function, winning no great plaudits but providing the back-up so essential to a modern army. For a brief period in 1944 the battalion was renamed the 119th Infantry Brigade, an exaggeration designed to conceal the withdrawal of troops from Italy for D-Day.

By this stage, the 2nd Battalion had joined the Italian campaign, having spent the first half of the war in the garrison at Gibralta. Its greatest test came at the crossing of the Rapido in the breakthrough at Cassino. Despite heavy artillery fire from both sides and despite a faster than anticipated current, a bridgehead was successfully established; it then had to be held for 36 hours until tank support could be brought forward. 153 casualties were sustained in the operation, including the Commanding Officer, Lieutenant-Colonel J R I Platt, who lay wounded for 30 hours before being rescued.

In Northern Europe the 10th Battalion had been redesignated a parachute battalion, dropping on D-Day and fighting in the first intense phase of the Normandy campaign. By the beginning of July 1944, the battalion was down to just 16 officers and 366 men. It was to be called upon again at the crossing of the Rhine.

Also in Normandy were the 4th and 7th Battalions, serving together in the famous 43rd (Wessex) Division. On 10 July 1944 the 4th Somersets were thrown into the assault on the German stronghold of Hill 112. Advancing over 1,500 yards of open country, horrendous casualties were incurred; the next two days saw the figures escalate, and the battalion virtually wiped out. In the aftermath, it was re-built with some 500 reinforcements, and continued the fight.

Perhaps the most important moment came at the battle to take the Reichswald Forest. On 16 February 1945 the 7th Battalion took 3,000 yards of ground, capturing 400 prisoners in the process, and then held their position whilst the 4th came through to take the escarpment overlooking Goch. Lieutenant-General Horrocks was later to pay tribute to the regiment's contribution: 'The Somersets had burst open the door of the Reichswald and the crisis of battle was over.' [1]

[1] Popham *The Somerset Light Infantry* p.8

The West Yorkshire Regiment
(The Prince of Wales's Own)

Principal Battle Honours 1939-45

Keren – Defence of Alamein Line – Pegu 1942
Yenangyaung 1942 – Maungdaw – Defence of Sinzweya
Imphal – Bishenpur – Meiktila – Sittang 1945

Raised 1685; amalgamated to form The Prince of Wales's
Own Regiment of Yorkshire 1958.

Although two battalions of the West Yorkshires had formed part of the British Expeditionary Force, they played little part in the fighting, being posted in the rear of the force, and the regiment served for the most part outside the European theatres.

Stationed in Palestine, the 2nd West Yorkshires moved to the Sudan in 1940 and thence to the Abyssinian border, where they had their first brush with the Italian army. It was a complete success. An enemy advance, potentially threatening Egypt, was halted, with intelligence reporting the presence of '5000 heavily armed regular British troops with many tanks'; it was in fact 120 West Yorkshires with a couple of Bren-gun carriers. [1]

In March the following year, they joined General Platt's forces in Eritrea in time to participate in the assault on Keren, one of the key battles of the East Africa campaign. With a massive effort, the supposedly impregnable position at Fort Dologorodoc, the key to Keren, was taken and for ten days was held against a series of counter-attacks that effectively represented the last gasp of the Italian forces in Eritrea.

From East Africa, the 2nd Battalion went on to see service in Egypt, Iraq and in the Western Desert, still as part of the 5th Indian Division with whom they had fought at Keren. In late 1943 the Division was posted to India to join the British and Empire troops who were preparing to re-launch the offensive against the Japanese in Burma.

Amongst these were the men of the 1st West Yorkshires, who had arrived in Rangoon in January 1942 to serve with the 7th Armoured Brigade in the retreat from Burma.

The period between that retreat and the launching of the Allied offensive was one of recovery and preparation. Although not engaged in military action, the 1st West Yorks were still kept busy: the fact that so many of the men had been miners in their civilian lives was put to good use in the cutting of mountain rock faces during the construction of the Tiddim Road.

Amongst the battles in which the regiment was to distinguish itself was the defence of Sinzweya in the Arakan. The 2nd Battalion had advanced with the 5th and 7th Indian Divisions in January 1944, and were making gains when the Japanese launched their own offensive. The 2nd West Yorkshires' position was surrounded, and for 25 days the men held on until they were relieved. The heroic defence was a major factor in breaking the Japanese initiative. 'Never has any Regiment,' said General Christison, 'counter-attacked so successfully and so often as in that battle. It is rare in history that one Regiment can be said to have turned the scale of a whole campaign.' [2]

The two battalions were to meet up in April 1944 in Imphal. The Japanese assault was concentrated on trying to break the defence of the city and for more than three months the fighting was desperate and determined. The Allied forces, however, remained strong and on 22 June the siege was lifted. By happy coincidence, that day was the anniversary of the formation of the regiment, and in honour of both battalions having served together, it was resolved to keep 22 June as a regimental celebration to be known as Imphal Day.

The war, of course, was still far from over, and the subsequent advance of the Allies was met with continued resistance from Japanese troops, disinclined to cede any ground without a fight. By the end of 1944 the 2nd Battalion, by now reduced to the size of a company, was withdrawn from the frontline to regroup.

In March 1945 both battalions again saw service alongside each other in the capture of Meiktila. Then began the long march on Rangoon. In Pegu, north of Rangoon, British prisoners were liberated, including men of the 1st West Yorkshires captured during the retreat from Burma some three years earlier.

When Japan surrendered on 15 August 1945, the 2nd Battalion was preparing for the invasion of Malaya. In the event, it became the first British battalion to land in Singapore after the hostilities.

Sergeant Harold Turner of the 1st Battalion was awarded a posthumous Victoria Cross for his gallantry during the protracted struggle around Bishenpur in June 1944.

[1] Maule *The Great Battles of World War II* p.76
[2] Spencer *A Short History of the Prince of Wales's Own Regiment of Yorkshire 1685-1966* p.24

The East Yorkshire Regiment
(The Duke of York's Own)

Principal Battle Honours 1939-45

Dunkirk 1940 – Normandy Landing – Odon – Schaddenhof
North-West Europe 1940, 44-45 – Gazala – El Alamein
Mareth – Sicily 1943 – Burma 1945

Raised 1685; amalgamated to form
The Prince of Wales's Own Regiment of Yorkshire 1958.

The 2nd, 4th and 5th Battalions of the East Yorkshire Regiment formed part of the British Expeditionary Force. The 2nd saw heavy fighting both in Belgium and in the retreat to Dunkirk, sustaining nearly half its casualties on the beach itself, whilst the 4th and 5th were also drawn into the later stages of combat.

The 4th and 5th East Yorkshires were to serve together for the next couple of years as elements within the 50th Division. During the second half of 1941, they were posted to various points in the Middle East – the Western Desert, Egypt, Cyprus, Iraq, Syria – to forestall potential problems, before returning to North Africa.

February 1942 saw 50 Division dug in on the Gazala Line in the Western Desert. They were still there in May when Rommel's Afrika Korps launched a major offensive. For a week, the fighting was so intense and the supplies to the beleaguered British troops so scarce, that by the end the 4th East Yorkshires no longer existed.

The 5th Battalion, however, remained in the front line of the British forces, a position doubly dangerous in such conflict, facing not only the enemy but also risking being caught in what has now come to be termed 'friendly fire'. It was a problem that afflicted the 5th in October 1942. Ordered to hold up the Germans while the British forces gathered for El Alamein, the battalion launched a raid one night, but under fire from both sides were obliged to pull back.

The 50th Division participated in the advance toward Tunis, winning a battle honour at Mareth in April 1943. The regimental history tells us that in the battle:

'Courageous work was . . . done by the stretcher bearers – dressing and evacuating casualties under extremely heavy fire, particularly [by] Pte. Andersen, who, after carrying three casualties over an exposed forward slope, was himself killed in the fourth attempt.' [1]

Eric Andersen was awarded a posthumous Victoria Cross.

In the Sicily landings, the 5th Battalion fought a series of rear actions against German parachute troops, before returning to Britain.

Both the 2nd and 5th East Yorkshires landed in Normandy on D-Day and fought with great distinction in those first desperate few weeks. The sense of history that accompanied the invasion of Europe was epitomized by Major C K King; the text for his pep talk to 'A' Company as the ships approached France was taken from the Shakespearian account of Henry V's speech on the eve of Agincourt.

Also landing in Normandy was the 7th Battalion, though it was not to see service as a unit, being used instead to provide replacement troops for other regiments.

The 5th Battalion, still with the 50th Division, advanced through Northern France to take Antwerp in September 1944. It was subsequently to see action in the fighting that surrounded the Arnhem landings, before the Division – much weakened by three years of warfare across two continents – was disbanded.

For the 2nd East Yorkshires, the advance continued. Also involved in the struggle around Arnhem as part of the 3rd Division, it pushed forward into Germany, meeting determined SS opposition in the final battle at Bremen in April 1945.

The 1st Battalion, meanwhile, had arrived in Burma in 1945 in time to assist the drive toward Rangoon, serving alongside the 1st West Yorkshires. The association between the two regiments was of course to be sealed in 1958 when they amalgamated to form The Prince of Wales's Own Regiment of Yorkshire.

1,024 men of the regiment were killed in the war.

[1] Nightingale *A History of The East Yorkshire Regiment in the War of 1939-45* p.126

The Bedfordshire and Hertfordshire Regiment

Principal Battle Honours 1939-45

Dunkirk 1940 – North-West Europe 1940 – Tobruk Sortie
Belhamed – Tunis – North Africa 1941, 43 – Cassino II
Trasimene Line – Italy 1944-45 – Chindits 1944

Raised 1688; amalgamated to form The 3rd East Anglia Regiment 1958;
redesignated 3rd Battalion, The Royal Anglian Regiment 1964.

The 1st Battalion, The Bedfordshire and Hertfordshire Regiment was stationed in the Middle East at the end of the '30s and spent the first years of the war in Palestine and Egypt. It was not until March 1941 that it was sent to a potential war zone, as garrison of the Aegean island of Lemnos during the crisis in Greece. Given the catastrophic nature of that campaign, it is perhaps fortunate that the men were evacuated before the arrival of the Germans.

A period of service in Syria, assisting the suppression of the Vichy forces there, followed. Then, in October 1941, the battalion was despatched to Tobruk to relieve the garrison.

A battle honour was to be won in the sortie that broke out of the besieged town, but the more common experience was the seemingly endless round of patrolling and skirmishing. A typical action was 'B' Company's capture of a sandhill named Tugun, a conflict that cost 25 casualties from a 45 man attack and that brought back 60 enemy prisoners. The conduct of the Beds & Herts throughout the siege can be gauged by enemy documents citing Corporal Goodship, who had been taken prisoner while leading a patrol, as an example of how to behave in captivity.

This was to be the one contribution the battalion made to the North African war, but the regiment was to return in the form of the 2nd Battalion. Having already won a battle honour on the Dunkirk perimeter, the 2nd Beds & Herts landed at Algiers in March 1943 and almost immediately found itself involved in fighting. Two early battles saw the taking of Sidi Nisr and Djebel Aoud, but at the price of eight officers, including the Commanding Officer, and some 230 men.

Even heavier fighting was to come in Italy at the crossing of the Rapido and in the final thrust at Cassino, before the battalion was sent to the civil war in Greece. It left behind a territorial battalion – the 1st Hertfordshires – which had arrived from Gibralta to join the assault on the Gothic Line.

The men of a further territorial battalion, the 2nd Herts, were the regiment's sole representatives in the Normandy campaign, landing on D-Day as a beach group to consolidate the bridgeheads that had been gained.

1944 also saw the return of the regiment to the war against the Japanese, avenging the capture of the 5th Battalion in the fall of Singapore. From April until August, the men of the 1st Battalion fought as Chindits around Indaw deep in enemy territory, before linking up with the Allied forces advancing from Kohima. As at Tobruk, the battalion served alongside the 1st Essex Regiment, with whom the regiment was later to amalgamate.

The conditions in the jungle were described by Lieutenant-Colonel T J Barrow:

'The weather was exceedingly hot. Water was scarce. The jungle was burnt up over very large areas. We had not been able to wash for many days. We had to move fast. Routine was . . . . nine and a half hours marching [a day] during which we would cover about eighteen to twenty miles.' [1]

Under such conditions, disease was of course always a danger and it was malaria rather than the enemy that took the life of the Commanding Officer, Lieutenant-Colonel Eason.

[1] Peters *The Bedfordshire and Hertfordshire Regiment* p.105

The Leicestershire Regiment

Principal Battle Honours 1939-45

North-West Europe 1944-45 – Sidi Barrani
North Africa 1940-41, 43 – Salerno – Gothic Line
Italy 1943-45 – Crete – Malaya 1941-42 – Chindits 1944

Raised 1688; redesignated 4th (Leicestershire) Battalion,
The Royal Anglian Regiment 1964; disbanded 1970.

With the two regular battalions overseas, it fell to the territorials of The Leicestershire Regiment to strike the first blows against Nazism. The 1/5th Battalion landed at Andalnes in Norway, though typically of the times it did so without transport, which had been lost in a U-boat attack, and with an acute shortage of ammunition and supplies. Under these circumstances, it is to the credit of the men that the brief campaign, covering the withdrawal of Norwegian troops, was conducted with some efficiency. Even so there were losses, most significantly the capture of the Commanding Officer, Lieutenant-Colonel German.

The 2/5th Battalion was also plunged into a conflict for which it was ill-prepared. Sent to France in April 1940 to work on the construction of a railway in Brittany, it found itself posted forward as the Allied front collapsed. When the enemy was encountered at the Canal de la Haute Deole, the men fought valiantly, but with little combat-training and a desperate shortage of weapons, stood no chance and were over-run.

Better news for the regiment was to come later in the year when the 2nd Battalion was part of the Allied thrust against the Italians in North Africa. The first battle of that campaign, at Sidi Barrani on 11 December 1940, marked the beginning of a year that was to see the battalion serve on three fronts.

The success of that first drive across the western desert brought major logistical problems, and the men were called upon not only to fight but also to deal with the huge numbers of Italian prisoners: in just two days, the numbers being guarded by 'A' Company alone rose from 3,000 to 10,000.

The tour of duty was broken by a brief period of leave in Alexandria in February 1941 (where Christmas was belatedly celebrated) and was then abruptly terminated in May with a posting to Crete.

Operating in a mobile reserve capacity, the 2nd Leicesters assisted a variety of other units on the north coast in an attempt to stem the German invasion. It was a costly exercise; by the time the survivors were evacuated, almost 150 were reported dead or wounded of an original complement of some 580 all ranks. 'D' Company was effectively wiped out, having been surrounded whilst aiding a beleaguered battalion of Argyll and Sutherland Highlanders.

There was, however, to be little time for recovery. Bolstered by reinforcements, the battalion was plunged into the Syrian conflict the following month – another tough struggle in hostile conditions, albeit one that resulted in victory for the Allies.

The final involvement in the Mediterranean theatre came in September 1941, with a spell in Tobruk leading up to the final break-out. When the Leicesters were finally relieved in December, the Adjutant commented that 'it was almost with a sense of regret that the troops said goodbye. The spirit of defiance that the Australians had bred in Tobruk passed into them, and they felt they had not let them down.' [1] Indeed it appears that the men's major complaint was not the enemy, but the lack of cigarettes, rationed to just 50 per week.

With the departure of the 2nd Leicesters from Africa, it was the 2/5th who again maintained the regiment's presence in the war with Germany. Landing at Algiers in January 1943, the battalion was soon in the thick of the fighting at the Kasserine Pass. Soon after, at Montaigne Farm, 'C' Company held a position under repeated German attack for seven days, taking 54 enemy prisoners and winning a battle honour that, though it is not amongst those born on the regiment's banners, was as hard won as any.

The 2/5th were later to serve in Italy and Greece.

The 1st Battalion had been in India at the commencement of hostilities and had been sent to the Malaya/Siam border in late 1941 in anticipation of Japanese attack. When the invasion did come, a long fighting withdrawal down the length of the country ended with capture at Singapore. Casualties were so heavy that a composite battalion was formed with survivors of the 2nd East Surreys. Known as The British Battalion, its strength stood at 786 all ranks; by the time that Singapore surrendered, this number had fallen to just 265.

The 8th Battalion was reconstituted as the 1st in June 1942 and served in Normandy, whilst the honour of the regiment in the Far East was restored by the 2nd and 7th Battalions in the 1944 Chindits campaign. During that operation, the 2nd staged a march over the Naga Hills to the Chindwin that earned them the congratulations of General Wingate himself: 'Well done, Leicestershire Regiment – Hannibal eclipsed.'

[1] Underhill *The Royal Leicestershire Regiment 1928 to 1956* p.87

The Green Howards
(Alexandra, Princess of Wales's Own Yorkshire Regiment)

Principal Battle Honours 1939-45

Norway 1940 – Normandy Landing
North-West Europe 1940, 44-45 – Gazala – El Alamein
Mareth – Akarit – Sicily 1943 – Minturno – Anzio

Raised 1688.

The 1st Battalion of The Green Howards served in the first British campaign of the war, the failed expedition to Norway. Landing at Andalsnes on 25 April, the battalion remained in the country for less than a week before being evacuated from the same port, but in that time fought successfully enough to hold back the German advance and to claim a battle honour for its contribution.

The 1st Green Howards had been withdrawn from the British Expeditionary Force for Norway, but left behind the 4th and 5th Battalions, who saw active service in defence of the Dunkirk perimeter, emerging with the boast of being the last British formations out of the port. Also at Dunkirk were the 6th and 7th Battalions, sent to France as pioneers but called upon to fight in the general collapse of the Allies.

These same four territorial battalions were all to serve in North Africa in 1942 in the battle at Gazala. The 4th and 5th formed part of the 150th Brigade that was captured by the Germans but whose courage was paid tribute to by Rommel himself, who wrote later of 'the toughest British resistance imaginable'.

The 6th and 7th, however, fared better and escaped the heat of the Cauldron to fight again at El Alamein. Their role in that battle was unspectacular – staging a diversionary attack to the south, whilst the main thrust broke through in the north – but costly, with half the men in the rifle companies of the 6th lost.

The greatest contribution was yet to come. The German retreat from Alamein came to a halt at the Mareth Line, where one of the bitterest battles of the western desert were fought. Both here and at Wadi Akarit a fortnight later, the two battalions – fighting side by side in the 50th Division – distinguished themselves. Casualties were again high, with 500 dead and wounded between the battalions, but so too was the courage displayed, with 30 awards for gallantry being won.

Falling into both categories was the Commanding Officer of the 7th,

Lieutenant-Colonel D A Seagrim, who personally led his troops under enemy fire at Mareth, accounting for two machine-gun posts and some 20 Germans, for which he was awarded the Victoria Cross. Sadly he never learnt of the award, for he was killed at Akarit.

Moving on to Sicily, the 5th and 6th were joined by the 1st Battalion. Early progress proved deceptive when the full might of the German army was met, and the advance was stalled on the Catanian Plain. One of the casualties in that struggle was one of the great losses of the war: the legendary Yorkshire and England fast bowler Captain Hedley Verity was wounded leading his company, and died in captivity some three weeks later.

Some of the sternest resistance was met at Mt Pancali, where the efforts of the 6th and 7th were acknowledged by a German veteran of the desert wars: 'I have been against many British attacks, but that was the finest I have ever seen. I congratulate you.' [1]

The 1st Battalion pressed on to Italy where it fought through the slow war in the south, before being sent in to reinforce the bridgehead at Anzio in February 1944. For 11 weeks, the men held the notorious position at The Fortress, where the enemy was so close that it was reported the German morning roll-call could be heard. In the break-out, the battalion staged a diversion that cost some 155 men.

Meanwhile the 6th and 7th had been withdrawn to serve in the Normandy landings, where Company Sergeant-Major Hollis of the 6th Battalion won the first Victoria Cross of the campaign, taking out a pill-box single-handed and capturing 25 prisoners on D-Day itself. His Commanding Officer later described this extraordinary soldier as being 'absolutely personally dedicated to winning the war – one of the few men I ever met who felt like that.' [2]

The two battalions fought through the different challenges of the North-West European war into Holland, where the 50th Division – having been in almost continuous action for two and a half years – was finally disbanded. There was still, however, regimental interest in the campaign, for the 1st Battalion arrived in Germany in April 1945 for the last days of the war.

Far away in India, meanwhile, the 2nd Green Howards had been patiently awaiting orders to move forward for some considerable time. When they were at last sent into Burma in September 1944, the main action had already passed, and the battalion was anyway much weakened by the departure of men for other units. Amongst them was Lieutenant W B Weston who won a VC whilst serving with the 1st West Yorkshires at Meiktila.

[1] d'Este *Bitter Victory* p.357
[2] Hastings *Overlord* p. 110

The Lancashire Fusiliers

Principal Battle Honours 1939-45

Defence of Escaut – Caen – Medjez el Bab – Sangro
Cassino II – Argenta Gap – Malta 1941-42 – Kohima
Chindits 1944 – Burma 1943-45

Raised 1688; amalgamated to become 4th Battalion, The Royal Regiment
of Fusiliers 1968; disbanded as 4th Battalion 1969.

The 1st Battalion of The Lancashire Fusiliers made a brief but significant contribution to the war effort, serving in action for just four months in 1944.

The second Chindits campaign introduced the concept of blocks to Burma – temporary strongholds at strategic points in enemy-held land that could be held against attack and supplied by air – and The Lancashire Fusiliers, having been flown in by glider in March 1944, assisted in the building of the most famous of these blocks, known as White City.

As expected, White City soon came under heavy Japanese pressure and for two weeks the fighting was bloody and bitter. A sergeant serving through the encounter later described the tenacity of the opposition:

'One particular incident impressed itself upon me – a British officer in the bayonet charge spared and passed a wounded man, who immediately shot him dead from behind. The man was at once shot by the officer's batman, who was in turn shot by yet another casualty lying apparently helpless. 'Never pass a wounded Jap' was now on everybody's lips.' [1]

The onslaught only ended when the battalion staged an attack from the stronghold on the enemy's base. By then, however, there were wider problems. The original plan had been for Chinese troops under the command of General Stillwell to advance from the north to link up with the Chindits. In the light of the Japanese U-Go offensive, with Kohima and Imphal under siege (the former garrison including the 1/8th Lancashire Fusiliers), this proved impossible, and the battalion instead advanced north toward Stillwell.

Progress was difficult, hampered by the monsoon and by the Japanese system of bunkers, notoriously well-built and defended, that could only be penetrated by machine-gun and grenade attack at close quarters, sometimes as close as 15 yards. Nonetheless contact was made with the Chinese and a joint operation staged to recapture Mogaung, before the men were withdrawn. Casualties in those four months amounted to 305 dead, wounded or evacuated sick.

The 2nd Battalion had a lengthier experience of the war, serving in the British Expeditionary Force alongside three territorial battalions, one of which – the 1/8th – was badly damaged at the Escaut; when it re-grouped in England, only four officers and 200 men were left. That battalion, as mentioned above, was later to fight in the Far East, but the 2nd joined the 1st Army in North Africa, landing in November 1942.

Together with a battalion of The Northampton Regiment, the 2nd Lancashire Fusiliers fought their first major battle at Medjez-el-Bab against three German parachute battalions. Though the attack failed to break through, it was enough to force the enemy to vacate the position under cover of night. It was a battle that cost the Commanding Officer, Lieutenant-Colonel L A Manly, his life.

With popular images of North Africa dominated by the 8th Army, it is worth noting Major Fred Majdalany's comments on the bleakness of the war in Tunisia:

'One just went on and on – no tents, no rest camps, no reliefs, no buildings that could be used in that utterly bare battle area.' [2]

The battalion followed the campaign through to Sicily and on to Italy. Much of the fighting was in mountainous country, as at Cassino, a terrain described memorably by Maj Majdalany: 'The monastery . . . brooded over the battlefield like a curse.' [3] But much also was concerned with crossing rivers. At Sangro, where earlier attempts to force a crossing had failed, the men waded through the chest-high, fast-flowing icy water, carrying just one day's ration and their personal arms, to establish a bridgehead and await the arrival of the tanks.

And at the Rapido, where the advance was held up by Panzers, Fusilier F A Jefferson launched a one-man attack with a PIAT gun that turned the tide of the combat and won him a Victoria Cross.

The 11th Battalion also fought in Italy, having spent 18 months under siege in Malta. Even the journey to that island was eventful, with a 60 hour defence of the convoy carrying the troops from Gibralta.

Of the other territorial battalions, the 10th served in the Arakan in 1942/43, whilst the 2/5th landed in Normandy on 29 June 1944 and won a battle honour in the taking of Caen.

[1] Ray *Regiment of the Line* p.161
[2] ibid. p.170
[3] ibid. p.175

The Royal Scots Fusiliers

Principal Battle Honours 1939-45

Ypres-Comines Canal – Odon – Falaise – Scheldt – Rhine
Bremen – Landing in Sicily – Garigliano Crossing
North Arakan – Pinwe

Raised 1678; amalgamated to form The Royal Highland Fusiliers (Princess
Margaret's Own Glasgow and Ayrshire Regiment) 1959.

Unusually for an infantry regiment in the Second World War, both regular
battalions of The Royal Scots Fusiliers fought side-by-side in a single action;
in this case in the invasion of Madagascar. Prior to that, the 2nd Battalion had
already encountered the enemy in the British Expeditionary Force, winning a
battle-honour at the Ypres-Comines Canal. The men took over a farmhouse near
Vimy Ridge and held the position for 24 hours against ferocious enemy assaults
before being forced back.

Also in the BEF was the 6th Battalion, one of the few components of the 51st
(Highland) Division to escape capture. The sense of anger at the mismanagement
of that division's campaign was, however, felt just as keenly by those who escaped;
the battalion's war diary records of the final evacuation: 'Inevitable end to attempt
for six weeks to hold a Corps front with a depleted division. Many first-class men
sacrificed to indecisive orders or none at all.' [1]

The 1st Battalion, meanwhile, was called back from India in 1940. Its first
conflict was the May 1942 sea-borne invasion of Madagascar, a Vichy-held colony
that was a potential target for the Japanese.

The 1st and 2nd Scots Fusiliers landed some 20 miles south of the key town of
Antsirane on the northern tip of the island, and proceeded to fight their way
through dense jungle. It was a far from one-sided campaign; the French troops
were equipped with 75mm field guns powerful enough to destroy armoured
support. Nonetheless a series of bayonet charges succeeded in clearing the
opposition, and the Scots Fusiliers entered Antsirane with pipes playing.

At the conclusion of the campaign, the island was handed over to the Free
French for administration, and the 1st Battalion departed for India, whilst the 2nd
spent some time in the Middle East.

From this beginning, the 2nd Scots Fusiliers made something of a speciality of
sea-borne operations. They were the first formation ashore in the landing on Sicily

– later fighting at Priolo and Catania – and they were amongst the first Allied troops in Italy, landing on 3 September 1943.

Rapid progress was made in the first week in Italy – some 70 miles covered – but later stages proved more difficult, particularly the bloody battle to cross the Garigliano. The battalion also served as reinforcements at Anzio, before being withdrawn to fight in North-West Europe, arriving in time to contribute to the crossing of the Elbe.

Already involved in that campaign were territorial battalions of the regiment. The 6th Scots Fusiliers had returned to the continent on 15 June 1944 and made several significant interventions in the struggle. Of particular note was Sergeant Rees, who soon acquired a reputation as a man without fear. In the course of intense fighting around Broek in November, with the four supporting tanks knocked out, Sgt Rees disappeared, only to return some while later driving 14 prisoners before him, all of whom he had personally captured and disarmed. When asked why he had taken such extreme risks, he is reported to have answered that he was keen to get his hands on a watch and a Luger pistol.

Great courage was also demonstrated by 19-year old Fusilier Dennis Donnini of the 4th/5th Battalion, who was posthumously awarded a Victoria Cross for his actions on 18 January 1945. The final paragraph of his citation read:

'The superb gallantry and self-sacrifice of Fusilier Donnini drew the enemy fire away from his companions on to himself. As the result of this, the platoon was able to capture the position, accounting for thirty Germans and two machine guns. Throughout the action, fought from beginning to end at point blank range, the dash, determination and magnificent courage of Fusilier Donnini enabled his comrades to overcome an enemy more than twice their own number.' [2]

The 1st Battalion served in the North Arakan and in Burma.

[1] *The 6th Battalion Royal Scots Fusiliers 1939-46* p.43

[2] *A Soldier's History: The Royal Highland Fusiliers (Princess Margaret's Own Glasgow and Ayrshire Regiment)* p.48

The Cheshire Regiment

Principal Battle Honours 1939-45

St Omer-La Bassée – Normandy Landing
Capture of Tobruk – El Alamein – Mareth – Sicily 1943
Salerno – Rome – Gothic Line – Malta 1941-42

Raised 1689.

The 2nd Battalion, The Cheshire Regiment arrived in France in September 1939 in its capacity as a machine-gun unit, and spent the winter preparing for the coming war. When orders were received the following May to advance into Belgium, its experiences were typical; the regimental history records of 'D' Company:

'In Brussels, the road was blocked with cheering crowds and flowers, chocolates, cigarettes and fruit were thrown into the truck. A very different experience awaited the Company a week later.' [1]

It is as succinct an account as exists of the rapid reversal of fortunes in 1940 that led back to Dunkirk.

Also in the rank of the British Expeditionary Force were the 4th and 7th Battalions, the latter laying claim to being the first territorial unit to fire on the enemy.

Most of the remainder of the regiment's involvement was centred on the Mediterranean. The 1st Cheshires, also a machine-gun battalion, was stationed in Mersa Matruh as the war with Italy commenced, and was in the early stages of the desert campaign, fighting at Sidi Barrani, Tobruk and Benghazi.

Though the opposition was swept aside more easily than anticipated, conditions were still difficult. This was particularly so when the terrain became impassable for vehicles or when an approach to a battlefield had to be conducted discreetly; at these times, a 'long carry' was called for, each man being loaded up with some 100 pounds of equipment to be transported by foot, sometimes for 12 miles or more.

In February 1941 the battalion was despatched to Malta, where it remained for the duration of the siege of that island. Work here was hard and relentless, with low rations and often no electricity. Among the men's tasks was unloading those convoy ships that managed to break through the Axis blockade, including SS *Pampas*, which staggered into dock badly damaged in March 1942. Up to their waists in water, and under enemy bombing, the men worked in shifts to get the oil and petrol drums from the sinking vessel ashore. More spectacular was the repulsing of an Italian sea-borne assault in July 1941, when a battalion gun sunk at least one and possibly two E-boats.

Meanwhile the 2nd Battalion had landed in Africa in June 1941, and the following February moved forward to Gazala, where the companies were distributed across the front-line. In the Afrika Korps' offensive that year, the battalion was so badly hit that it was forced to restructure as two companies of four platoons apiece, and then suffered further losses in the retreat to Alamein, including all the platoon commanders of 'A/C' Company.

The 2nd Cheshires fought alongside the newly-arrived 6th Battalion at Alam Halfa and El Alamein, before being withdrawn to rebuild and train its reinforcements. As the struggle for the Mareth Line intensified, it was rushed forward (over 920 miles in four and a half days) to serve at Medenine and Akarit, in the company of The Green Howards.

From Africa, the men proceeded to Sicily, joining the battle to secure the Primosole bridgehead. The function of machine-gun companies was to support infantry action, but occasionally they found themselves out-stripping other troops, as when Captain Martin of 'A' Company captured the village of San Antonio, and only narrowly managed to avoid being killed by The Royal Berkshires, advancing behind.

The 2nd Battalion returned to England in November 1943 and enjoyed three weeks leave – their longest spell since the war began – before commencement of training for D-Day. It served in France until November 1944 and was then withdrawn. The 1st Battalion arrived in Holland the following February to keep the regiment's name in the front-line of Northern Europe.

In Italy the same function was being fulfilled by the 7th, which had also been in Sicily, and the 6th Battalions. Both spent time at Anzio, and the 6th also distinguished itself in establishing the bridgehead at Salerno, in the taking of Monte Camino, and in crossing the Garigliano.

[1] Crookden *The History of The Cheshire Regiment in The Second World War* p.44

The Royal Welch Fusiliers

Principal Battle Honours 1939-45

St Omer-La Bassee – Caen – Lower Maas – Reichswald
Weeze – Rhine – Madagascar – Donbaik
North Arakan – Kohima

Raised 1688.

The 1st Battalion of The Royal Welch Fusiliers sailed for France in September 1939 as part of the 2nd Division. Even before contact was made with the enemy, tragedy struck with the death of the Commanding Officer, Lieutenant-Colonel Garnons-Williams in a 'plane crash.

On 11 May 1940 the battalion moved forward into Belgium to the river Dyle, but like so many British units, it soon found that its actions and its localized successes in checking the German advance were undermined by the collapse of the line elsewhere. A series of positions were taken and then abandoned, with wearying marches between: in one 30 hour period, 40 miles were covered on foot.

The major encounter was to come at La Bassée Canal. On 24 May, the Royal Welch were sent in to retake bridges seized by the enemy, but found themselves overwhelmed by greater forces. 'D' Company was ambushed at night and suffered heavy casualties, whilst 'B' Company was surrounded and forced to split into small groups in an attempt to rejoin the British lines. The remnants re-grouped and, aware that the evacuation from Dunkirk demanded that as much time be bought as possible, stood their ground. On 27 May the survivors finally withdrew, though the Commanding Officer, Lieutenant-Colonel H S Harrison was killed as he tried to delay the progress of German tanks following them across a bridge over the Bourne Canal.

When the battalion returned to England, just five officers and 263 other ranks were left of an original complement numbering over 1,000.

Rebuilt, the 1st Royal Welch sailed for India in April 1942, their journey enlivened by a concert party organized by 2nd Lieutenant Jack Hawkins, later to achieve international stardom in films portraying the archetypal British officer.

In March 1943 an intervention in the assault on Donbaik in Arakan failed, though it did provide valuable experience in fighting the Japanese. This was to be utilized the following year when the battalion was sent forward to Kohima. The first two weeks showed how costly the Far East war could be; though no heavy fighting was seen, 59 casualties were sustained and a further 70 cases of sickness reported.

At the end of April a position was taken over at Garrison Hill, then under heavy siege. With supplies having to be dropped in by air, water was rationed and no washing or shaving permitted for 12 days. Almost as vital as water was chloride of lime, used to keep the masses of flies off the corpses. During the break-out toward Imphal, another problem was encountered with a plague of leeches, small enough to crawl through a boot-lace hole; as they swelled with blood, the only remedy was to burn the creatures off with a lighted cigarette.

Despite these horrors and the near-suicidal Japanese opposition, Imphal was reached, and the tide of the war turned. The battalion fought on to Mandalay.

Also in the 1944 battle in the Arakan was the 2nd Battalion. Its most distinctive campaign, however, had come earlier in Madagascar.

The men landed on the northern tip of the island on 4 May 1942 with the 29th Brigade Group, and soon swept aside the Senegalese and Vichy troops to take Antisrane within a few days, For four months they remained in the north, building defences against the feared Japanese attack, though time was also found for recreation with football matches, horse-racing, choir-singing and crocodile shoots.

The southern half of Madagascar, however, remained unoccupied, and in September sea-borne assaults were launched against Majunga and Tamatave to secure the whole island for the Allies.

Casualties throughout the campaign had been thankfully light, but disease was more prevalent, with 90% of the men contracting malaria.

The 4th, 6th and 7th Battalions fought together in the 158th Brigade in Normandy. Prior to that, they had been posted in Northern Ireland from September 1939. A major bombing campaign by the IRA on the British mainland had culminated in an explosion in Coventry that killed five and injured 50. When two IRA members were executed in April 1940 for the killings, it sparked a wave of strikes and civil unrest, and the Fusiliers found themselves engaged in another conflict a long way from the struggle against Nazism.

The South Wales Borderers

Principal Battle Honours 1939-45

Norway 1940 – Normandy Landing – Sully – Caen
Le Havre – North West Europe 1944-45 – North Africa 1942
Mayu Tunnels – Pinwe – Burma 1944-45

Raised 1689; amalgamated to form The Royal Regiment of Wales
(24th/41st Foot) 1969.

The disorganisation that tainted so much of the early British war effort is exemplified by the experience of the men of the 1st Battalion, The South Wales Borderers.

Having spent the latter years of the '30s in India, they were posted to Iraq in November 1941 in anticipation of a German attack. When it became apparent that no such attack was coming, they moved overland the following May to a position just outside Tobruk, which they were ordered to hold in cover of the general British withdrawal of forces from the area. This order, however, was almost immediately countermanded and a chaotic retreat ensued, exacerbated by lack of transport and the capture of the battalion's reconnaissance officers by the Germans. Under heavy attack, and in unfamiliar and hostile terrain, over 500 men were lost, most taken prisoner.

The remainder regrouped, only to be informed shortly afterwards that the battalion was being disbanded. The name of the 1st South Wales Borderers was subsequently revived to designate a training squadron back home.

Mention should be made, however, of a mass escape from an Italian prisoner-of-war camp by members of the battalion in September 1943. Many were re-captured or killed in the attempt, but four officers and 30 men were successful in reaching freedom.

The 2nd Battalion had already seen its first action by this stage, having been sent on the aborted mission to Norway in 1940.

It was later to achieve the distinction of being the only Welsh battalion to land on D-Day. And by the end of that fateful day, it could boast of having covered more ground than any other battalion.

Further progress was more difficult. The struggle around the German-occupied town of Caen was protracted and bitter; in a month's fighting, alongside the 2nd South Wales Borderers, the battalion gained only 4,000 yards of ground. Victory was eventually won, and the men pressed on across Northern France and into the Low Countries.

In common with other infantry regiments, The South Wales Borderers raised additional battalions in 1940 in response to the catastrophe of the BEF. One such was the 5th Battalion, intended to serve as Home Defence and disbanded in 1943 when the threat of invasion had receded. Another was the 7th, later to be attached to the Royal Artillery.

The story of the 6th Battalion, like that of the 1st, was typical of the confusion of the British Army. Trained initially as an infantry battalion, it was posted in 1942 to India in a new role as a tank regiment, only to be retrained the following year as an amphibious assault unit. When it did eventually see active service, it was once again a regular infantry battalion.

And, of course, when they were called upon to serve, the men responded magnificently. In July 1944, they were sent to North Burma to assist the American and Chinese forces who were rolling back the Japanese gains. The next 15 months, as they advanced down the Myitkina-Mandalay-Rangoon road and beyond, was a period of intense jungle fighting. The battalion would claim by the end that they had covered 5,000 miles, much of it on foot since the monsoon precluded the use of vehicles, clearing pockets of resistance as they progressed. Following the Japanese surrender, it was sent to Sumatra as part of the army of liberation.

By the end of the War, the regiment had incurred 1,024 casualties.

The King's Own Scottish Borderers

Principal Battle Honours 1939-45

Dunkirk 1940 – Odon – Caen – Arnhem 1944 – Flushing
Rhine – Bremen – Ngakyedauk Pass – Imphal – Irrawaddy

Raised 1689.

In common with so many other units, the 1st Scottish Borderers moved to France in late 1939, and spent the winter there waiting for the Germans to make a move. When war came, they advanced to a position near Louvain on the river Dyle, and proceeded to spend three weeks in a fighting retreat to Dunkirk.

The failure of the British Expeditionary Force was followed by a second lesser known attempt at a British intervention in mainland Europe. Lieutenant-General Alan Brooke, who had just returned from Dunkirk, was ordered to return to the continent in command of what was conceived of as a new BEF. Accordingly the 52nd (Lowland) Division, including the 4th and 5th Battalions of The Scottish Borderers, landed at St Malo on 13 June 1940 to reinforce the troops still in France.

The intention was to establish an Allied stronghold in Brittany, and thus keep the French battle alive, or at the very least to make a token attempt to do so, but it was immediately apparent that the venture was misguided. Brooke himself condemned the plan as 'a wild one which was quite impossible' [1], and the troops were evacuated. The 5th Battalion, covering the withdrawal, was the last British infantry unit out of France, leaving on 18 June.

All three of these battalions were to return to France four years later, fighting through the North-West European campaign and ending the war in Bremen. A particularly significant contribution was made by the 4th and 5th Battalions in an assault landing at Walcheren on 1 November 1944 in the operation to open the port of Antwerp. The Divisional Commander was later to write:

'Both battalions went into it with such determination and sheer guts that nothing could have stopped them . . . . their losses were extremely light in relation to the strength of their objectives.' [2]

The 4th sustained 75 casualties, with a further 62 in the 5th.

Also present during the campaign was the 7th Battalion who landed with the 1st Airborne Division at Arnhem. Of the 40 officers and 700 men who landed (including, of course, the obligatory pipers), just 76 all ranks escaped the disaster.

Whilst most of the regiment was serving in Europe, the 2nd Battalion was in the Far East. Stationed at Waziristan on the North-West Frontier, the men did not see combat with the Japanese until August 1943 when they were sent into North Arakan.

The first action was near Maungdaw in October, and from then on, they fought through to the end of the war. A series of tough encounters with the enemy was undertaken at places whose names have passed into regimental lore: Horseshoe Hill, Able Hill, Allwynbin, Ngakyedauk Pass. They were also in the famous Admin Box that held out under heavy assault in early 1944. During this latter action, two successive Commanding Officers were killed.

Conditions during the campaign were atrocious, with the monsoon compounding the dangers posed by the Japanese and by disease. During a short break for recovery in August 1944, with the Battalion at less than half-strength, a medical inspection found that 80% of the troops considered to be fit were actually suffering from dysentery and malnutrition.

An improved diet and exercise programme did much to improve the situation and the 2nd Borderers returned to the front-line in December, marching some 170 miles to the Irrawaddy. A succession of mopping up operations ended at Prome in July 1945. By the end, just five members of the battalion were still serving from those who had been present at the outset.

1,325 men from The King's Own Scottish Borderers gave their lives during the course of the war.

[1] Glover *The Fight For The Channel Ports* p.207

[2] Gunning *Borderers in Battle* p.150

The Cameronians (Scottish Rifles)

Principal Battle Honours 1939-45

Odon – Scheldt – Rhineland – Rhine
North-West Europe 1940, 44-45 – Sicily 1943 – Anzio
Italy 1943-44 – Chindits 1944 – Burma 1942, 44

26th Cameronian Regiment raised 1689; 90th Perthshire Light Infantry
raised 1794; these two regiments amalgamated to form The Cameronians
(Scottish Rifles) 1881; disbanded 1968.

The 1st Battalion of The Cameronians fought through both stages of the war in Burma. Stationed in India at the outset, it was rushed forward to Rangoon in February 1942 with the intention of helping the defence against the advancing Japanese. In the event, defence turned rapidly to withdrawal and to the longest retreat in British military history.

Though there was no doubt that the enemy had the upper hand in 1942, there were moments of success and many individuals distinguished themselves. One such was Corporal Sayle, who in three days wiped out three enemy machine gun crews, capturing two of the guns for the battalion's use.

The retreat from Burma was a long painful operation, and when the battalion assembled for inspection by General Wavell on 26 May just prior to leaving the country, there were only 14 officers and 120 other ranks left, organized into three platoons. Even so, the standards of the regiment were proudly upheld, each survivor being sure to make use of the battalion's one razor before going on parade. In his address that day, General Wavell told the men:

'You have already shown that you can beat the Jap when everything is in his favour; when next you meet him it will be under conditions much more favourable to you, and I have no doubt you will display again those fighting qualities which have marked your actions in Burma, and to more effect.' [1]

It was a prescient remark for, rebuilt and back up to strength, the 1st Cameronians were to return to Burma in the Chindits campaign, flying in by glider in March 1944.

For just over four months, the battalion operated within hostile territory, disrupting the Japanese lines of communication and tying up large numbers of the enemy forces. Though supplies were dropped by air, the men were largely dependent on their own resources to survive, marching for hundreds of miles to keep ahead of the enemy, and carrying their wounded with them. By the end, when both the monsoon and the Japanese caught up with them at Namkin and a withdrawal to India ordered, the battalions had 50 men on stretchers and a further 150 walking wounded. Even with these handicaps, a march back over jungle terrain and hills up to 3,500 feet high, was successfully undertaken.

The 2nd Battalion fought exclusively in Europe, though it was on occasion posted further abroad. Arriving in France in September 1939, it established positions on the Ypres-Comines Canal, where it remained through the winter. Like most of the BEF, it advanced and retreated in May 1940, fighting its major battle back on the Ypres-Comines Canal whilst covering the withdrawal. It was an effective action: the Germans crossed the canal, and the 2nd Cameronians pulled back some 1,500 yards before launching a sudden counter-attack that took the enemy by surprise and stalled the advance.

By the time the Battalion was evacuated, some 360 casualties had been sustained.

Also in France were the 6th and 7th Battalions, serving in the 52nd (Lowland) Division in the brief attempt to create a second BEF.

Having rebuilt in Scotland, the 2nd Cameronians left again in March 1942 to spend the next 18 months in a succession of postings. They were held in reserve in Madagascar and spent some time in India, Persia and Transjordan, before being called up for Sicily.

They were also present in Operation Baytown, the landing on the toe of Italy in September 1943. In the first month the battalion made good progress, advancing 260 miles, some of it by sea, but thereafter the campaign slowed.

In March 1944 the men were sent in to reinforce the Anzio bridgehead, a two and a half month struggle culminating in the break-out and the march on Rome. In keeping with Scottish regimental tradition, the entry into the city was accompanied by the swirl of pipes.

A further period in the Middle East ensued and then in February 1945, the 2nd Cameronians made their return to Northern Europe to serve in the later stages of that campaign. Already present were the 6th, 7th and 9th Battalions.

1,222 men of the regiment died in the war.

[1] Barclay *The History of The Cameronians (Scottish Rifles) Vol III: 1933-1946* p.96

The Royal Inniskilling Fusiliers

Principal Battle Honours 1939-45

North-West Europe 1940 – Djebel Tanngoucha
North Africa 1942-43 – Centuripe – Sicily 1943
Garigliano Crossing – Cassino II – Italy 1943-45
Yenangyaung 1942 – Burma 1942-43

27th Foot raised 1689; 108th Regiment raised 1854; these two regiments
amalgamated 1881 to form The Royal Inniskilling Fusiliers 1881;
amalgamated to form The Royal Irish Rangers 1968; amalgamated to form
The Royal Irish Regiment (27th (Inniskilling) 83rd and 87th and The Ulster
Defence Regiment) 1993.

The 1st Inniskilling Fusiliers, stationed in India at the outbreak of hostilities, were sent forward to Prome as the Japanese invaded Burma in early 1942. Contact was made with the enemy in late-March but by 1 April Prome had been evacuated as the battalion rushed north to defend the oil-fields at Yenangyaung. It arrived to find that the installations had been destroyed by Chinese troops to prevent them falling into enemy hands.

Surrounded by the rapidly advancing Japanese forces, the men had to fight out, at great cost, to join up with the Chinese, and then to retreat back to India.

Returning to Burma in December 1942, the battalion joined the attempt to clear the Mayu Peninsula. Despite massive efforts – at one village the men of 'A' Company attacked naked, shedding their clothes to enable them to swim a river unencumbered – the drive to Donbaik failed. Again surrounded by the enemy, the battalion split into twos and threes to try to escape. About half the men managed to reach the safety of Kyaukpanduywama.

In the war against Germany, the 6th Battalion had landed with the 38th (Irish) Brigade at Algiers in November 1942. Though it was primarily engaged in patrolling rather than in the major engagements of the time, casualties were still serious and included the Commanding Officer, Lieutenant-Colonel Allen who was shot in the drive to Tunis. In that final push, the battalion won a major battle honour at Tanngoucha Hill.

For the invasion of Sicily, the 6th was joined by the 2nd Battalion, veterans of Dunkirk, who had spent the intervening period on non-combatant duties in Madagascar, India and Persia.

The initial opposition in Sicily came from dispirited Italian forces, their lack of will to fight demonstrated when Corporal Stephen Hughes took a machine-gun post armed only with a grenade. At Catania, however, the German army was encountered and determined opposition was met once more. Prepared to try anything, the Germans met the 2nd Battalion at the Simento river with cries of 'Don't fire! This is the Jocks.' The regimental history notes drily that the men 'were not deceived and directed their fire to the place where the sporrans ought to be.' [1]

The 6th Battalion made its greatest contribution at Centuripe, reported by Reuters as 'one of the greatest achievements in storming almost impregnable heights'. [2]

Both battalions went on to fight in Italy, again often being used for patrolling purposes. The 2nd Battalion, having landed in the first wave at Reggio on 3 September 1943, scored a morale-boosting first in reaching the key road and rail junction at Isernia ahead of all units. 'D' Company under Lieutenant Long advanced to the town on 4 November and proceeded to stencil the regimental cap badge on every available wall.

At the crossing of the Garigliano, in a more notable military accomplishment, the 2nd Inniskilling made the first breach in the Gustav Line.

Following the subsequent Allied break-through to Rome, men of the 6th Battalion attended a Mass given by the Pope. Later, the pipes of the Irish Brigade played for the Pontiff at his specific request.

Soon after, however, in July 1944 the 6th Battalion was disbanded and the men used as reinforcements for the 2nd Battalion. Joining the Irish Brigade, the 2nd Inniskillings fought through to the end of the Italian campaign.

[1] Fox *The Royal Inniskilling Fusiliers in The Second World War* p.74
[2] ibid. p.78

The Gloucestershire Regiment

Principal Battle Honours 1939-45

Defence of Escaut – Cassel – Mont Pincon
Falaise – North West Europe 1940, 44-45 – Taukyan
Paungde – Pinwe – Myitson – Burma 1942, 44-45

28th Foot raised 1694; 61st Foot raised 1756; these two regiments amalgamated to form The Gloucestershire Regiment 1881; amalgamated to form The Royal Gloucestershire, Berkshire and Wiltshire Regiment 1993.

The battalions of The Gloucestershire Regiment fought in two major theatres of war, North-West Europe and Burma, and the pattern was essentially the same in both – defeats in early campaigns followed by a victorious second coming.

The 2nd and 5th Battalions were in the British Expeditionary Force, often fighting side by side. The mood of the time was summed up by Major Anthony Scott of the 5th:

'A great many were puzzled at the vagueness of the orders during this hectic period, but, looking back at the complexity and fluidity of the situation, one wonders that units kept together and carried out their difficult tasks as well as they did.' [1]

For the 5th Battalion those tasks included a fighting withdrawal, marching for three and a half days over 95 miles. It sustained 87 casualties over the campaign, though the remainder were to escape from Dunkirk.

The 2nd Battalion was less fortunate. In the most severe bombing raid of the campaign at Tournai, the battalion suffered 194 casualties. And when it retreated to Cassel, some 15 miles south of Dunkirk, it was ordered to hold the town. A withdrawal was finally authorized, but by then Cassel was surrounded and, though some men reached safety, 484 were taken prisoner. The order to withdraw was hand-delivered and might have been received earlier, had the battalion not been ordered to destroy its ciphers, thus rendering coded radio messages unintelligible.

Elsewhere, the 1st Battalion had been posted to Burma in 1938, stationed just outside Rangoon. It took the opportunity of the chaos surrounding the Japanese offensive to salvage as many vehicles as it could, converting itself into a highly mechanized unit. It was consequently not only better acquainted with the country, but also better equipped than most of those who faced the long retreat from Burma in 1942. It fought a number of actions including successful encounters at Letpadan and Paungde. Field-Marshal Slim was to write of the former, with typical British under-statement:

'The 1st Gloucesters, at about the same time, surprised a Japanese battalion in billets in the small town of Letpadan, eighty miles south of Prome, inflicted severe losses upon it, and chased it into the jungle – a most sprightly affair.' [2]

By the time the battalion arrived at Kohima, eight officers and 156 other ranks were dead, many from disease. One platoon was later to serve in the re-taking of Burma, but the remainder stayed in India, helping to maintain civil order in the wave of protest that followed the arrest of Gandhi in 1942.

The 2nd Battalion, re-formed after Dunkirk, returned to mainland Europe on D-Day. The first two months were relatively incident-free, but the battalion was to play a key role in the attack on Le Havre, and later in taking Arnhem in April 1945. It sustained over 700 casualties.

The 5th Battalion also re-formed after Dunkirk and in 1941 was converted to become the 43rd Reconnaissance Regiment. It too was part of the Normandy fleet in 1944, but the ship carrying it was sunk by a mine on the crossing, killing 189 men. Undeterred, it re-formed again and finally returned to Europe later in the year.

The 10th Battalion was to restore the regiment's tradition in the Far East. Posted to India in October 1942, it was sent into the fighting in the Arakan for 16 weeks in early 1944. In July of that year it flew into Myitkyina with the 36th Division, ordered to advance down the railway to Mandalay. In the midst of the monsoon, the casualties came almost as much from malaria and dysentery as they did from the enemy.

Christmas 1944 was spent at Katha on the banks of the Irrawaddy. Geese, pork, Christmas pudding and beer were airlifted in, and a service held in the village church, which had been restored by the battalion during their stay. It was a far cry from the last Christmas the regiment had spent in Burma three years earlier, when the 1st Battalion had been bombed.

In February 1945 the 10th Battalion occupied Myitson. During the Japanese counter-attack, 'D' Company was cut off whilst holding a vital position. For five days it held firm, before the rest of the battalion could join them.

Amongst the other battalions raised during the war was the 8th, which guarded Queen Mary whilst she was staying at Badminton House.

[1] Daniell *Cap Of Honour: The Story of The Gloucestershire Regiment (The 28th/61st Foot) 1694-1950* p.251

[2] Slim *Defeat Into Victory* p.38

The Worcestershire Regiment

Principal Battle Honours 1939-45

Mont Pinchon – Seine 1944 – Geilenkirchen – Goch
North-West Europe 1940, 44-45 – Keren – Gazala
Kohima – Mandalay – Burma 1944-45

29th Foot raised 1694; 36th Foot raised 1702; these two regiments
amalgamated to form The Worcestershire Regiment 1881; amalgamated
to form The Worcestershire and Sherwood Foresters Regiment
(29th/45th Foot) 1970.

The first troops from the Worcestershire Regiment to encounter the enemy in
the Second World War were the men in two territorial battalions. Both the 7th
and 8th Battalions were part of the British Expeditionary Force in 1940, the 7th in
Belgium as the German offensive began, and the 8th in the south of the line
amongst the French army. The casualties were heavy for both, just 400 of the 800
men of the 7th made it back from Dunkirk, whilst the whole of the 8th's 'B'
Company was lost.

Better news was to come from Africa. In January 1941 the 1st Battalion,
stationed in the Sudan, was sent into Eritrea with the 5th Indian Division. In the
protracted but successful capture of the enemy stronghold at Keren and the equally
successful siege of Amba Alagi in Abyssinia, the battalion helped deal the two
decisive blows that brought down Italy's East African empire.

July 1941 saw the 1st Worcesters transferred to the Western Desert for a period
of training on wholly new terrain.

The German offensive of May 1942 forced the British withdrawal from the
Gazala line, and the battalion established a defensive box some 20 miles west of
Tobruk to cover the retreat. Within a square 1,000 yards across, surrounded by
minefields, the men met an attack of such overwhelming strength and numbers that
the box could hold out for no more than a day. Leaving behind the wrecks of 35
enemy tanks, an orderly retreat to Tobruk was made on the evening of 14 June.
Within a week, however, Tobruk too had fallen and of nearly 500 men left in the
battalion, all but 68 were captured.

On the other side of the Empire, the 2nd Battalion had been stationed
in Rawalpindi at the start of the War, but moved to Madras when the fall of
Singapore suggested the possibility of an assault on India by sea. That threat never

materialized, and in November 1944 the battalion – as part of the 19th Indian Division – crossed the Chindwin river in the drive against the Japanese.

In the first month, the 2nd Worcesters advanced some 400 miles with little evidence of the enemy, by now withdrawing. In January 1945 there was a meeting with the 7th Battalion.

Re-formed after the losses of Dunkirk, the 7th had arrived in India in 1942 and had been posted to the front in April 1944. It formed part of the force sent to relieve the beleaguered garrison at Kohima and then pressed on south down the Manipur road to Imphal. It had also achieved the distinction of becoming the first battalion to cross the Burma border since the occupation; it had reached the village of Tama to find a ghost town wiped out by typhus, cholera and malaria.

The two battalions pursued separate but parallel paths in the last months of the British offensive in Burma. During the crossing of the Irrawaddy river, the 2nd met virtually no opposition, though the bridgehead they helped established was to come under heavy attack. The 7th meanwhile found themselves with more problems; during one attack whilst they had yet to cross the river, four officers including the CO were killed.

The heaviest fighting probably came during the siege of Mandalay, in which both battalions were involved, albeit from different sides of the city. With the monsoon approaching, and with serious supply problems for the Allied forces, the 7th were withdrawn from Burma shortly after the fall of Mandalay, whilst the 2nd continued its advance, meeting fierce resistance at Kalaw.

Back home, the 1st Battalion had re-formed in January 1943 with two officers and ten NCOs who had escaped Tobruk, and with the remainder mostly drawn from the 11th Battalion. It landed in Normandy in June 1944, its subsequent experiences following the typical pattern of the British forces advancing across Northern Europe.

Whilst the Worcestershire Regiment played its full part in the combat, it also made two further contributions to the war effort. The 8th Battalion, veterans of Dunkirk, appeared in the 1942 film *Next of Kin* with Mervyn Johns and Jack Hawkins, illustrating the saying that careless talk costs lives. And the 10th Battalion were involved in Operation Quicksilver, the attempt to persuade the enemy that the D-Day landings were to come from Kent and Essex, an operation so successful that the Luftwaffe bombed the fleet of dummy ships and landing craft.

The East Surrey Regiment

Principal Battle Honours 1939-45

Dunkirk 1940 – North-West Europe 1940 – Oued Zarga
Longstop Hill 1943 – North Africa 1942-43 – Sangro
Cassino – Italy 1943-45 – Malaya 1941-42

31st Foot raised 1702; 70th Foot raised 1756; these two regiments amalgamated to form The East Surrey Regiment 1881; amalgamated to form The Queen's Royal Surrey Regiment 1959; redesignated 1st Battalion, The Queen's Regiment 1966; amalgamated to form The Princess of Wales's Royal Regiment 1993.

Of the three battalions of The East Surrey Regiment serving in the British Expeditionary Force, the 2/6th was to suffer the worst fate. As part of Beauforce, the men were caught up in the retreat of the 51st (Highland) Division, eventually surrendering at St Valéry on 12 June 1940. By this time, just 15 officers and 261 men were left of the battalion, so determined had been their resistance.

The 1st and 1/6th Battalions had shared the experience of the main body of the BEF. The latter fought a resolute two day defence at Oost-Dunkirke to facilitate the evacuations, in which both battalions were brought back to Britain.

The contradictory nature of that campaign is illustrated by two stories concerning soldiers from the 1st Battalion. During the defence of the line at the Escaut, Private Lenihan was obliged to perform an emergency amputation of a comrade's shattered leg using the only tool available to him: a standard issue clasp-knife. The horror is in stark contrast to Private Hersey's concern that his French wife, whom he married during the 'Phoney War' should also escape; a battledress was obtained and the woman, a qualified nurse, was smuggled out of Dunkirk.

The 1st and 1/6th Battalions went on to see action in the same theatres for the remainder of the war. The 1st was landed with Operation Torch in Algeria in November 1942, and joined the drive to take Tunis that was eventually halted at Tebourba.

When the Germans launched their final counter-offensive of the campaign in February 1943, the 1st Surreys were again in the thick of the fighting. A particularly devastating action saw 'D' Company take a feature known as Fort McGregor; it was subsequently retaken by the Germans, with just four Surreys returning to tell the tale. Soon after, the battalion fought in the final battle to take the much-disputed Longstop Hill. It was while occupying the position that a final shell landed and killed the Commanding Officer, Lieutenant-Colonel Wilberforce, the only battalion CO involved to have survived the battle.

In March the 1/6th arrived and were immediately plunged into the fighting at Hunt's Gap. Different problems were to arise after the Axis collapse, with some 19,000 prisoners to administer.

The 1st Surreys fought in Sicily, where at Centuripe, Lance Corporal D Chadwick won a Military Medal for his capture of a German officer carrying plans of the German forces.

Both battalions also fought in Italy. At Cassino, the 1st spent a nerve-wracking month in positions so close to the enemy lines that it was reported that the singing of 'Lili Marlene' could be heard at night.

Key parts were later played by the 1st at Argenta Gap and the 1/6th at Forli. The 1/6th later served in Athens, sustaining eight casualties in the civil war.

In Shanghai at the outbreak of war in 1940, the 2nd Battalion was posted to Singapore and then – as the Japanese threat loomed ever closer – sent forward to North-West Malaya. The anticipated invasion was met at Jitra on 11 December 1941, and the Allied forces driven back some 60 miles to Gurin. It was there that the 2nd Surreys faced the full brunt of the Japanese assault. Reduced to just 10 officers and 260 men, it formed a composite 'British Battalion' with the 1st Leicesters, a unit that was to pass into history as an embodiment of the fighting spirit of the British Army.

Perhaps the most distinguished action was at Kampar where the battalion held two Japanese divisions for four days before being again forced back. The end came in Singapore, and the survivors were taken into captivity; 149 were to die before the end of the war.

Mention should also be made of Captain Wilson of the regiment, who won a Victoria Cross in 1940 whilst serving with the Somaliland Camel Corps. Commanding a machine-gun post, he held out against an Italian advance for four days despite being wounded and despite a bout of malaria. The award was believed to be posthumous, but reports of his death happily turned out to be inaccurate.

The Duke of Cornwall's Light Infantry

Principal Battle Honours 1939-45

Hill 112 – Mont Pincon – Nederrijn – Geilenkirchen
Rhineland – North-West Europe 1940, 44-45 – Gazala
Medjez Plain – Cassino II – Incontro

32nd Foot raised 1702; 46th Foot raised 1741; these two regiments
amalgamated to form The Duke of Cornwall's Light Infantry 1881;
amalgamated to form The Somerset & Cornwall Light Infantry 1959;
amalgamated to form The Light Infantry 1968.

The 1st Battalion, The Duke of Cornwall's Light Infantry had a particularly disastrous war, denied the chance to make a meaningful contribution and suffering heavy losses. Stationed in India from 1922, it was posted to Iraq in November 1941 at a time when it was feared that Germany would strike at the Middle East.

That threat did not materialize, and the following May the battalion was suddenly despatched to Egypt. With no time for training, the men were sent into the thick of the fighting at Gazala but, in the absence of adequate equipment and artillery support, could do little to halt the German advance then sweeping the Allies before it. Some 150 survivors of the first encounter regrouped and rendered service in the withdrawal, but it was effectively the end of the battalion. 11 men returned to Britain to join a new 1st Battalion formed from the former 6th.

Thereafter, though they were involved in the preparations for D-Day, the 1st Cornwalls played no active part in the war.

The 2nd Battalion, in contrast, fought in two major theatres. In France soon after the declaration of war, it took up a position on the Maginot Line. It was a difficult line to hold, for the men were stretched very thin and communications were problematic. On 6 March 1940 No. 17 Platoon was caught in a skirmish with German troops, though what actually happened is uncertain, for there were no survivors.

Soon afterwards, the battalion was moved to the north to join the main body of the BEF, subsequently advancing into Belgium in mid-May. Several actions were fought in the retreat, most notably preventing an enemy crossing of the Escaut on 21 May, but it was a hopeless cause; by the end of the month, the men were in the queues on the beaches of Dunkirk.

After 18 months of training, the 2nd Cornwalls were chosen to join the troops in North Africa, reinforcing the 1st Army. The campaign was coming to a close, but the fighting was still intense, as the battalion found at Medjez el Bab, where the first major battle honour was won.

The Cornwalls did not fight in Sicily, but rejoined the Allied campaign in February 1944 in Italy. Between then and November the fighting was almost continuous. They served in the final push to dislodge the enemy from Monte Cassino, and managed the rare achievement at Incontro of winning a battle honour that was awarded to no other unit. The Incontro monastery was on a 600 foot high hill near Florence and was occupied by crack Panzer Grenadiers. The battalion stormed the hill in a daylight assault that was a total success.

The Cornwalls were also involved in the subsequent struggle to break through the Gothic Line. During the crossing of the river Ronco, two companies were separated from the rest of the battalion and suffered a full-scale counter-attack. Though the enemy had the better of the battle, the resistance was such that the Germans reported they had been confronted by an entire division.

In late November, the battalion was withdrawn and departed for Greece, where it remained until the end of the war.

The regiment contributed the 5th Battalion to the campaign in North-West Europe. Landing in the second wave of the invasion, the battalion saw its first action on 27 June 1944 near Bayeux. It was reported that in the first half hour five Panzers were knocked out at the cost of just 20 casualties. Amongst the dead was the Commanding Officer, Lieutenant-Colonel Atherton, to be replaced by his second-in-command Major R W James, then aged 26.

As part of the 43rd (Wessex) Division, the 5th Cornwalls fought in the battle on 10 July to take Hill 112, a key point in the ridge between the Odon and Orne rivers. Initially held in reserve, the 5th did not join the attack until mid-evening. The hill was eventually taken, but by the time the battalion came back down, the casualty rate had reached 300. One of them was Lieutenant-Colonel James, killed whilst commanding the action from a vulnerable observation post in a tree.

Reinforced by men from the 4th Battalion, the 5th Cornwalls continued the advance across Europe, ending up on the Elbe as Germany surrendered.

The Duke of Wellington's Regiment

Principal Battle Honours 1939-45

Dunkirk 1940 – St Valéry-en-Caux – Fontenay Le Pesnil
North-West Europe 1940, 44-45 – Djebel Bou Aoukaz 1943
Anzio – Monte Ceco – Sittang 1942 – Chindits 1944
Burma 1942-44

33rd Foot raised 1702; 76th Foot raised 1787; these two regiments
amalgamated to form The Duke of Wellington's Regiment
(West Riding) 1881.

The 1st Battalion, The Duke of Wellington's Regiment, stationed at home as war was declared, was soon posted to France with the British Expeditionary Force. It acted in a rearguard capacity at Dunkirk.

After a period of regrouping and re-training back in the UK, the 1st returned to the fray in 1943 in North Africa, where it made a decisive contribution at the battle around Djebel Bou Aoukaz. It later served through the Anzio landing and the ensuing Italian campaign. It was during this time that Private Burton was awarded the Victoria Cross, the citation stating that his 'magnificent gallantry and total disregard of his own safety during many hours of fierce fighting in mud and continuous rain were an inspiration to all his comrades.'

The 1st Battalion was accompanied in the North African and Italian struggles by territorial battalions of the regiment.

The 2nd Battalion, meanwhile, spent the war in the Far East. From its posting in India, it was despatched in some haste in early 1942 to Rangoon in response to the Japanese invasion of Burma. It was, of course, to prove a futile attempt to hold back the enemy, and the men of the regiment spent the next four months retreating back through the country to India under the most dispiriting of conditions.

If they were offered little opportunity to shine in the early hostilities in Burma, however, the men were soon to be given a chance to help rebuild morale, both their own and that of the whole Army. In 1944 the battalion became part of the famous Chindits campaign, operating successfully behind enemy lines and helping to break the myth of Japanese invincibility.

Like much of the rest of the infantry, The Duke of Wellington's Regiment saw the role of some of its battalions transformed during the course of the war. The 4th converted to Royal Artillery, and the 5th first to the Royal Engineers and later to

Artillery. The 8th and 9th Battalions, raised in response to wartime demands, became RAC regiments, while the 10th served in England as Home Defence.

Two territorial battalions, the 2/6th and the 2/7th, were sent to France in the wake of the BEF to perform guard duties in the Lines of Communication. With the unexpected rapidity of the German advance, they were called upon to act as front-line troops and, despite lack of training and equipment, distinguished both themselves and their regiments. The 2/7th was evacuated from St Valéry, one of the last battalions to escape the fiasco of the BEF, and one of the very few to get out from that port.

Territorial battalions – the 6th and 7th – were also involved in the Normandy landings. A report dated 30 June 1944 from the officer commanding the 6th gives some indication of the conditions under which such units found themselves operating:

'In 14 days there have been some 23 officer and 350 OR casualties. Only 12 of the original officers remain and they are all junior. Since I took over I have lost two second-in-commands in successive days and a company commander the third day. Majority of transport, all documents, records and a large amount of equipment was lost.' [1]

One of the members of the regiment who lost his life during the conflict was the 6th Duke of Wellington, descendant of the Iron Duke who gave the regiment its name.

[1] Hastings *Overlord* p.148

The Border Regiment

Principal Battle Honours 1939-45

Dunkirk 1940 – Arnhem 1944 – North-West Europe 1940, 44
Tobruk 1941 – Landing in Sicily – Imphal
Myinmu Bridgehead – Meiktila – Chindits 1944
Burma 1943-45

34th Foot raised 1702; 55th Foot raised 1755; these two regiments
amalgamated to form The Border Regiment 1881; amalgamated to form
The King's Own Royal Border Regiment 1959.

Three battalions of The Border Regiment – the 1st, 4th and 5th – fought in the British Expeditionary Force in Flanders and France. Most of the men were to be evacuated from Dunkirk and Le Havre though there were, of course, casualties. The 1st Battalion lost 250 killed, wounded or taken prisoner, whilst the 4th, a territorial battalion sent to France to carry out guard duties, lost the whole of 'D' company. Ordered to hold the town of Incheville, just east of Dieppe, to protect the flank of the doomed 51st Highland Division, it was surrounded and, despite an heroic six day defence, was eventually over-run.

Despite these losses, the 4th Battalion was the first to return to action, serving in Syria in July 1941 – in the struggle against Vichy French troops – and in Tobruk, where it helped relieve the beleaguered Australian garrison, and then fighting in the subsequent break-out from the city.

Meanwhile the 1st Battalion was being converted to an airborne unit, forming the 1st Air Landing Brigade with the 2nd South Staffords. On the night of 9/10 July 1943, these two battalions staged the first ever military invasion by glider. The intention was to land ahead of the sea-borne invasion forces at Syracuse in Sicily, to seize a key bridge and to attack the town from behind. In the event, logistical problems reduced the scale of the operation – of 137 gliders, some 80 or so landed in the Mediterranean, and only 30 men, led by Lieutenant Welch of the 1st Borders, were involved when the bridge was taken – but it was nonetheless successful enough to warrant further exploration of the role gliders could play in modern war.

The key contribution, of course, was to come the following year at Arnhem. The 1st Battalion was amongst the forces dropped on 17 September 1944, landing with instructions to hold the landing grounds for the second wave of lifts and then to take up positions on the west of the town the next day. By that time, it was apparent that the plan was not running to schedule; the resistance had been fiercer than anticipated, and the Second Army had so far been unable to break through to relieve the airborne forces. On the third day, with no relief apparent, the 1st withdrew to a position around Oosterbeck, and it was here that the order to withdraw was finally received, eight days after the landing; it had originally been expected that they could only last two without ground support.

The commanding officer of the battalion, Lieutenant-Colonel Haddon, had been involved in a glider crash before the Arnhem convoy had even left the UK, and, finding instead a place in the second day of lifts, had been shot down. Meeting up with units of the Second Army, he had joined battalions of the Dorset Regiment crossing the Rhine in a vain attempt to break through to Arnhem. When they were unable to progress, Lt-Col Haddon advanced alone and did eventually make it to Oosterbeck, but was captured by the Germans before he could join up with his men.

Men of the 1st Battalion later served in the peaceful liberation of Norway, but the rest of the regiment's fighting was done in the Far East. The 2nd, 9th and 4th Battalions all fought in the Burma campaigns, the first two being stationed in Imphal during the three-month siege of that city, whilst the 4th – newly arrived from North Africa – fought in the Chindits operation behind enemy lines in the vicinity of Kohima.

The regiment could thus boast of having played a central part in repulsing the Japanese attack on India in early 1944, and in converting that fighting into a British counter-offensive that was ultimately to sweep the Japanese from Burma. Both the 2nd and 9th Battalions served in the advance across Burma.

The 5th Battalion, on its return from Dunkirk, was engaged in home defence, as were the 6th and 7th Battalions.

The Royal Sussex Regiment

Principal Battle Honours 1939-45

North-West Europe 1940 – Abyssinia 1941 – Omars
Alam el Halfa – El Alamein – Akarit
North Africa 1940-43 – Cassino II – Italy 1944-45
Burma 1943-45

35th Foot raised 1701; 107th Foot raised 1854; these two regiments amalgamated to form The Royal Sussex Regiment 1881; redesignated 3rd Battalion, The Queen's Regiment 1966; amalgamated to form The Princess of Wales's Royal Regiment 1993.

The 2nd, 4th and 5th Battalions together formed the 133rd (Royal Sussex) Brigade, fighting in the first North-West Europe campaign, though seldom as a coherent unit; the 2nd Battalion, which saw the majority of the action, was for the most part detached from the Brigade and sustained heavy casualties.

Also in the British Expeditionary Force were the 6th and 7th Battalions, the latter attacked by a Panzer Division outside Amiens and holding out for half a day before being over-run.

The 1st Battalion meanwhile was stationed at Suez and joined the 7th Brigade of the 4th Indian Division in time for the East African campaign of 1941. It took the two frontier towns of Karora and Mersa Taclai in Eritrea before moving on to Abyssinia.

Unlike the North African war, where the vast battlefield was mostly uninhabited, the fighting here did affect some local populations, though disruption was kept to a minimum; when two camels belonging to herdsmen were killed, replacements were provided from captured Italian garrisons.

The most famous of the 1st Sussex's battles was to come later in the year at the Omars in the Western Desert. Omar Nuovo was seized and held, despite desperate efforts by the Germans to recapture the position – two days of artillery bombardment were followed by a Panzer assault and Luftwaffe bombing, all to no avail. The American war correspondent, Quentin Reynolds, described the battalion's resistance as revealing 'the ruthless, spartanlike army that Britain has been waiting for.' [1]

In July 1942 the 133rd Brigade arrived in North Africa to join the struggle. Stationed at the western end of Alam el Halfa ridge when Rommel launched an attack the following month, the men held the position in an encounter that saw the end of the Afrika Korps' advance.

There were thus four battalions available to fight at El Alamein. The 1st was to win the congratulations of Churchill for a daring night raid on a German position, whilst the Sussex was also involved in the Supercharge operation that broke through the enemy lines. In the sequel to the battle, the 2nd Battalion captured General Frattini, the chief of the Italian paratroops.

The 1st was later to take the surrender of an even more celebrated foe in the form of General von Arnim, commander of the Afrika Korps after Rommel's departure, following the defeats inflicted on the enemy at Wadi Akarit and Medjez el Bab.

Early in 1944 the 1st Battalion sailed for Italy to join the stalemate at Cassino. For six weeks the men held a line so close to the enemy that even the battalion headquarters were within 200 yards of the German positions. Eric Linklater wrote of these desperate times:

'And still it rained, and snow fell on the mountain heights, where week after week, the 7th Indian Brigade held their grim sangars, despite German mortars, German machine-guns and all the malignity of nature.

Never have troops endured with more patient valour the perils and abominations of war than did these men of the Royal Sussex, the 4/16th Punjab Regiment and the 1st/2nd Gurkha Rifles.' [2]

In those six weeks, the battalion lost 22 officers and over 300 men.

The battalion fought on to the Gothic Line, where the padre distinguished himself when, armed with just a pitchfork, he took 14 prisoners.

The 9th Battalion, meanwhile, was posted forward from India in the Arakan campaign of 1944. It fought through to Mandalay and on to Malaya.

[1] Martindeau *A History of The Royal Sussex Regiment* p.248

[2] ibid. p.274

The Hampshire Regiment

Principal Battle Honours 1939-45

Dunkirk 1940 – Normandy Landing – Rhine – Terbouba Gap
Hunt's Gap – Salerno – Cassino II – Gothic Line
Malta 1941-42

37th Foot raised 1702; 67th Foot raised 1758; these two regiments
amalgamated to form The Hampshire Regiment 1881; amalgamated to
form The Princess of Wales's Royal Regiment 1993.

The 1st Hampshires were involved in the first British offensive in the Western Desert, serving at Sidi Barrani, until they were sent to Malta in February 1941. Here they were to remain throughout the subsequent siege.

It was one of the more challenging tasks of the war with the men engaged in heavy labour, filling in bomb craters and unloading ships whilst being constantly under threat from enemy attack. Nonetheless the spirit of defiance remained strong so that when, for example, monthly petrol rations were reduced to 30 gallons per battalion at the height of the siege in 1942, the Hampshires responded by cutting consumption to less than ten gallons, using bicycles instead for transport.

The level of work involved is evidenced by the figures when two ships, the *Orari* and the *Troilus,* broke through the blockade in June 1942 – the men unloaded 8,000 tons of supplies in just two days.

With the ending of the siege, the Malta Brigade, to which the battalion now belonged, joined the assault on Sicily. It was a bloody struggle, costing the Hampshires over 300 casualties in three weeks, but in October 1943 permission was finally given to return to Britain after a full 22 years service abroad.

The Malta Brigade was to fight again on D-Day and in the ensuing campaign in Northern Europe, where 'C' Company had the distinction of being the first British infantry to return to Belgian soil. Also in the campaign was the 7th Battalion.

Four other battalions, meanwhile, were engaged in the Mediterranean war. The 2nd Hampshires, veterans of Dunkirk, landed in Algeria in November 1942 and took up a position at Terbourba, between Tunis and the Allied stronghold of Medjez el Bab. On 1 December a German force, outnumbering them by four to one, attacked. Four days of bitter fighting saw the battalion forced to relinquish the position, having sustained 70% casualties, but the resistance was sufficient to halt the enemy advance intended to strike at Medjez el Bab.

Amongst the casualties was Major H W Le Patourel, whose heroism in continuing a charge despite the fall of his comrades was rewarded with a Victoria Cross. The award was made as a posthumous gesture, but happily this proved eroneous; Maj Le Patourel had been wounded and captured, but survived to collect his honour.

The next month the 1/4th, 2/4th and 5th Battalions, who between them constituted the 128th (Hampshire) Brigade also landed in Algeria. Almost immediately they too felt the full onslaught of a German offensive. Swept back from a position at Sidi Nisr, a stand was taken at the companion feature of Hunts Gap, which was held despite massive pressure. Fighting alongside was a unit of Royal Artillery, though such was the level of combat that of 130 Gunners, only nine remained after the first day.

Further heavy losses were to be incurred in Italy. With the 2/4th Battalion withdrawn to form Beach Groups, the 2nd joined the Hampshire Brigade and was present at the landing at Salerno. The first day of that operation saw the 5th Battalion lose 340 men dead, wounded or missing.

Even when the fighting was not at this intense pitch, danger was ever-present. The 5th Battalion's padre, Rev C G Baalam was killed by a mine in January 1944 whilst attempting to retrieve German dead for a Christian burial.

The Brigade fought at Monte Ornito and at Cassino, where Captain R Wakeford won a Victoria Cross for the successful capture of enemy machine-guns, despite being wounded.

A third VC was awarded, this time to Lieutenant G R Norton of the 1/4th Battalion, at Monte Gridolfo during the attempt to break through the Gothic Line. Badly wounded, Lt Norton was taken back to an RAMC hospital, where the nurse appointed to care for him turned out to be his twin sister. They celebrated their birthday the day after his arrival.

2,094 men of the regiment were killed during the war.

The South Staffordshire Regiment

Principal Battle Honours 1939-45

Caen – Noyers – Falaise – Arnhem 1944
North-West Europe 1940, 44 – North Africa 1940
Landing in Sicily – Sicily 1943 – Chindits 1944
Burma 1944

38th Foot raised 1705; 80th Foot raised 1793; these two regiments
amalgamated to form The South Staffordshire Regiment 1881;
amalgamated to form The Staffordshire Regiment
(The Prince of Wales's) 1959.

The 1st Battalion of The South Staffordshire Regiment saw brief service in the early campaign in the Western Desert, though its role was more supportive than active. Amongst its tasks were the digging of cemeteries and the escorting of prisoners of war to India.

In 1942 the battalion returned to India where it was initially employed on internal security duties. One major exception was a platoon under Lieutenant Thomas, which was sent into Japanese-held territory around Tiddim. During a three and a half month action, the men travelled 3,000 miles, 600 miles on foot, reconnoitring and patrolling. It was in effect a prelude to the Chindits operations.

The whole battalion was to join the second of those operations in 1944. The initial phase of the Chindits was the establishment and occupation of a block codenamed White City near the Myitkina-Mandalay railway. This railway was an essential supply line linking the Japanese units in the north of the country to the main body of the enemy; the immediate military objective of the operation was therefore to cut that line, whilst the wider aim was to inspire a British and Empire army much demoralised by the Japanese advances.

On both counts, it was a success. Though White City was under constant attack from the Japanese, and though conditions within the block were extremely harsh, it was held for 15 days, long enough to disrupt the occupying forces, and was then abandoned to enable the Chindits to move on to help take Mogaung.

Amongst those distinguishing themselves at White City was Lieutenant G A Cairns of the 1st South Staffords, who lost an arm to a Japanese officer's sword, but continued to lead his men until his death. He was posthumously awarded the Victoria Cross, though the award was delayed when the citation was destroyed in the 'plane crash that killed Wingate. The Chindits campaign cost the battalion 584 dead, wounded and sick with just two men reported missing.

The 2nd Battalion of the regiment returned from a posting in India to be transformed into an air-landing battalion of the 1st Airborne Division. They were amongst the forces landing in Sicily – thus becoming with the 1st Border Regiment the first troops to stage a glider invasion of a country – and served briefly in the Italian campaign.

It was in Northern Europe, however, that the 2nd South Staffords were to see their most famous action. On 17 September 1944 the 1st Airborne Division, together with two American divisions, took off in aeroplanes and gliders to land in advance of the front line as part of Operation Market Garden. 1st Airborne Division landed at Arnhem, but despite its heroic endeavours was unable to hold off the enemy long enough for the support troops to overcome the obstacles in their path. That operation saw the 1st South Staffords achieve the distinction of being the only British battalion to win two Victoria Crosses in a single battle during the war: awarded to Lance Sergeant J D Baskeyfield and to Major R H Cairn (attached from the Royal Northumberland Fusiliers).

With its airborne partner, the 1st Border Regiment, the 2nd Battalion was later involved in the peaceful liberation of Norway.

The 1st/6th South Staffords territorials formed part of the British Expeditionary Force, and were to return to the continent in 1944 in the company of the 5th, 2nd/6th and 7th Battalions.

The Dorsetshire Regiment

Principal Battle Honours 1939-45

St Omer-La Bassée – Normandy Landing – Caen
Arnhem 1944 – Aam – Geilenkirchen – Landing in Sicily
Malta 1940-42 – Kohima – Mandalay

39th Foot raised 1702; 54th Foot raised 1755; these two regiments
amalgamated to form The Dorsetshire Regiment 1881; amalgamated to
form The Devonshire & Dorset Regiment 1958.

For the most part, the men of the 1st Battalion of The Dorsetshire Regiment shared the experience of their colleagues in the Malta Brigade: the 2nd Devons and the 1st Hants.

As part of the garrison of Malta between June 1939 and March 1943, the battalion served through the siege of the island, providing vital support for the front-line contributions of the RAF and the Royal Navy. Their tasks were hazardous though uncelebrated, centring around the need to repair bomb-damaged airstrips and the unloading of supply ships.

The last two years of the war, however, were spent on more active service in Sicily, Italy and North-West Europe, leading sea-borne invasions in each instance.

Landing in Sicily on 10 July 1943, the 1st Dorsets took all the immediate objectives that first day, and for a short while afterwards found the opposition by Italian forces presented few obstacles to their advance. On 14 July the situation changed when the battalion encountered the famous Herman Goering Division for the first time. Thereafter the campaign, though ultimately successful, slowed considerably; it took the Dorsets a week of hard fighting to capture Agira.

The Italian operation was also successful, with the brigade landing at Pizzo in advance of the 8th Army that was then fighting its way up the country.

The following year, the battalion again led an invasion by sea, this time on D-Day. As a motor battalion, it led the break-out from the bridgehead that had been established at such heavy cost. It subsequently fought in the battle to take Villers Bocage, with a patrol from 'C' troop becoming the first Allied forces into the town.

On 29 September 1944 a Dorset patrol achieved an even more noteworthy first, becoming the first British soldiers on German soil since the BEF. Two months later the battalion was withdrawn to the UK.

The 2nd Battalion had been in the BEF, making its major contribution at La Bassée Canal. For four days the men held a position on the canal in the face of enemy attacks, before being withdrawn and ultimately evacuated from Dunkirk.

Having been transferred to the Far East, the 2nd Dorsets were sent into the desperate struggles to relieve Kohima in March 1944. On 26 April two companies took up positions around the District Commissioner's bungalow on Garrison Hill, in what was to become one of the key battles of the campaign. For 18 days, wave after wave of Japanese counter-attack were repulsed in close hand-to-hand fighting, with the enemy's positions sometimes just 15 yards away. Eventually the remainder of the battalion arrived as reinforcements and the Japanese were thrown back. A decisive element in the victory was the firepower provided by a tank, which had had to be dragged up Garrison Hill by men from the Royal Engineers.

Further fighting followed to re-open the Manipur Road to Imphal, and then began the chase of the retreating enemy across Burma. On 21 December 1944 the Dorsets crossed the river Chindwin and proceeded to make rapid progress through the jungle, covering the 150 miles to Shwebo in just 21 days. By March 1945 they were on the outskirts of Mandalay.

The men were destined to travel yet further, for with the Japanese surrender, they were selected to form part of the British Commonwealth Occupation Force in Tokyo, finding themselves in the Emperor's Palace itself.

Of the territorial battalions, both the 4th and 5th served in North-West Europe, arriving on 23 June 1944 with the 43rd (Wessex) Division. This was the division largely responsible for taking the famous Hill 112.

Both battalions also played key roles in the fighting around Arnhem. The 5th held positions on the south side of the Neder Rijn, beating back enemy counters, whilst the 4th crossed the river to assist those troops from the 1st Airborne Division who managed to escape the disaster of Operation Market Garden.

In the subsequent advance into Germany, both battalions were continually active, operating as kangaroo-borne infantry. The final campaign was on the Bremerhaven Peninsular, where they were still fighting on the eve of the German surrender.

The South Lancashire Regiment (Prince of Wales's Volunteers)

Principal Battle Honours 1939-45

Dunkirk 1940 – Normandy Landing – Bourguebus Ridge
Falaise – Rhineland – North-West Europe 1940, 44-45
Madagascar – North Arakan – Kohima – Nyaoungu Bridgehead

40th Foot raised 1717; 82nd Foot raised 1793; these two regiments amalgamated to form The South Lancashire Regiment (Prince of Wales's Volunteers) 1881; amalgamated to form The Lancashire Regiment (Prince of Wales's Volunteers) 1958; amalgamated to form The Queen's Lancashire Regiment 1970.

The unreal calm before the blitzkrieg in West Europe is nowhere better illustrated than in a War Diary entry of the 1st Battalion, The South Lancashire Regiment for 9 May 1940, the eve of the war: 'Ensa concert in Lille with Will Hay attended by large numbers of men.' [1]

In the event, it was not until the closing stages of the campaign that the regiment was to become heavily involved in the fighting. During the defence of the perimeter of Dunkirk, the men held a position at the Nieuport Canal for four days before finally being evacuated on 1 June.

Two years later, the 2nd South Lancs landed in Madagascar to serve in one of the less celebrated actions of the war. The opposition from Vichy French and local troops was swept aside with admirable efficiency and rapidity, but it was by no means an easy campaign that saw the taking of Antisrane in three days. The South Lancs had the particularly difficult task of staging a night march over sands and through mangrove swamps to attack the enemy's rear.

87 casualties were sustained in that action, though ultimately the major problem on the island was to prove to be disease; in a six month stay, 500 cases mainly of malaria and dysentery were hospitalized.

With Antisrane, one of the finest harbours in the world, secured against Japanese attack, expeditions were undertaken in September 1942 to take control of the rest of the island.

The battalion was then transferred to India, where it fought in the Arakan campaign of early 1944. In April of that year it moved north to join the fighting in the Naga Hills around Kohima, clearing the last Japanese elements from the area.

A period of intensive training was followed by a remarkable march through the jungle that commenced in December and did not end until the Irrawaddy was reached in February 1945. The fact that the Allies' objective was the Irrawaddy was no secret, but the direction of the force containing the 2nd Battalion was; whilst the main body was to aim at Mandalay, a southern surprise assault was to be made at Nyaungu. The march through the jungle therefore had to be made with some discretion. Consequently the men often found themselves acting in a pioneer capacity, developing obscure tracks into roads capable of taking vehicles. In the course of the advance, six elephants were acquired.

The bridgehead at Nyaungu was successfully established on Valentine's Day 1945, but it was a far from smooth operation. A night crossing, supposedly unopposed, attracted the attention of Japanese machine-gunners and was complicated by the failure of several boats' engines. The men were obliged to paddle and even to swim boats full of wounded across the river under enemy attack. The operation's success, however, proved the key to the war in Burma and to the continuation of the advance, in which the battalion continued to serve. By the time it reached Rangoon, its strength had been reduced to three rifle companies.

By this stage, the 1st Battalion was also driving back the enemy. Landing on D-Day, the 1st South Lancs sustained 127 casualties on the first day, including the death of the Commanding Officer, Lieutenant-Colonel R P H Burbury, but took all its objectives. It also claimed the very English honour of being the first unit to brew up tea in France.

Fighting continuously for the first nine days, the battalion was then withdrawn for a short break, before returning to fight in Operation Goodwood and at Falaise.

Tough battles were also to come in October 1944 in Operation Aintree, the clearing of the Overloon-Venraij area, and in February 1945 in the Rhineland. The battalion was in Bremen when the war ended.

846 men of the regiment lost their lives in the conflict.

[1] Mullay *The South Lancashire Regiment* p.363

The Welch Regiment

Principal Battle Honours 1939-45

Falaise – Lower Maas – Reichswald – Croce
Italy 1943-45 – Canae – Kyaukmyaung Bridgehead
Sittang 1945 – Burma 1944-45

41st Foot raised 1719; 69th Foot raised 1756; these two regiments
amalgamated to form The Welch Regiment 1881; amalgamated to form
The Royal Regiment of Wales (24th/41st Foot) 1969.

Comprising two regular and four territorial battalions in 1939, The Welch
Regiment raised a further five battalions during the course of the war, making
a total of 11. Of these, four were to see active service overseas: the 1st and 2nd
(the two regulars), and two of the existing territorials – the 4th and the 1/5th.

The 1st Battalion was stationed in Palestine at the start of the war, and was
posted to North Africa in 1940, serving in the opening campaign in the Western
Desert. Before the end of the year, however, the men were ordered to Crete in
preparation for the defence of the island.

When the expected German invasion came on 20 May 1941, the 1st Welch were
in the west of the island, and for a week fought a valiant though ultimately doomed
battle around Canae and Suda Bay. On 27 May, the decision to evacuate the island
was taken, and the British and Allied troops made a fighting retreat to Sphakia on
the south coast. The men of the 1st Welch formed the rearguard covering the
withdrawal, finally embarking on Royal Navy ships on 1 June to sail to Egypt.

Much of the next year was spent in the Western Desert, fighting in the front line
around Benghazi against the Afrika Korps. Having regrouped in Egypt and Sudan,
the 1st Welch joined the 50th Division in the invasion of Sicily in July 1943.

Most of the 50th Division returned to Britain to prepare for the Normandy
landings, but the 1st Battalion linked up with the 1st Canadian Division to land at
Reggio in the first wave of the assault on Italy.

A break in the active service role of the battalion came in November 1943,
when it formed the guard for Chiang Kai-Shek and President Inoenu of Turkey at
the Mena conference in Egypt.

In May the following year, the battalion returned to Italy and spent the
remainder of the war in that country, ending up in Tarvisio as part of the 6th
Armoured Division.

During most of this time, the 2nd Battalion, The Welch Regiment, had been stationed in India, awaiting the relaunch of the campaign against the Japanese.

In October 1944 the 2nd Welch, by then with the 19th (Indian) Division, advanced as part of the offensive that was finally to sweep the enemy from Burma. While the rest of the division advanced on Rangoon, an infantry brigade containing the 2nd Welch was detached to capture Maymyo.

The heaviest fighting, however, was still to come, in the action around Toungoo, some 200 miles north of Rangoon. A combination of mountainous, jungle terrain and uncompromising resistance from the Japanese kept the 2nd Battalion fully occupied up until VJ-Day.

Of the territorial battalions, the 4th Welch landed in Normandy in 1944 and saw heavy fighting around Caen, before advancing all the way to Hamburg. At one point during the progress through Holland, a section of the battalion found itself totally surrounded by German forces. A determined effort, however, broke through the enemy ranks, leaving an estimated 500 casualties amongst the opposing German paratroops.

The battalion later played its part in the intense fighting around the Reichswald Forest.

The 1/5th Battalion also landed at Normandy. In the struggle around Falaise, Lieutenant Tasker Watkins (later to be promoted to Major) won a Victoria Cross, the citation in the *London Gazette* concluding that his 'superb leadership not only saved his men's lives but decisively influenced the course of the battle.'

The Black Watch
(Royal Highland Regiment)

Principal Battle Honours 1939-45

Falaise Road – Rhine – Tobruk – El Alamein – Akarit
Tunis – Sicily 1943 – Cassino II – Crete – Burma 1944

42nd Foot raised 1739; 73rd Foot raised 1786; these two regiments
amalgamated to form The Black Watch (Royal Highland Regiment) 1881.

Three battalions of The Black Watch served in the British Expeditionary Force. Of these, the 6th had the familiar experience of fighting in Flanders and withdrawing through Dunkirk, but the 1st and the 4th were both part of the 51st (Highland) Division, stationed in the south with the French army. This was the division that met the Germans at the Somme and was forced back through the country to end up at the tiny port of St Valéry-en-Caux, where the planned evacuation failed to happen. Fighting valiantly to the end – and even beyond, for not all heeded the order to surrender and some, out of ammunition, resorted to using their bare fists before capitulating – the 1st Battalion was taken prisoner; only one officer and 18 other ranks escaped.

The 4th Battalion was more fortunate. Sent ahead of the division to establish defences at Le Havre, it managed to get out of the country. It spent the remainder of the war in Gibralta on garrison duties. The 1st meanwhile was re-formed and, together with the 5th and 7th Battalions, joined the reconstituted 51st (Highland) Division.

The division was sent to North Africa in 1942 and, at El Alamein, met again the old foe General Rommel, who had taken the surrender at St Valéry. Honour was restored with a decisive intervention in the battle, forcing a path through the minefields to allow the armour of the 8th Army to break the enemy positions. The price was high, with the 7th Battalion losing over 250 men on the first night alone.

Further heavy casualties were sustained in the campaign to throw the Germans out of Africa, particularly in the intense one-day battle at Wadi Akarit. Always however, the losses were more than outweighed by the gains; at Akarit, for example, the 7th took 1,000 prisoners and captured 50 big guns.

The 51st Division continued the chase into Europe, fighting in Sicily and then briefly in Italy, before being withdrawn to prepare for the Normandy landings. In the subsequent campaign, major engagements were fought at Falaise and the Reichswald Forest. The 1st Black Watch went on to claim the distinction of being the first British battalion to set foot on German soil. It is an indication of the demands of war that the then commanding officer of the 1st had just five years earlier been a private in the regiment.

In the crossing of the Rhine The Black Watch again displayed great heroism. Platoons of the 1st Battalion were surrounded by the enemy for a whole day, under tank and artillery attack but, when relieved, emerged still holding 25 enemy prisoners. A subaltern in the 7th, having had the revolver shot from his hand by a machine gun, charged alone, armed only with a shovel, and succeeded in taking out the enemy post; he was awarded the DSO for his bravery.

Whilst the 1st and other battalions were thus pursuing the enemy, the 2nd Black Watch were also making a significant contribution. It served in the 1941 East African campaign against the Italians in Somaliland, the major action coming at Barkasan. With inadequate resources, 'A' Company resorted in desperation to traditional infantry methods, with a full-frontal bayonet charge; 260 casualties were sustained, but 1,800 inflicted upon the enemy in a notable victory.

Pulled out of Africa to defend Crete, the 2nd Battalion again found themselves with poor and insufficient equipment. Nonetheless, when the expected German invasion materialized in May 1941, the men held their positions for ten days until ordered to evacuate the island. Despite the enemy's total air superiority that made daylight movement impossible, the battalion piper insisted on playing reveille on the airfield every morning during the battle.

The withdrawal from Crete was disastrous, with German divebombers attacking the ships and accounting for 200 battalion deaths. On arrival in Africa, however, little time was available for recovery, and the men were soon moved forward to reinforce the besieged garrison of Tobruk.

In November 1941 the battalion staged a break-out from Tobruk to link up with the 8th Army. But the promised tank support failed to make the rendezvous and again the men had to fall back on the bayonet charge as the only tactic available. This time, the enemy was too strong and the casualties were catastrophic; a battalion strength of over 600 men was reduced within two hours to just 68.

So ended the 2nd Battalion's war with Italy and Germany. Rebuilt, it transferred to the Far East, where it again distinguished itself under hostile conditions in the Chindits campaign of 1944.

The 6th Black Watch served in North-West Africa and later in Italy. It won a battle honour at Cassino, where one of the casualties was Sergeant William Wilson. Descended from a member of one of the Independent Companies that gave birth to the regiment, Sgt Wilson had joined up in 1908 and been badly wounded in the Great War; despite being nearly 50 in 1939, he had again heeded his country's call and re-enlisted.

Fighting in Italy was so severe that in June 1944 alone, the battalion saw the Commanding Officer replaced on seven occasions.

The Oxfordshire And Buckinghamshire Light Infantry

Principal Battle Honours 1939-45

Cassel – Ypres-Comines Canal – Normandy Landing
Pegasus Bridge – Reichswald – Rhine – Enfidaville
Salerno – Anzio – Gemmano Ridge

43rd Foot raised 1741; 52nd Foot raised 1755; these two regiments
amalgamated 1881 to form The Oxfordshire and Buckinghamshire Light
Infantry; amalgamated to form The Royal Green Jackets 1966.

The 1st Battalion of The Oxfordshire & Buckinghamshire Light Infantry served in the British Expeditionary Force, advancing on 17 May 1940 in time to cover the general withdrawal from the front-line positions. The battalion's Commanding Officer, Colonel Whitfield, has left an account of the venture that surely sums up the experience of many at the time, with its emphasis on the sheer exhaustion the men experienced:

'[T]he men were very tired. For five days in section posts they had been guarding vulnerable points which entailed constant vigilance and little sleep . . . . I did not know it was possible to go so long without proper sleep.' [1]

The major battle of the campaign was to be fought at the Ypres-Comines Canal, where the battalion had taken up a defensive position. This 'canal' being dry did not provide a substantial obstacle to the Germans, and when the attack came on 26 May, a high level of casualties was sustained. One of those wounded was Colonel Whitfield, whose misfortune did not end there; the ambulance in which he was being treated was captured by the enemy and he was taken prisoner.

Nine officers and 320 other ranks of the battalion were finally evacuated from Dunkirk on 1 June.

The 1st Ox & Bucks returned to Northern Europe four years later in the follow-up to D-Day. They were initially held in reserve and did not see action until 16 July 1944, though when they were called upon, it was again in the thickest of the fighting, during the battle for Cahier.

An action even more fraught with danger was the storming in late November of an enemy position on the river Maas. In a full-frontal attack, the battalion risked everything, but emerged successful with a tally of some 200 prisoners.

As the Allies advanced into Germany itself, the 1st Ox & Bucks served in two of the most difficult encounters of the later stages of the campaign. They helped in the operation to clear the Reichswald Forest, and met heavy opposition from German marines defending the bridgehead on the Aller.

Whilst the 1st had been fighting as orthodox infantry, the 2nd Battalion was branching out into new areas of warfare. Returning from India in July 1940, it became the following year part of the 1st Air Landing Brigade (subsequently moved to the 6th Air Landing Brigade).

A long period of training as glider-borne infantry was to bear fruit in the first operation of D-Day. During the night of 5 June 1944, the best part of two companies, together with a detachment of Royal Engineers, was towed over to France in six gliders. The men's task was to seize vital bridges ahead of the sea-borne forces, with the rest of the battalion to fly in the following day in support.

It was an operation that gripped the public imagination and has remained a key part of the memory of D-Day. Both Benouville and Ranville Bridges were successfully taken – the first parts of North-West Europe to be liberated from the Nazis. In honour of the Air Landing Brigade, the former was renamed Pegasus Bridge.

The 2nd Ox & Bucks fought through the subsequent campaign in their capacity as infantry, though their ability to act as air-borne troops was always available. The danger inherent in such a role was amply demonstrated in the last massive battle of the front, the crossing of the Rhine. A glider operation succeeded in taking key bridges across the Issel but the anti-aircraft gunners exacted a heavy toll. The density of enemy fire was such that in one glider both pilots were hit, and the battalion's quartermaster had to land the craft himself. Casualty rates reached 50% in this final air-borne operation.

[1] Booth *The Oxfordshire & Buckinghamshire Light Infantry* pp.129-130

The Essex Regiment

Principal Battle Honours 1939-45

Zetten – North-West Europe 1940, 44-45 – Palmyra
Tobruk 1941 – Defence of Alamein Line – Enfidaville
Sangro – Villa Grande – Cassino I – Chindits 1944

44th (West Essex) Foot raised 1741; 56th (West Essex) Foot raised 1755;
amalgamated to form The Essex Regiment 1881; amalgamated to form
3rd Battalion, The Royal Anglian Regiment 1968.

The 1st Battalion, The Essex Regiment moved to Sudan soon after war was declared on Germany, and spent the first year on garrison duties in Khartoum and Atbara. With the opening of the East African campaign, it joined up with the 5th Indian Division then concentrating near the border with Italian-held Abyssinia.

The first operation was the re-taking of Gallabat, just within Sudan, from where the Essex were to attack Metemma, a small town in Abyssinia. A lack of air-cover, however, and the stranding of supporting tanks in a mine-field, left the men trapped on an open hillside, where 68 casualties were sustained before an order to withdraw came.

The propaganda value of driving the Italians off Sudanese soil was enhanced by the arrival of drummers loyal to Haile Selaisse. These drummers beat out a steady message of resistance across the border, a tactic that produced a stream of African deserters from the Italian forces.

In December 1940 the 1st Essex left for Palestine. From there, the following April, they participated in the suppression of Rashid Ali's uprising in Iraq. It was a brief campaign but one, commented Lieutenant-Colonel Nichols later, 'which called for continual improvisation, considerable endurance, and ability to put up with great discomfort.' [1] Although one straightforward encounter was fought at Falluja, it was effectively a guerilla war against a mobile enemy whose tactics largely comprised sniping and sabotage.

During the fighting, the Essex managed to supplement a somewhat restricted issue of equipment, picking up a brand-new enemy Bren carrier, which was smuggled out of the country and on to the next campaign in Syria. Another brief campaign saw Palmyra taken in a tough battle against hardened French Foreign Legion troops.

In October 1941 the scene changed again, with a posting to Tobruk, where the

Essex were just in time to assist the break-out from the besieged town. At the end of November, in nearly two weeks of constant action, the men took and held El Duda ridge just outside Tobruk to facilitate a link-up with the advancing Allied army. More than 200 casualties were sustained.

Having in little more than a year fought in four theatres against four enemies – Italy, Iraq, France and Germany – it was time for the 1st Essex to move on. Its next action was to come in the Arakan in May 1943, to be followed in 1944 by an involvement in the Chindits campaign. The intense sacrifice demanded by that expedition, particularly toward its end as the monsoon broke, was evocatively depicted by Captain P P S Brownless:

'The extreme misery of the march is impossible to describe. The incessant rain, the monotonous drips from the trees . . . . The men staggered through the mud and up the slopes, borne down by the weight of their great packs. All were tortured with exhaustion because all were sick . . . . We had been sodden for weeks, were covered with mud, and we stank. Hollow-eyed, wasted, hungry.' [2]

Back in Africa the 1/4th and 2/5th Battalions were representing the regiment in the war against Hitler. Both spent much of 1941 in Sierra Leone, where the main enemy was disease – over 300 cases of malaria in the 1/4th alone – but moved to the Western Desert before Alamein.

The 1/4th Battalion faced a particularly difficult series of battles, at El Alamein, Akarit and Enfidaville in Africa, and then in Italy the first failed attempt to break through at Cassino. So heavy was this last encounter that two minor battle honours – Castle Hill and Hangman's Hill – were won in addition to the one borne on the colours.

The 5th Battalion was also in Italy, serving notably at the crossing of the Sangro and at Villa Grande, where seven days in December 1943 cost 279 casualties.

The 2nd Battalion, meanwhile, fought in both North-West Europe campaigns. Emerging with comparatively few casualties from Dunkirk, it returned to France on D-Day. The first 14 days saw constant action, including a bitter contest over Verriäres Wood, with casualties rising to above a third of the men.

A battle honour was awarded at Zetten in January 1945, when a German attempt to take the Island between Nijmegen and Arnhem was defeated.

(1) Martin *The Essex Regiment 1929-1950* p.58
(2) ibid. p.118

The Sherwood Foresters (Nottinghamshire and Derbyshire Regiment)

Principal Battle Honours 1939-45

Norway 1940 – Gazala – El Alamein – Tunis
Salerno – Anzio – Campoleone – Gothic Line – Coriano, Singapore Island

45th Foot raised 1741; 95th Foot raised 1823; these two regiments amalgamated to form The Sherwood Foresters (Nottinghamshire and Derbyshire Regiment) 1881; amalgamated to form The Worcestershire and Sherwood Foresters Regiment (29th/45th Foot) 1970.

The first Sherwood Foresters to meet the enemy were the men of the 8th Battalion, who landed at Andalsnes in Norway, some 230 miles north-west of Oslo, on 18 April 1940. Advancing inland by train, they took up positions at Tretton alongside Norwegian troops, where, following a few skirmishes, the expected German attack came on 23 April. It was a hopeless cause; the Foresters were not trained for combat on a snow-covered terrain, and were without the appropriate clothing and equipment. They were also tired and hungry, having not slept or eaten properly for 36 hours.

The result was inevitable. 25 men were killed, others captured while the rest dispersed, with some escaping over the border to Sweden. A small group, however, under the leadership of the quarter-master, Captain J F Hallam, made its way back to Andalsnes to be evacuated; Capt Hallam was awarded the Military Cross, the first decoration the regiment won in the war.

Elsewhere the 2nd, 2/5th and 9th Battalions were soon to meet much the same fate in the retreat of the BEF. The dominant experience was one of total confusion: at one point the Adjutant of the 2nd Battalion had to rush back to prevent Royal Engineers from blowing a bridge until the men had passed, whilst at Haisette the Burgomaster, dressed up in his robes of office, came out to hand over the keys to the town, believing that they were the Germans. Nonetheless, all the battalions were successfully evacuated.

Beyond Europe, however, the regiment was to incur much greater losses. In October 1941 the 1/5th Battalion left the UK for Singapore, arriving there on 29 January, at a time when the retreat from Malaya was already underway. Positions were prepared in the centre of the island, but the battalion was not called upon to fight; barely a fortnight after its arrival, Singapore surrendered and the men were taken into captivity. 450 of them were to die, mostly whilst working on the infamous Burma-Siam railway.

Disaster was also to strike the 1st Battalion. Brought from the Middle East in January 1942 to serve as a motor battalion in North Africa, it was sent forward a few months later, and plunged into the battle of Gazala. Two companies served in the Knightsbridge box, and others fought on the perimeter of Tobruk, but when that town was over-run on 20 June, all the survivors – including the Foresters – were taken prisoner. The 16th was later reconstituted as a new 1st Battalion but never saw service abroad.

It was left to the 2nd and the 5th Battalions (the latter re-numbered from the 2/5th) to strike back at the enemy. Arriving at Algiers in early 1943 to join the 1st Army, both battalions fought through the final stages of the African war, mostly in a series of small-scale but hazardous encounters.

With the fall of Tunis, the 2nd Sherwood Foresters participated in the capture of Pantelleria, an island between Tunisia and Sicily being used by the Italians as an E-Boat base. It was a bloodless operation, in which the only reported casualty was Corporal Sanderson, bitten by a mule.

The next challenge was Italy, and the 5th Battalion arrived with the first wave at Salerno. The initial landing went smoothly, but the holding and extending of the position proved more difficult, with the battalion enduring a week of heavy mortar and sniper fire before breaking out.

Typical of the engagements in Italy was the crossing of the Volturno river. The 5th Battalion was on the far right of the line, the plan being for two companies to establish and hold a bridgehead whilst the other two companies attacked the town of Cancello to the west. As with so many other actions, however, the opposition was fiercer than anticipated and the men in Cancello were cut off, able to communicate with HQ only by a man swimming across the river, walking upstream and then swimming back. In the face of 50% casualties the whole battalion was eventually forced to withdraw.

At Anzio the 2nd Sherwood Foresters were sent forward to take Campoleone on 31 January 1944, a day the battalion history was to describe as 'one of the most distinguished but most sorrowful days in the battalion's history'. [1] The enemy was hurt but only at such a heavy cost that the men were pulled back into reserve. By the end of Anzio, the 2nd Battalion claimed the highest casualty rate of any British unit.

Both the 2nd and 5th Battalions were later to serve in the assault on the Gothic Line, where they were joined by the 14th Battalion. The 14th had a brief but distinguished history. It had fought at El Alamein and all through Italy, including a stint as reinforcements at Anzio. By the time it was disbanded in January 1945, it had sustained a total of 632 casualties.

[1] Masters *The 2nd Battalion The Sherwood Foresters 1939-1945* pp.28-29

The Loyal Regiment (North Lancashire)

Principal Battle Honours 1939-45

Dunkirk 1940 – Djebel Kesskiss – Gueriat el Atach Ridge
North Africa 1943 – Anzio – Fiesole – Monte Grande
Italy 1944-45 – Johore – Singapore Island

47th Foot raised 1741; 81st Foot raised 1793; these two regiments
amalgamated to form The Loyal North Lancashire Regiment 1881;
amalgamated to form The Queen's Lancashire Regiment 1970.

The initial war experience of the 1st Battalion, The Loyal Regiment was far from unique: they wintered in France, advanced into Belgium in response to the German invasion, and were withdrawn to Dunkirk.

It was at Dunkirk itself that The Loyals fought their major conflict. As part of the 2nd Brigade of the 1st Division, the battalion was waiting to be evacuated on 29 May 1940 when word came that the Germans were putting heavy pressure on the town's perimeter defences at Bergues. The 1st Loyals were ordered back to hold the line while the evacuation continued.

For two critical days, Bergues was held firm under persistent German fire. Even when the order to abandon the position was received on 1 June, one final action saw an enemy incursion across the Bergues-Furnes Canal repulsed. The battalion did not finally escape until early evening on 2 June, one of the last battalions to get out.

When the 1st Loyals returned to active service, it was in the very different environment of North Africa. They landed at Algiers on 9 March 1943, part of the second wave of Operation Torch, the Anglo-American campaign to pincer the Afrika Korps.

Almost immediately they were plunged into a series of bloody encounters. At the beginning of April, battalion strength stood at 33 officers and 801 other ranks; by the end of that month, casualties had reduced this to 14 and 520 respectively. One of the officers who died was Lieutenant W A S Clarke, posthumously awarded the Victoria Cross for his part in the fighting around Guiriat.

Tunis fell on 7 May 1943, and with it collapsed the Axis opposition in North Africa. There were still however pockets of enemy forces, one of which was cleared without opposition by the 1st Loyals on the island of Pantellaria.

The following year the battalion was again called upon to assist a seaborne invasion, landing at Anzio on 22 January 1944. Taking up a position on the left flank, the 1st Loyals were held in reserve around the Flyover Bridge, the last line before Anzio itself. It soon became the frontline when a German counter-attack broke through US ranks on 17 February. Two days of fierce combat were needed to save the vital position.

The succeeding stalemate also took its toll, but two and a half months later the victory at Cassino allowed the forces at Anzio finally to advance. By the end of May, the 1st Loyals were in the Roman suburbs, counting the cost of a campaign that had killed or wounded more than 450 soldiers.

The ranks were rebuilt and when George VI inspected the battalion on 30 July, the strength was up to 730 all ranks.

The 1st Loyals later fought in Northern Italy, defending Monte Grande against a German counter. When they were subsequently posted to Palestine, they were relieved by men of the 2nd Battalion.

This was not, however, the same 2nd Battalion that had existed at the start of the war, for that unit had had the misfortune to find themselves in Singapore when the Japanese advance swung south through Malaya.

Initially held in reserve, the 2nd Loyals were brought forward on 13 January 1942 as the retreat reached Johore. Two weeks of fighting saw the battalion – much reduced in number – forced back over the Johore Causeway, and ultimately back to Gillman Barracks, where it had been stationed pre-war. It was there that the order to surrender was received.

Also in Singapore was the 18th Regiment, The Reconnaissance Corps, previously the 5th Loyals. Arriving on the liner *Empress of Asia,* which was struck by enemy fire even before it docked, the 18th Recces were involved in just the final phase of the battle, though they successfully held their position for the last two days.

Both battalions were taken prisoner, the 2nd Loyals being sent to Korea and the 18th Recces to work on the Burma railway. Nearly 300 men from each unit died in action or while imprisoned. One who did return was Captain M L Webber who made and operated a secret wireless set whilst in captivity, and was later awared an OBE for his services in the camp.

The 10th Battalion was later renamed the 2nd Battalion, and it was this body that relieved the 1st Loyals at Monte Grande in 1944.

The Northamptonshire Regiment

Principal Battle Honours 1939-45

North–West Europe 1940, 45 – North Africa 1942-43
Garigliano Crossing – Anzio – Cassino II
Italy 1943-45 – Yu – Imphal
Myinmu Bridgehead – Burma 1943-45

48th Foot raised 1740; 58th Foot raised 1740; these two regiments
amalgamated to form The Northamptonshire Regiment 1881;
amalgamated to form The Royal Anglian Regiment 1960.

B oth the 2nd and 5th Battalions of The Northamptonshire Regiment were in the British Expeditionary Force and fought in the front-line before being evacuated. The 2nd Battalion, instructed to hold the enemy at Arras, successfully did so in the face of greater numbers and arms. But when the French forces on the immediate right fell back, the position became untenable and a withdrawal was ordered; 'C' Company, out on the right flank, was unable to obey the command and were over-run. The same fate overtook 'A' Company a couple of days later at St Eloi on the Ypres-Comines Canal.

By the time the battalion got out from Dunkirk, it was reduced to some 150 men, whilst the 5th Battalion was down to just two companies.

Rebuilt at home, both battalions were to return to action in 1942. The 2nd Northants were in the second wave of landings at Madagascar in May of that year. They faced little resistance, but the episode helped restore morale, particularly since it met with total success under less than perfect conditions: at night, with the men having spent seven weeks on a crowded ship followed by a 20 mile march over difficult terrain.

The 5th Battalion arrived in Algiers in November 1942 to join the 1st Army. By the end of that month, having helped take Medjez, it had reached Djedeida, the furthest any unit got in the drive toward Tunis before the German counter-offensive pushed the Allies back. The following April, the battalion was again in the thick of the fighting. In the battle for Tanngoucha, 'A' Company, having advanced under cover of a night fog, found itself in the morning isolated and virtually surrounded by the enemy. The men faced shelling from both friend, foe and German infantry assault before extricating themselves. As Captain Emery, commanding the company, wrote: 'We were given a demonstration of the maxim that in the infantry nothing is ever so bad that it couldn't be worse.' [1]

The 2nd and 5th Battalions served together again in the Sicily campaign and then in Italy, where the 5th found itself required to police the streets of Foggia to quell an outbreak of looting. Around the same time, it was joined by three escaped prisoners of war, including Captain Truckle of the regiment who had been captured in Tunisia in November 1942.

The 2nd Northants were sent in to reinforce the Anzio bridgehead in early 1944, spending ten days in a particularly notorious position known as The Fortress. With the forward enemy positions just 30 yards away, the struggle reduced to endless exchanges of grenades, light mortars and sniper fire, with no element of surprise possible.

The 5th meanwhile were involved in the battle at Cassino, and later at Monte Spalduro, which was captured and held for ten weeks. The conditions were described by Captain Giblett:

'Slit trenches were full to the brim with muddy water which had to be baled out, while shelling and mortaring were so frequent it was sometimes difficult to know whether to risk lying in the open or jump into the trench full of water, Everyone was covered from head to toe in mud, all were thoroughly soaked to the skin and the cold freezing nights caused the utmost discomfort.' [2]

The 5th Battalion remained in Italy, while the 2nd were pulled out to serve in the last stages of the North-West Europe campaign. Also arriving in that theatre was the 4th Battalion of the regiment, landing in Holland in February 1945.

On the other side of the world, the 1st Northants were sent forward into Burma in December 1943. They began the new year with an assault on a Japanese-held river bunker at Kyaukchaw. Typical in many ways of the jungle war, Kyaukchaw was a ten day battle to dislodge the enemy from a position so strong that it took only 100 men to hold it. Lieutenant A G Horwood was awarded a posthumous Victoria Cross for his part in breaking the enemy stronghold.

With the Japanese offensive of March 1944, the position was abandoned and the battalion switched to the fighting around Imphal. By the time it was withdrawn in July, it had sustained 450 casualties, but was back in the front-line a few months later, capturing Budalin in January 1945, and later crossing the Irrawaddy.

[1] Barthorp *The Northamptonshire Regiment* pp.76-77

[2] ibid. pp.79-80

The Royal Berkshire Regiment (Princess Charlotte of Wales's)

Principal Battle Honours 1939-45

North-West Europe 1940 – El Alamein – Medjez Plain
Centuripe – Sangro – Cassino – Trasimene Line
Argenta Gap – Malta 1940-42 – Defence of Kohima

49th Foot originally raised 1742; 66th Foot raised 1755; these two regiments amalgamated to form The Royal Berkshire Regiment (Princess Charlotte of Wales's) 1881; amalgamated to form The Duke of Edinburgh's Royal Regiment (Berkshire and Wiltshire) 1959; amalgamated to form The Royal Gloucestershire, Berkshire and Wiltshire Regiments.

The 1st Berkshires advanced with the British Expeditionary Force in May 1940 to take up the pre-ordained positions on the river Dyle in Belgium, and it was there that the first contact was made with the enemy. Under fire on 15 May, the order came to retire, but with the telephone system destroyed, communicating the command to the companies was not easy. A lieutenant was sent out, but was killed before he could complete his task, and the Commanding Officer eventually went out himself on a motor-cycle to pass on the instructions. Even then the withdrawal was difficult: a night operation accompanied by enemy shelling and up a steep hill carrying heavy equipment.

The men were evacuated from Dunkirk, alongside those of the 4th Battalion, who had suffered greater losses, reduced to just 50 still fighting fit.

Less than a year later, the 1st Battalion departed for the Far East, where it was to serve in the ten-week North Arakan campaign in 1943.

In April 1944 it was again in action, staging a nine-day march to Kohima, fighting all the way against the advancing Japanese forces. The following five weeks, with the battalion forming part of the garrison of Kohima, were even more intense. Supplies were so short that water was rationed to a pint per day for each man, with shaving and washing forbidden. The inevitable consequence was disease and sickness. By the time the town was relieved, two officers and 56 other ranks were dead, more than 250 were wounded and a further 60 sick.

The fighting continued with the breaking of the Japanese offensive and the advance through Burma. The 1st Berkshires were eventually withdrawn to prepare for Operation Dracula, the assault landing on Rangoon that turned out to be a bloodless exercise, but the regiment's presence was maintained by the 2nd Battalion. The 2nd had arrived in Burma in December 1944 and went on to assist the taking of Mandalay.

Back in Europe, the 10th Battalion had moved from the Middle East to join the assault on Sicily. In the subsequent Italian campaign, a typical encounter came at Monte Damiano in January 1944.

Coming out of 20 days of continuous fighting that included the crossing of the Garigliano, the 10th stormed an enemy-held ridge only to come under artillery fire from the next ridge as the Germans tried to recapture the lost ground. Low on supplies and ammunition, the battalion spent five days holding the position before being relieved. At one point, stretcher-bearers were sent out into no-man's land to collect the dead and wounded, at which point the enemy fire ceased, and a German voice called out in English: 'Gentlemen, will you please stop firing while we also bring in our wounded.' [1] A short truce ensued whilst humanitarian needs were seen to.

The following month saw the battalion sent into Anzio to reinforce the bridgehead that had been established. Taking up a front-line position, the 10th were caught in the German attack that began on 7 February. Within 24 hours, the battalion was down to 340 men still fighting. By 9 February it had been further reduced to just 40 men and had reached the end of its capacity to resist when the attack suddenly ceased, the Germans having also suffered massive casualties and being unable to continue.

The 10th Berkshires were withdrawn and subsequently disbanded.

With the senior battalions engaged in the war against the Japanese, it was left to the 5th to represent the regiment on D-Day. Having fought to establish its position on the beach, the 5th's major task was the unloading of equipment as the invasion forces continued to arrive. It was not the most spectacular of roles, but an absolutely critical one, and the battalion was called upon to repeat it for the crossing of the Rhine the following year.

The 30th Battalion also served in North-West Europe, arriving in January 1945 and seeing some action in Holland, though it was mainly intended as an occupation force.

[1] Blight *The History of The Royal Berkshire Regiment (Princess Charlotte of Wales's) 1920-1947* p.282

The Queen's Own Royal West Kent Regiment

Principal Battle Honours 1939-45

North-West Europe 1940 – El Alamein – Medjez Plain
Centuripe – Sangro – Cassino – Trasimene Line – Argenta Gap
Malta 1940-42 – Defence of Kohima

50th Foot raised 1757; 97th Foot originally raised 1759; these two regiments amalgamated 1881 to form The Queen's Own Royal West Kent Regiment; amalgamated to form The Queen's Own Buffs, The Royal Kent Regiment 1961; redesignated 2nd Battalion, The Queen's Regiment 1966; amalgamated to form The Princess of Wales's Royal Regiment 1993.

The Royal West Kent Regiment was well represented in the British Expeditionary Force, with the 1st, 4th and 5th Battalions coming together to form the Queen's Own Brigade; from this force of some 2,400 men, over 1,000 casualties were sustained. Even more were lost from the 6th and 7th Battalions, sent to France in a pioneer capacity but caught up in the fighting. It was a foretaste of the bitter war the regiment was to experience.

Before further contact with the enemy, however, there was the pressing issue of defending Britain against the anticipated invasion. Kent being underneath the front-line of the Battle of Britain, there was also the duty of keeping souvenir hunters from the wreckage of 'plane crashes.

The 4th and 5th were to serve together again at Alam el Halfa in the Western Desert, where Rommel's final advance was halted. It was another damaging encounter, with an attempt to cut off the supply line and escape route of the Afrika Korps heavily repulsed. Even so, both battalions were present at El Alamein.

On the other side of the battle-zone, the 1st and 6th West Kents fought with the First Army. The former spent three costly days at Sidi Abdallah, whilst the latter scored some spectacular hits against an enemy tank attack at Djebel Abiod. Even before the landings in North-West Africa, the regiment had visited the scene, with Captain Courtney escorting the American General Mark Clark on his secret mission to Algeria to prepare for Operation Torch.

In the subsequent invasion of Italy, the 6th again distinguished itself at Centuripe, and in Italy made a decisive contribution in the nine day battle to cross the Sangro in November 1943.

The 1st, 5th and 6th Battalions all served at Cassino, whereafter the latter two remained in Italy for the duration of the war, whilst the 1st was withdrawn to assist the suppression of the Greek rising.

Meanwhile, the 4th West Kents had been despatched to the Far East in October 1943, where they were to write one of the most glorious chapters in British military history.

January 1944 saw the battalion sent forward to the Arakan region to fight at Razabil and then at the Mayu Tunnels. In April the men were transferred north to Kohima, as the Japanese U-Go offensive swept toward India.

On 6 April the Japanese assault reached the battalion's position at the District Commissioner's bungalow. For over two weeks the men held off an attack of immense ferocity under conditions of terrible hardship. The main water supply was a spring outside the main compound, just 30 yards from the Japanese lines, and a daily water ration of half a mug per man had to be imposed. So close were the Japanese that even the wounded came under fire, many being killed as they lay in the cramped hospital area. Sleep was nigh-on impossible as breaks in the fighting were filled with propaganda offensives in an attempt to undermine the heroic resistance of the West Kents.

The resistance, however did not falter. The incongruity of the situation made for almost surreal combat at times, with the tennis court being the scene of grenade battles, and with men having to resort literally to hand-to-hand fighting at times. But the courage was unparalleled, symbolized by the posthumous Victoria Cross awarded to Lance-Corporal Harman. When the battalion was finally relieved after 15 days, casualties from the 500 men stood at 61 killed, 125 wounded and 13 missing. Even this did not tell the whole story, for so limited were the medical facilities that only the most seriously wounded could be accommodated – many more returned to the fighting.

The stand of the West Kents at Kohima effectively halted the gravest threat yet posed to India, and remains one of the most significant and stirring actions of the war.

Even more severely damaged was the 2nd Battalion. When the Italian surrender opened up the possibility of taking control of the Aegean, the men – veterans of the siege of Malta – were sent to occupy the island of Samos. The Germans responded with an invasion of the Dodecanese, and the West Kents were rapidly moved to Leros to try to hold the island. Five days of heavy fighting ended with the unexpected surrender of Leros on 17 November 1943. All but 43 of the men were killed or captured.

The King's Own Yorkshire Light Infantry

Principal Battle Honours 1939-45

Norway 1940 – Fontenay le Pesnil – North-West Europe 1944-45
Argoub Sellah – Sicily 1943 – Salerno – Minturno – Anzio
Gemmano Ridge – Burma 1942

51st Foot raised 1755; 105th Madras Light Infantry raised 1839; these two
regiments amalgamated to form The King's Own Yorkshire Light Infantry
1881; redesignated 2nd Battalion, The Light Infantry 1968.

Two battalions of The King's Own Yorkshire Light Infantry – the 1st and the
1st/4th – were involved in the Norwegian campaign of 1940, though in truth
neither of them had the equipment, training or strength to make much difference to
the rapid German capture of the country. The regular battalion fared slightly better
than most units in Norway, emerging with 85 dead or wounded, but even so it lost
a further 135 men captured.

The 1st Battalion had been called back from France for the expedition, leaving
just the 2nd/4th as the regiment's contribution to the western front. Situated in the
lines of communication, the 2nd/4th was not expected to fight and was thus poorly
equipped, with scarcely any vehicles at its disposal and with one third of the
recommended Bren-gun complement. When the battalion was caught up outside
Rouen on the fringe of Rommel's sweep through Western France, it made a
commendable showing, and managed to inflict some damage on the enemy before
being evacuated from Cherbourg.

Also short on the essentials of warfare were the men of the 2nd Battalion,
stationed in Burma as hostilities began. Such was the level of complacency in
decision-making circles that, despite the Japanese expansionism evident since the
early '30s, the men were untrained in jungle warfare. They were also without
helmets to protect against small arms fire, without the tools to cut through
undergrowth and even without machine-guns, taken away for another unit shortly
before the invasion of Burma in February 1942.

The odds thus stacked against them, the men nonetheless conducted a fighting
withdrawal from the Salween river back to the Sittang, with a particularly stiff
encounter at Magwe. After four months of retreat, three officers and 85 men
reached Imphal in a relatively fit condition. 130 were dead, 68 had been taken
prisoner – in many cases a worse fate – and approximately 400 had been wounded,

with a similar number having been evacuated sick.

It was left to the 2nd/4th Battalion to score the first substantial victory in the war. Landing at Algiers in January 1943, the men were sent forward to a position on Grenadier Hill in the Medjez Plain in time for the German offensive the following month. The first major battle honour was won at Argoub Sellah in a brief campaign that cost some 300 casualties, including the Commanding Officer, Lieutenant-Colonel L F E Wieler, who lost his right arm in the shelling at Sellah.

As the fighting moved to Sicily, the 1st Battalion rejoined the fray. Its first target was the village of Villasmundo; a comparatively minor affair in the broad sweep of the wa. However, it was still a harrowing experience, with promised artillery cover not materializing until the attack had been underway for 45 minutes, leaving the men exposed and vulnerable.

During the five and a half weeks of the Sicilian campaign, it was later calculated, the average private in the battalion covered some 300 miles on foot, with company and platoon commanders easily exceeding that figure. It was also reckoned that malaria accounted for more casualties than the enemy.

Both the 1st and 2nd/4th fought in Italy. Even before the armistice, the Italians had effectively conceded defeat, as Quartermaster-Sergeant Turton discovered to his surprise when, in the course of bringing rations forward, he found the village of Santa Eufemia surrendering to him.

Thereafter, the German army became the sole enemy, and life became more difficult, as the 2nd/4th found at Salerno. The 1st Battalion, meanwhile, won a battle honour at Minturno. Crossing the Garigliano without vehicles, and therefore carrying all necessary equipment by hand, its night-time advance through enemy mine-fields proved especially difficult. A platoon of 'B' Company was caught in a shrapnel mine-field with heavy losses.

Conditions in general were harsh in Italy. It was a cold, damp winter and, with so much of the campaigning taking place in the mountains, supplies were often scarce, whilst disease was still rife. The 1st Battalion served for a while in Anzio and then advanced to Rome, before being withdrawn to assist the war in Northern Europe.

Already active in that theatre was the 1st/4th Battalion. Its major encounter came on 25 June 1944, when it advanced through recently captured Fontenay le Pesnil to storm Tessel Wood, a position it held for 25 days.

The King's Shropshire Light Infantry

Principal Battle Honours 1939-45

Dunkirk 1940 – Normandy Landing – Antwerp – Venraij
Hochwald – Bremen – North-West Europe 1940, 1944-45
Tunis – Anzio – Italy 1943-45

53rd Foot raised 1755; 85th Light Infantry originally raised 1759; these two regiments amalgamated to form The King's Shropshire Light Infantry 1881; redesignated 3rd Battalion, The Light Infantry 1968.

The 1st Battalion of The King's Shropshire Light Infantry arrived in France in September 1939, and sustained its first fatality during a brief tour of the Maginot Line when Private Priday was killed by a mine. It went on to defend the perimeter of Dunkirk, despite the exhaustion produced by the long withdrawal from Belgium. Lieutenant-Colonel Bryans, the Commanding Officer, was to write of that retreat:

'This final march . . . was an amazing feat of endurance. The total distance covered must have been well over sixty miles, of which forty miles was completed on foot. After the first all-night march, after less than one and a half hour's rest, they were on the road again.' [1]

Safely evacuated, the battalion was to return to the war in March 1943. Landing at Bône in Algeria, it was rushed forward even before its transport had arrived. In its first action, it took Hill 170 in the Djebel Bou Aoukaz range, and then seized the southern feature of Bou Aoukaz itself, the key to the advance to Tunis.

Following the victory in Africa, the men were involved in the unopposed landing at Pantellaria. The next landing, at Anzio in January 1944, was to prove more costly, however. This was the scene of some of the bitterest fighting of the war, but as time went on conditions improved a little. By April a Mobile Cinema Unit had arrived, and the battalion had built a canteen, the only one of its kind in the bridgehead, furnished from the town and equipped with shower-baths.

Even so, it was a costly campaign. When a memorial stone was unveiled on the men's arrival in Rome, it recorded 572 casualties including prisoners of war.

The battalion fought on to the Gothic Line, before finally being withdrawn from Italy in February 1945.

The 2nd Battalion, meanwhile, had spent the first years of the war far from the action. Stationed in the West Indies at the outbreak, its first task was guarding the Royal Dutch Shell Oil Company refineries in Curaçao and Aruba, the status of which was uncertain following the occupation of Holland. With the belated entry of the United States into the war, these duties were taken over by American troops and, following a regrettably brief tour of the States, the battalion returned to Britain to train for D-Day.

The landing at Normandy was successful and comparatively incident-free, though the Commanding Officer, Lieutenant-Colonel Maurice was killed the following day by a shell. His replacement, Lieutenant-Colonel Millet fared little better, being killed in December in Holland.

It was in the Low Countries that the major contributions of the 2nd and 4th Battalions – the latter having arrived a week after the initial invasion – were to come. Three days of fighting in Antwerp saw 'A' Company of the 4th cut off and virtually wiped out.

At Overloon in October 1944 an advance through an orchard was held up by machine-gun fire, and Sergeant Eardley won a Victoria Cross for his actions in taking out three enemy posts single-handed. It was the first of two such awards to the regiment, the second coming at Kervenheim the following February, when Private Joseph Stokes lost his life clearing buildings in the street fighting.

With the crossing of the Rhine, however, the back of the enemy's resistance was broken, and the 4th Battalion covered 295 miles in a rapid advance, halted only by the stiff opposition provided by a Hitler Jugend SS Training Regiment, described by the CO as 'undoubtedly the most unpleasant and vicious young men I have ever met.' [2]

The last battle of the 2nd came at Bremen. The campaign had cost the battalion 144 dead, 552 wounded and 66 missing.

Though the 1st, 2nd and 4th Battalions were the only ones to see action, the contribution of others should not be forgotten. In particular, the 5th, as a training battalion, provided some 100 officers and 4,000 men for the active units, whilst the 6th – converted to the 181st Field Regiment, RA – served in the battle of the Rhine.

[1] Moulsdale *The King's Shropshire Light Infantry* p.64

[2] ibid. p.73

The Middlesex Regiment
(Duke of Cambridge's Own)

Principal Battle Honours 1939-45

Dunkirk 1940 – Normandy Landing – Caen – Mont Pincon
Rhine – El Alamein – Akarit – Sicily 1943
Anzio – Hong Kong

57th Foot raised 1741; 77th Foot originally raised 1756; these two
regiments amalgamated to form The Middlesex Regiment (Duke of
Cambridge's Own) 1881; redesignated 4th Battalion, The Queen's
Regiment 1966; disbanded 1970.

The 2nd, 7th and 8th Battalions of The Middlesex Regiment all served in the British Expeditionary Force in 1939-40. The 2nd suffered its first casualty at Louvain on 11 May 1940, when a soldier was wounded, apparently by shots fired by the Belgian Army. It was at Louvain too that the battalion brought down a dive-bomber and fired what it claims were the first shots at the advancing German army.

Withdrawing to the Escaut on 16 May, the 2nd was joined by the 7th and 8th Middlesex. Perhaps the greatest contribution came from Sergeant Burford of the 7th who, on a patrol across the Lys, captured the car of a senior German officer and with it the enemy's order of battle. The documents were passed to Lord Gort who adapted his plans accordingly. The successful evacuation from Dunkirk, in which all three battalions were brought back, was greatly helped by the information obtained by Sgt Burford.

The 1st Battalion, meanwhile, had been posted to Hong Kong in 1937 in response to the Sino-Japanese war that potentially threatened the colony. When the war did come in December 1941, the men put up a spirited defence but the enemy was too strong for an island so difficult to defend. 105 men of the battalion died during the siege.

The end came on Christmas Day, though 'B' and 'D' Companies, still defending the southern tip of the island, refused to join the surrender until they had written orders to do so. Amongst those fighting was 2nd Lieutenant Cheesewright, who had broken out of a surrounded position to bring his men, guns and ammunition to the last remaining forces; the need for silence was such that their escape was undertaken without boots. Lt Cheesewright was later to die as a prisoner of war.

Success, however, was to come to the regiment in another theatre. The 7th Battalion served as a machine-gun battalion with the 51st Highland Division at El Alamein, in the very thickest of the fighting, and was later to distinguish itself at Mareth and Wadi Akarit. The scale of fighting here can be gauged by the 33 casualties that 'D' Company alone sustained at Akarit; the commitment of the men by the fact that the same company received four decorations for courage.

The 7th was joined by the 2/7th for the Sicilian campaign, bringing a new weapon, the 4.2" mortar, to add to the regiment's now established machine-guns. The 2/7th was to see action too in Italy, serving in the Anzio landing.

The 51st Division including the 7th Battalion, meanwhile, had followed the 2nd Battalion into Normandy. By the end of July, four battalions were active in France, with the new 1st (formerly the 2/8th) and the 8th landing in later waves. The latter, as part of the famous 43rd (Wessex) Division won a battle honour at Mont Pincon.

All four battalions were involved in the prolonged battle to take Caen, and in the subsequent advance through Belgium and Holland into Germany. The 1st, 7th and 8th all fought in the epic fight to clear the Reichswald and to take Goch. During this battle the Commanding Officer of the 1st, Lieutenant-Colonel P Hall, was killed, seemingly by a friendly mine. All were involved in the crossing of the Rhine, the 1st and 7th in an amphibious capacity.

The Middlesex Regiment could also boast in the North-West European campaign one of the most famous generals: Lieutenant-General Brian Horrocks, then commanding XXX Corps, had been a battalion commanding officer in 1940.

1,117 men of the regiment were killed or died of wounds during the war.

The King's Royal Rifle Corps

Principal Battle Honours 1939-45

Calais 1940 – Rhineland – North-West Europe 1940, 44-45
Egyptian Frontier 1940 – Sidi Rezegh 1941
Alam el Halfa – El Alamein – North Africa 1940-43
Italy 1943-45 – Greece 1941, 44-45

60th Foot raised 1755; redesignated 2nd Battalion,
The Royal Green Jackets 1958.

The scale of casualties suffered by the King's Royal Rifle Corps during the war – 159 officers and 986 men dead with a further 8,000 or more wounded or missing – reflects its perpetual presence in the thick of the action. Time and again, its battalions were virtually destroyed, only to be re-built and to re-enter the fray.

The pattern was set early on, when the 2nd and 7th Battalions (the latter being a TA unit better known as the 1st Queen Victoria Rifles) were sent into the defence of Calais. For four days from 23 May 1940 the Germans were held off and valuable time bought for the evacuation of the BEF, before the position became untenable and was over-run.

The following year the 9th Battalion was involved in the ill-advised adventure in Greece, where a front at Florina Gap proved too long to hold, and in the ill-prepared defence of Crete. More than 150 men were taken prisoner in the retreat through Greece, and only one officer and 13 men escaped in the evacuation from Crete.

In November 1941 the 1st Battalion also suffered heavy losses. An initial full-blooded charge over 2,000 yards of open ground at Sidi Rezegh was a complete success, with 700 enemy taken prisoner. The next day, however, a tank and lorried infantry counter-attack swept over the position, and barely 55 members of the battalion returned. One of those who died was Rifleman John Beeley, who was awarded a posthumous Victoria Cross for his action in eliminating an anti-tank gun post. The citation reflects so many acts of courage, saying that to protect his unit, he 'went to certain death'.

By the time the 1st, 2nd and 9th Battalions of the King's Royal Rifle Corps fought at Gazala in May 1942, all three had been reduced to a handful of men and re-built. Again the battle was costly, and by the end the 9th was disbanded to provided sufficient recruits to bring the 1st and 2nd back up to strength.

Thus reinforced, both battalions served at Alam Halfa – on the disputed southern front – and then at El Alamein. In the latter struggle, the 1st were involved in the early fighting in the south, whilst the 2nd staged two important night attacks; the first saw the capture of 100 prisoners of war, the second, on 2 November, took a key position at El Aqqaquir, where the breakthrough was to come.

In the pursuit across the Western Desert to Tunis, the 1st saw action at Mareth and the 2nd at Akarit.

North Africa alone cost the regiment more than 500 dead, many from the 11th Battalion, which had also been present at El Alamein and had suffered so many casualties that it was withdrawn to Syria for a period. By October 1943, however, it was strong enough to re-enter the campaign, which now moved on to Italy. It was joined there by the 1st and 2nd.

Perhaps the greatest challenge faced in Italy was the crossing of the Ronco. Three companies were caught on the wrong side of the river without adequate support and were over-run; only one officer managed to swim back to the Allied lines.

The 2nd Battalion was withdrawn from Italy to serve in North-West Europe, landing the day after D-Day. The 12th Battalion arrived soon after, and both fought at Falaise. A later battle honour was won at the Rhineland.

The Wiltshire Regiment (Duke of Edinburgh's)

Principal Battle Honours 1939-45

Defence of Arras – Hill 112 – Maltot – Mont Pincon
Seine 1944 – Cleve – Garigliano Crossing – Anzio
Rome – North Arakan

62nd Foot originally raised 1743; 99th Foot originally raised 1760; these two regiments amalgamated to form The Wiltshire Regiment (Duke of Edinburgh's) 1881; amalgamated to form The Duke of Edinburgh's Royal Regiment (Berkshire and Wiltshire) 1959; amalgamated to form The Royal Gloucestershire, Berkshire and Wiltshire Regiment 1993.

In common with many infantry battalions stationed in India in the late '30s, the 1st Battalion of The Wiltshire Regiment was not immediately called upon to serve in the front-line. When its time did come, it was suffering from severe personnel problems: 150 men were sent to join other units in 1943, whilst a further 270 of the longest-serving were repatriated. Reinforcements did arrive in 1944, but it was difficult to maintain any sense of stability when, in an extreme case, one of the new arrivals had been in ten regiments in the previous three years.

Nonetheless, the battalion was posted forward in February 1944 to relieve the 7th Indian Division, then under siege in the Sinzweya Box in North Arakan. A hazardous advance through the jungle, supplied from the air and under enemy attack, was rewarded with success. The men's major battle was fought in April in the assault on Point 551, a strategic position commanding the Maungdaw-Buthidaung road. The battalion objectives were two approach features – known as Camel and Hump – which demanded an attack up steep, bamboo-covered slopes under mortar and sniper fire. The summits were taken and held whilst the next stage of the operation was prepared.

By the time the battalion was withdrawn in October, it had suffered 200 casualties and 600 cases of malaria.

Back in Europe, the 2nd Battalion was one of the first units to move to France in 1939. Its most distinguished action came during the counter-attack at Arras, when for the only time in the campaign, the initiative was briefly seized from the Germans. When that offensive failed, the Wilts came under heavy pressure, holding their position on the Scarpe for three days and being reduced to just 300 men. A further defensive stand was made at Ypres-Comines prior to evacuation.

Re-built, the 2nd Wilts spent some time in the Middle-East – including a brief stay in Madagascar – before joining the campaign in Sicily. In the assault crossing of the Simento, the battalion successfully established a bridgehead despite determined opposition from the famous Herman Goering Division.

The most intense fighting the battalion was to face came in Italy in early 1944. Battle honours were won in the crossing of the Garigliano and at Anzio, where the Wilts served for the last two months. These battles almost finished the battalion, with 600 casualties and cases of sickness.

Withdrawn to the Middle East, the battalion re-built again and – completing some 25,000 miles of travel during the war – joined the final stages of the North European campaign.

Already active in that theatre were the 4th and 5th Battalions, both in the 43rd (Wessex) Division. Two famous honours were won in Normandy: at Hill 112 and Mont Pincon.

In the latter conflict, both battalions were heavily engaged in the early stages. Separate attempts to cross the river Druance at the foot of the hill were met with enemy machine-gun and mortar fire. In an astonishing display of leadership, Lieutenant-Colonel Pearson of the 5th advanced directly on the bridge, in full sight of the enemy; though it cost him his life, his example inspired his men onto renewed efforts and a foothold was gained. By evening the battalion had been reduced to just 75 all ranks. The 4th Battalion, also severely depleted, came to the support of the tanks of the 13th/18th Hussars in the final taking of the summit.

The two battalions again displayed remarkable tenacity in the crossing of the Seine, where they were the assault battalions. It was through the bridgehead that they established that the armour of the Allied forces was to pass in the advance on the Low Countries.

Ending the war in Bremen, Major Pope of the 4th Wilts distinguished himself in capturing two German generals, a vice-admiral and the Bishop of the city, a known Nazi sympathiser.

The Manchester Regiment

Principal Battle Honours 1939-45

Dyle – Defence of Arras – Caen – Scheldt – Lower Maas
Roer – Reichswald – Gothic Line – Malta 1940 – Kohima

63rd Foot raised 1756; 96th Foot raised 1824; these two regiments amalgamated to form The Manchester Regiment 1881; amalgamated to form The King's Regiment 1958.

The first battle honour awarded to The Manchester Regiment during the Second World War was won by the 2nd Battalion at the river Dyle. As part of the 2nd Division within the British Expeditionary Force, it had advanced to the Dyle on 11 May 1940, following the German invasion of the Low Countries. Two days of fighting around the town of Wavre delayed the German advance, but with the front being penetrated in the south, the order to withdraw was given on 16 May and the retreat to Dunkirk commenced. The men were successfully evacuated.

The 1st Battalion was less fortunate. Stationed in Singapore at the start of the war, it was allocated the task of defending the eastern side of the island, in a coastal front stretching down from Changi. An attack from the Japanese was widely expected and the Manchesters spent some months constructing positions to hold the beaches in anticipation of a seaborne invasion. In the event, of course, the attack came from the north and west sides of Singapore and the battalion, though it was shelled and dive bombed, was effectively sidelined.

On 12 February 1941, with the Japanese having taken Johore Causeway, the Manchesters were ordered to abandon their carefully prepared positions without yet having fired a shot. On 14 February 'B' and 'C' Companies did engage the enemy for the first time, but the surrender of Singapore was announced the following day, and all the survivors were taken prisoner.

The regimental history tells us of the mood of the moment:

'Notwithstanding the desperate position in which they stood, the men were cheerful until the very end, and when they marched away into captivity they were still in good heart. Colonel Holmes, who led them, put a photograph of the King on his back where the men following him might see it, and the men sang as they marched.' [1]

The strength of the battalion before the invasion of Singapore stood at just over a thousand. 60 were killed; a further 378 died whilst in captivity.

The regiment was later to return to the Far East, with the arrival in India of the 2nd Battalion in June 1942. Now converted to a machine-gun battalion, though still with the 2nd Division, the Manchesters were sent forward into Burma in April 1944. At the time, the Japanese U-Go offensive had trapped the garrisons of Kohima and Imphal and, amidst intense action, the battalion assisted in clearing the road between the two towns in the relief of the sieges.

The subsequent advance to Malaya met with equal success, and in April 1945 – after a year of fighting – the division was withdrawn back to India.

Back at home in June 1942, the 1st Battalion had been reconstituted from the men of the 6th Battalion. Also a machine-gun unit, the battalion landed at Arromanches on 27 June 1944 with the 53rd (Welsh) Division, and was immediately plunged into the fighting around Caen.

The struggle consisted largely of a series of small, bitter actions in which the companies of the 1st Manchesters were often used separately to provide machine-gun cover for infantry attacks. Typical in most respects (though on this occasion the whole battalion was involved) was the taking of Point 112, a minor hill in the Mont Pincon feature. A raid on an enemy position comprising three machine-gun posts, artillery and mortars, resulted in 77 minutes of bloody exchange.

With the eventual collapse of the opposition, the advance across France was to prove easier, though that too was not without its own difficulties. The regimental history records the mixed emotions of that largely unopposed progress:

'The subsequent race through Northern France was chiefly remembered by the cordial welcome that was everywhere given to us, and by the mean and despicable acts of vengeance that the French and Belgians were taking upon those of their countrymen who they were pleased to call collaborateurs.' [2]

The battalion was involved on the outskirts of many of the most celebrated conflicts of the campaign, including the attempt to break through to Arnhem, and the German offensive in the Ardennes. In the latter, with the British flank potentially threatened, The Manchester Regiment again took up positions around the Dyle, with 'A' Company actually digging in on the historic field of Waterloo.

In February 1945 German troops in the Reichswald Forest posed another major challenge. 53rd Division was detailed to clear the northern part of the forest. The battalion contributed nearly 70,000 rounds of fire to the initial barrage, and then advanced – no easy task when carrying machine-guns in the winter mud of a forest battlefield. Nonetheless, Reichswald was duly cleared.

The 1st Battalion ended the war in Hamburg, where 15,000 prisoners were taken.

[1] Bell *History of The Manchester Regiment First and Second Battalions* p.80
[2] ibid. p.164

The North Staffordshire Regiment
(The Prince of Wales's)

Principal Battle Honours 1939-45

Dyle – Ypres-Comines Canal – Caen – Brieux Bridgehead
Medjez Plain – North Africa 1943 – Anzio
Rome – Marradi – Burma 1943

64th Foot raised 1756; 98th Foot originally raised 1760; these two regiments amalgamated to form The North Staffordshire Regiment (The Prince of Wales's) 1881; amalgamated to form The Staffordshire Regiment (The Prince of Wales's) 1959.

The first men of the North Staffordshire Regiment into battle were those of the 2nd Battalion who formed part of the British Expeditionary Force in 1940. Having advanced to the Dyle in Belgium, they spent 20 days retreating some 100 miles to Dunkirk, during which time they established ten positions, all of which were held until orders to abandon them were received. It was a source of some pride that the enemy had never managed to break through the battalion at any stage. 140 men were killed or wounded during the campaign.

Following a period of recuperation and re-organisation, the battalion was posted to North Africa with the First Army in March 1943, in time to assist the final blows against the Germans in North Africa. Their initiation into that conflict came in the fighting around Medjez el Bab in Tunisia. On 21 April they comprehensively defeated a battalion of the famed Herman Goering Division at Banana Ridge on 21 April, inflicting 85 casualties and taking 230 prisoners at the cost of just 26 casualties.

The most trying action was to come at Anzio in January 1944, an operation that achieved mixed results. For while the landing of a combined force of American, British and Free French troops took the German army by surprise and rapidly established a beach-head, the failure fully to exploit that early advantage left the troops vulnerable to counter-attack.

When the enemy response did come, the North Staffords were confronted by no less than three German battalions at Buonriposo Ridge on 7 February. With over 300 casualties that night, the position became untenable and was relinquished, though the battalion, re-grouped into two companies, was to remain at Anzio. Indeed it was one of these companies that made the decisive contribution in repulsing a two-day enemy attack on Flyover Bridge, the last defences on the outskirts of Anzio.

By the time the Allied advance retook the position at Buonriposo at the end of May, 43 officers and 741 other ranks of the North Staffords were reported as casualties.

The battalion was to return to the front-line later in the year, serving at Florence and winning a battle honour for taking the key town of Marradi, before being despatched to Palestine in January 1945.

The 1st Battalion of the regiment was stationed in India when war was declared, and there it remained for the next few years, performing the necessary though unspectacular task of policing the colony at a time of turmoil.

When they were summoned into battle, the 1st North Staffords joined the tail-end of the Arakan campaign that, though unsuccessful, saw Allied troops return to active conflict with the Japanese for the first time since the disastrous retreat from Burma. Holding the Ngakyedauk Pass for six days in May 1943 whilst the 26th Indian Division passed through, the mortar platoon was responsible for killing over 200 Japanese for minimal losses.

Territorial battalions of the North Staffordshire Regiment joined the forces landing in Normandy in 1944, as did territorial battalions of the South Staffords, with whom the regiment was later to be amalgamated.

The 6th Battalion was to serve in the taking of Caen in 1944 and subsequently win a battle honour at Brieux, holding a position under intense fire to enable a detachment of Royal Engineers to construct a bridge. The battalion was then broken up to provide reinforcements for other units.

The York and Lancaster Regiment

Principal Battle Honours 1939-45

Fontenay Le Pesnil – Antwerp-Turnhout Canal
Tobruk 1941 – Mine de Sedjenane – Sicily 1943 – Salerno – Minturno
Crete – North Arakan – Chindits 1944

65th Foot raised 1756; 84th Foot raised 1783; these two regiments
amalgamated to form The York and Lancaster Regiment 1881; disbanded
1968.

B y the end of the Second World War, the 1st Battalion, The York and Lancaster
Regiment could claim to be one of the most travelled of all units in the British
Army; in six years it covered more than 30,000 miles on an itinerary that took in
England, Scotland, Northern Ireland, Norway, France, Belgium, Germany, Italy,
South Africa, Egypt, Palestine, Syria, Iraq, Persia and India.

Initially posted to Northern France with the BEF, the 1st York & Lancasters
were transferred before the German offensive began, and sent to Norway in April
1940. They arrived in the second wave of British forces with the aim of
reinforcing the already beleaguered troops, but the lack of equipment and clear
leadership and the determined aggression of the enemy that characterized the entire
Norwegian expedition allowed for little chance of success in their mission. The
battalion was soon evacuated by the Royal Navy, with casualties from the brief
campaign standing at 29 dead, 23 wounded and 150 missing.

Re-formed back home, the battalion spent most of 1941 with the 5th Division
training in Northern Ireland in anticipation of its return to the fray. That return
was to be a long time coming. In January 1942 the 5th Division sailed for India via
South Africa, arriving only to be sent on to Persia. When it became evident that
the Middle East was unlikely to see an enemy attack, the division moved on to
Egypt, where the British were preparing for the Sicily landings.

The Sicily campaign and the subsequent invasion of Italy saw the battalion
engaged in fierce, protracted fighting for the first time. Through it all, the men
acquitted themselves with honour, particularly in the battle around Cassino.
Initially held in reserve, the battalion was called up in January 1944 to seize Monte
Natale; the position was held against immediate and sustained counter-attacks.

In April 1945 the 5th Division was posted to Germany, following on behind the
21st Army Group in the advance to the Elbe.

The 2nd Battalion of the regiment had been involved in the fighting considerably earlier. Arriving in Crete in November 1940 as part of 14th Brigade, it took up a position in Heraklion at the north of the island, where it was ordered to hold the harbour and the air-base in the event of a German assault.

That assault, of course, duly came in May the following year, and the 2nd York & Lancasters found themselves in the thick of battle. On the first day of the invasion alone, 1,000 enemy paratroops landed within the perimeter of the battalion's base, all of whom were accounted for. The attack, however, continued and though 14th Brigade held absolutely firm, the decision was taken that the defence of the island had become unsustainable. In the last week of May, the evacuation began from Heraklion harbour – still in Allied hands.

In early 1942 the battalion left the Mediterranean for India, reuniting briefly with the 1st Battalion, before that unit itself moved on. For most of their time in the colony, the men of the 2nd were employed on policing duties, but there was one more major operation to come. In 1944, as Chindit columns 65 and 84, the battalion advanced into Burma, where it remained for five months behind enemy lines, marching over 500 miles.

The territorial battalions of the regiment also played their part in the struggle. The Hallamshire Battalion also served in Norway and later landed in Normandy in 1944. Fighting through to Arnhem, the Hallamshires won the only Victoria Cross awarded to the regiment during the war.

The 6th Battalion saw perhaps more action than any other unit of the regiment, distinguishing itself at Dunkirk, in North Africa and in the long campaigns in Italy.

The 7th, 8th and 9th Battalions all made their contributions in India and Burma.

The Durham Light Infantry

Principal Battle Honours 1939-45

Dunkirk 1940 – Tilly sur Seulles – Defence of Rauray
Gheel – Tobruk 1941 – El Alamein – Mareth – Primosole Bridge
Salerno – Kohima

68th Foot raised 1756; 106th Bombay Light Infantry raised 1826; these two
regiments amalgamated to form The Durham Light Infantry 1881;
redesignated 4th Battalion, The Light Infantry 1968; disbanded same year.

The 2nd Battalion, The Durham Light Infantry fought with the British
Expeditionary Force and saw action at La Tombe on the river Dyle. A German
attempt to cross a partially demolished bridge was twice repelled by 'D' Company
under 2nd Lieutenant R W Annand, as described by Sergeant-Major Metcalfe:

'Mr Annand and Co. just belted them and they even got on to the parapet to be
able to pitch grenades. For two hours it was hell let loose, then Jerry gave it up
and withdrew . . . . [W]e'd only about 16 casualties. We fired well over 20,000
rounds and over 100 grenades had been used.' [1]

Eventually ordered to withdraw, Lt Annand returned to collect his wounded
batman, bringing him back in a wheelbarrow before collapsing with exhaustion and
his own wounds. He was later awarded a Victoria Cross.

Also in the BEF were the 6th, 8th and 9th Battalions, serving together in the
151st Brigade, and fighting with distinction in the Arras counter-offensive. All
battalions were evacuated from Dunkirk, though the 2nd was now down to just 150
men.

The 151st Brigade was back in the field the following year. Having moved to
North Africa, it was to be involved in three of the most critical battles of the
theatre at Gazala, El Alamein and Mareth.

Already in Africa was the 1st Battalion, which had transferred from China at
the beginning of the war. Early fighting around the Halfaya Pass was followed by
an intervention in the Syrian campaign. In August 1941 it joined the besieged
garrison of Tobruk, winning a major battle honour there.

The collapse of Tobruk the following year saw the 151st Brigade forced into
retreat back through enemy positions to Mersa Matruh. It was here that Private
Adam Wakenshaw won the regiment's second VC of the war. In a German attack
on 27 June 1942, Pte Wakenshaw lost his left arm whilst manning a 2-pdr in a duel

with an enemy light gun. With most of the gun's crew dead, he nonetheless continued to load the 2-pdr and, with the assistance of the gun-aimer, to fire. A further strike killed the aimer, but Pte Wakenshaw persevered in his efforts until he too was killed.

The 1st Battalion had left North Africa in 1942 to strengthen the garrison of Malta. With the ending of the siege of the island, the battalion was assigned an even more difficult task: the occupation of the Aegean island of Kos. The German invasion of October 1943 saw the swamping of Kos's defences, but 100 men did escape to Egypt to re-form the battalion.

With the ending of the African war, the 151st Battalion fought on into Sicily, where it won a major battle honour at Primosole Bridge. It also facilitated the capture of Catania, the city actually surrendering to Lieutenant Gardiner. It was joined by the 16th Battalion, which had earlier been in Tunisia with the 1st Army.

The 16th was to spend the rest of the war in Southern Europe, pursuing the enemy through Italy. The 1st Battalion too served in the later stages.

The 151st Brigade, meanwhile, had been withdrawn for the second campaign in North-West Europe. Yet more Durham battalions – the 10th and 11th – joined the war at this stage.

Elsewhere the 2nd Battalion fought in the Arakan Peninsular in 1943, and won a major battle honour at Kohima the following year.

Mention too must be made of the 5th Durhams who were redesignated 113th Light Anti-Aircraft Regiment, RA. In perhaps the most traumatic task any battalion faced, it was responsible in April 1945 for liberating the concentration camp at Belsen. Though Belsen was then still in enemy-held territory, Germany was fearful that a typhus epidemic could break out from the camp and requested assistance. Some 40,000 survivors of the Holocaust had to be moved from the camp for urgent medical treatment, whilst thousands of corpses had to be buried. A month after they had arrived in the nightmare, the Durhams had cleared and burnt the camp.

[1] Rissik *The D.L.I. At War* p.14

The Highland Light Infantry (City of Glasgow Regiment)

Principal Battle Honours 1939-45

Odon – Scheldt – Walcheren Causeway – Reichswald
Rhine – North-West Europe 1940, 44-45 – Keren
Cauldron – Landing in Sicily – Greece 1944-45

71st Foot raised 1777; 74th Foot raised 1787; these two regiments amalgamated to form The Highland Light Infantry (City of Glasgow Regiment) 1881; amalgamated to form The Royal Highland Fusiliers (Princess Margaret's Own Glasgow and Ayrshire Regiment) 1959.

The first soldiers of The Highland Light Infantry to see action were in a platoon drawn from the 5th and 6th Battalions who fought in Norway. The campaign was, of course, unsuccessful but the men fought courageously in an attempt to prevent a sea-borne assault on Hemmerberget before escaping back home.

The 1st Battalion served with the British Expeditionary Force, fighting at Lille and Armentieres. In a rearguard action at Rexpoede, covering the Dunkirk evacuation, the men found themselves surrounded by the enemy, but successfully fought their way out to be themselves evacuated, though three officers and 29 other ranks were killed in the break-out.

Soon after, two Battalions joined the so-called second BEF, landing at Cherbourg with the 52nd (Lowland) Division. Taking up an advanced position at Evereaux, they were attacked by the Germans on 13 June 1940 but held off the enemy before they too were withdrawn.

The focus of the regiment then transferred to Africa, where the 2nd Battalion was involved in the battle at Mersa Matruh, before moving to West Africa at the end of 1940 to join the struggle against the Italians in Eritrea.

The decisive battle was to come at Keren, but before that, on 21 January 1941, the battalion met the enemy at Barentu. Under heavy fire, one of the forward companies was halted short of the hill that was the objective, leaving a second company led by Captain Mark Hollis to advance alone. Casualties were severe and the position proved untenable, but the bravery of the Highlanders earned such respect from the enemy that when the hill was finally recaptured, the dead men were found to have been buried in a neat row of graves, with Capt Hollis' grave in front.

Whether this respect was reciprocated is doubtful. At Keren, it was joked that the Italians were issued with regulation white handkerchiefs to enable them to surrender, whilst the use of cologne was equally derided with the slogan: 'Shoot in the direction of the "hum"'. The humour was perhaps inevitable in the appalling conditions of Keren; General Donald Bateman who served both here and at Monte Cassino later wrote that: 'There is no doubt in my mind . . . that Keren was the tougher battle.' [1]

With the victory in East Africa, the 2nd HLI returned – via Iraq and Cyprus – to the Western Desert, in time to fight in the battle of the Cauldron.

Withdrawn to train as a specialist landing unit, the battalion missed the remainder of the campaign against Rommel, but returned as No. 2 Beach Brick for the invasion of Sicily. On both that occasion and the subsequent landing in Italy, the opposition was slight (though the Commanding Officer, Colonel Thorburn, was killed in the former), and the training proved unnecessary. Nonetheless, the battalion fought in the land campaigns, before being again withdrawn in October 1943 for specialist training.

This time its role was that of mountain troops, and it was used for the capture of the Kos Islands in the Adriatic in commando-style operations. The remainder of the war was spent in Greece, keeping order during the civil war.

The 1st Battalion returned with the Allied troops to North-West Europe in 1944, winning battle honours at Odon and at Reichswald, the latter the result of 30 days hard combat to clear the forest. It was joined in the campaign by further battalions of the regiment: the 5th and 6th both fought in the assault on Walcheren to open Antwerp, whilst the 10th distinguished itself at the crossing of the Rhine.

The only Victoria Cross won by a member of the regiment was awarded posthumously to Major Gerald Blaker whilst attached to the 9th Gurkha Rifles in Burma in 1944.

104 officers and 1,287 other ranks died during the war.

[1] Maule *The Great Battles of World War II* p.104

The Seaforth Highlanders (Ross-shire Buffs, The Duke of Albany's)

Principal Battle Honours 1939-45

St Valéry-en-Caux – Caen – Rhineland – El Alamein – Akarit – Sicily 1943Anzio – Madagascar – Imphal – Burma 1942-44

72nd (Highland) Regiment raised 1778; 78th (Highland) Regiment raised 1793; these two regiments amalgamated to form The Seaforth Highlanders (Ross-shire Buffs, The Duke of Albany's) 1881; amalgamated to form Queen's Own Highlanders (Seaforth and Camerons) 1961; amalgamated to form The Highlanders 1993.

The Seaforth Highlanders were particularly badly hit by the disaster of the first encounter with the enemy in North-West Europe, for while the 6th were successfully evacuated from Dunkirk, both the 2nd and 4th formed part of the 51st (Highland) Division. Stationed under French command on the southern end of the front, the 51st Division was left behind in the general retreat and was eventually forced to surrender at St Valéry. During that ill-fated campaign, however, the Seaforths did make honourable contributions at the Somme and at St Valéry itself.

Almost immediately, a new 51st Division was created back home, including both the 5th Seaforths and a newly-raised 2nd Battalion, and was deployed in North Africa. Together with the 5th Camerons, these two formed 152 Brigade, who made a vital intervention at El Alamein. A further battle honour was won at Akarit, where the men took and, for a whole day, held Roumana Ridge in fighting that was virtually hand-to-hand at times.

The surviving veterans of Dunkirk – the 6th Battalion – had meanwhile fought in the invasion of Madagascar in May 1942, helping to take the key port of Antrisam. It spent most of the next year as part of Paiforce, stationed in Iraq and Iran, before joining 152 Brigade in the taking of Sicily.

The level of the regiment's activity on that island is evidenced by the winning of five minor battle honours as well as the campaign honour 'Sicily 1943'.

The 6th Battalion continued the Allied push into Italy, where it was in the thick of the fighting at Garigliano and in the Anzio landings of January 1944. The 2nd and 5th Battalions were withdrawn for the victorious return to North-West Europe, still serving together in 152 Brigade. The men assisted in the capture of Le Havre,

207

whilst the 7th Seaforths – also active in the theatre – saw action in the assault crossing of the Seine. All three battalions later fought in the clearing of the Rhineland and in the battle to cross the Rhine itself.

The 6th Battalion was moved from Italy to Germany in the last few months of the war.

In the Far East, the 1st Seaforths had been in Shanghai in 1939. A period in Singapore followed, but the men were transferred again – this time to Assam – before the Japanese offensive came. Valuable time spent training in jungle conditions, augmented by contact with the enemy whilst aiding the final evacuation from Burma, gave the battalion a level of experience that was to be used to good effect throughout the ensuing war.

1943 saw much patrolling on the Chindwin, particularly in an encounter at Yetagan, and the following year, vital diversionary manoeuvres were staged on the same river to draw enemy forces away from the Chindits. In 1944 the taking of Kasom and the defence of Imphal helped turn the tide of battle and began driving the Japanese from Burma.

The 1st Seaforths were withdrawn in anticipation of an invasion of Malaya, but when that proved unnecessary with the surrender of Japan, the men instead staged an unopposed landing on Java.

It is appropriate too to mention the Seaforth Highlanders of Canada, an allied regiment that fought in Sicily, Italy and the later stages of North-West Europe. Private E Smith won a Victoria Cross for his heroism in the assault on the Gustav Line.

The Gordon Highlanders

Principal Battle Honours 1939-45

Odon – Reichswald – Goch – Rhine
North-West Europe 1940, 44-45 – El Alamein – Mareth
North Africa 1942-43 – Sferro – Anzio

75th Foot raised 1787; 92nd Foot raised 1794; these two regiments amalgamated to form The Gordon Highlanders 1881; amalgamated to form The Highlanders 1993.

The 1st Battalion, The Gordon Highlanders was stationed in England at the outbreak of war and was posted to France with the British Expeditionary Force in 1939, as part of the ill-fated 51st (Highland) Division. Sent to the southern wing of the Allied front-line, under the command of the French, the 51st were effectively isolated from the rest of the BEF. They not only faced some of the heaviest fighting against the German advance, but were also amongst the last to withdraw.

When they were eventually commanded to retreat, some four days after the evacuation from Dunkirk had been completed, they did so to the tiny port of St Valéry-en-Caux, from where they were due to be pulled out of the Continent. The sea approach to the town, however, was so narrow as to be almost impossibly difficult for the Royal Navy, particularly under the enemy air and artillery attack. The 51st were posted on the town perimeter to hold off the Germans, a task they performed so well that several thousand British and French soldiers were successfully evacuated despite the conditions.

For the 1st Gordons and their colleagues, however, there was no evacuation; desperately weakened, short of ammunition and supplies, and with the French troops alongside them already having capitulated, it became clear that there was no hope of rescue. On 21 June 1940, the order was finally given to surrender. The survivors of the battle were marched across Northern France and the Low Countries to be interned in prisoner of war camps in Germany.

The 2nd Battalion's plight was perhaps even worse. They had sailed for Singapore in March 1937, and were still there when the Japanese air attacks began in December 1941. By the end of January, the Japanese had overrun almost the whole of Malaya, and the 2nd Gordons were stationed with Australian troops on the road leading to Singapore island. There followed a desperately hard fighting withdrawal across the Johore Causeway. The Gordons retired to the east of the island in early February to prepare for a counter-offensive, but it never happened; the island surrendered to the Japanese, and the 2nd Gordons were taken prisoner. After several months providing work parties in Changi, they were sent in October 1942 to Siam to be used as slave labour in the construction of the Siam-Burma railway.

Though both battalions of the regiment were thus captured during the first half of the War, The Gordon Highlanders still had an important part to play.

The 1st Gordons were re-raised within a month of the original battalion being taken and took their place in the new Highland Division. They first saw action at El Alamein, where infantry were used to force paths through enemy ranks. The vanquished enemy were led, of course, by Rommel, who had accepted the surrender at St Valéry.

Even in the context of modern desert warfare, the Scottish character of the regiment was never far from the surface. The ruling in 1939 that battle-dress was to be worn rather than kilts had been resented by The Gordons as much as it was by other regiments, but at El Alamein they reasserted the traditions, being marched into battle by kilted pipers. The same pipers were later to steal the show at the Allied Victory Parade at Tunis. (It is also reported that much energy was exerted seeking out oatmeal in the hostile conditions of North Africa in order to make porridge for the soldiers.)

The Highland Division participated in the invasion of Sicily and returned to Britain shortly afterwards, having completed a 1,500 mile advance from El Alamein.

Both the 1st and the 2nd Gordons (the latter reconstituted in May 1942) played their part in the Normandy landings and the subsequent advance through France and North Germany, the 1st ending the War in Bremerhaven and the 2nd in Hamburg. One of the most emotional moments came in September 1944, when the 1st Gordons re-entered St Valéry, this time in triumph.

The Queen's Own Cameron Highlanders

Principal Battle Honours 1939-45

St Omer-La Bassée – Reichswald – Rhine – Keren
Sidi Barrani – El Alamein – Akarit – Gothic Line
Kohima – Mandalay

Raised 1793; amalgamated to form The Queen's Own Highlanders
(Seaforth and Camerons) 1961; amalgamated to form The Highlanders
1993.

B oth the 1st and the 4th Battalions of the Cameron Highlanders served in the disastrous first campaign in North-West Europe. The experiences of the two, however, were very different.

The 1st Camerons, in the main body of the British Expeditionary Force, fought their major conflict at St Omer-La Bassée, defending a position against a combined tank and dive bomber attack, before being evacuated from Dunkirk. In the battle Company Sergeant Major C T Mackintosh was awarded the Military Cross, the only NCO in the regiment to receive that honour. He was to spend much of the war in a prison camp in Poland, but returned to the regiment after the war and was subsequently commissioned.

The 4th Camerons, meanwhile, were amongst the ranks of the 51st Highland Division, the division that did not escape the Germans, and was taken prisoner at St Valéry.

A few months later, in another theatre, the 2nd Battalion were to restore the pride of the Camerons. Arriving in Egypt in time to join Wavell's offensive in late 1940, the battalion fought at the battle of Sidi Barrani, and became the first infantry to enter into the town itself. The prime objective – the Fortress of Nibeiwa – was taken in a bayonet charge reminiscent of great infantry encounters of the past. More than 2,000 Italian prisoners were captured.

Switched across the continent to Eritrea, the 2nd Camerons also distinguished themselves in the storming of the mountain stronghold at Keren. Short of supplies and under heavy fire, the men successfully took a feature that was to be renamed in their honour, Cameron Ridge. For a whole month the position became the front-line of the battle, with the enemy on another ridge some 800 feet above. Keren eventually fell on 26 March 1941.

This triumph to their credit, the 2nd Camerons later returned to the Western

Desert, but the run of victories was not to last. Attached to the 2nd South African Division, they were sent to Tobruk in June 1942 to defend the town against Rommel's second great campaign. Unfortunately Tobruk, which had held out for eight months the previous year, was this time unable to resist the onslaught of the Afrika Korps and fell on 22 June. Another battalion of Camerons was taken prisoner by the Germans.

During its time in Africa, however, the 2nd Battalion had earned itself a reputation second to none. Field Marshal Auchinleck himself commented: 'Their name had become a legend.' [1]

Also in North Africa were the 5th Camerons, who had joined the reconstituted 51st Highland Division. They fought at El Alamein and later in Tunisia and Sicily.

Back home, after the catastrophe of St Valéry, the 4th Battalion had been reformed in July 1940. Following a posting in the Dutch West Indies, guarding the oil refineries there, it had returned to Scotland and, on the fall of Tobruk, was renamed the 2nd Battalion.

Under this title, it joined the Allied forces in Italy in early 1944, during the attempts to break through the Gustav Line at Monte Cassino. It also participated in the liberation of the tiny independent state of San Marino. In November of that year, it was withdrawn and sent to Greece, where the civil war and threat of a communist revolution was causing concern to the British government.

1944, of course, was the year in which the prospect of an eventual Allied victory became inevitable, and the Camerons did their best to hasten its arrival. Apart from their representation in the Mediterranean, there was also the 1st Battalion, who served in Burma. Sailing for India in April 1942, it was part of the 2nd Division that fought with such distinction in the re-opening of the Kohima-Imphal road and breaking through the sieges of both towns.

And, landing the day after D-Day, there was the 5th Battalion. The veterans of North Africa fought right through the second North-West European campaign, serving in many of the most famous battles. Just as important, however, were the smaller, often uncelebrated actions, such as the crossing of the Uitwaterings Canal in November 1944, of which the Corps commander was to write:

'I would not, I think, be going too far to say that had not the 5th Camerons held on to their foothold on the East bank the advance of the whole Corps might well have been delayed for an appreciable time.' [2]

Perhaps the most satisfactory moment of all was the liberation of St Valéry.

[1] Baird *Whatever Men Dare* p.23

[2] Ewart *Queen's Own Cameron Highlanders* p.49

The Royal Ulster Rifles

Principal Battle Honours 1939-45

Dyle – Dunkirk 1940 – Normandy Landing – Caen
Rhine – Bremen

83rd Foot raised 1793; 86th Foot raised 1793; these two regiments
amalgamated to form The Royal Irish Rifles (later redesignated The Royal
Ulster Rifles) 1881; amalgamated to form The Royal Irish Rangers 1968;
amalgamated to form The Royal Irish Regiment (27th (Inniskilling) 83rd
and 87th and The Ulster Defence Regiment) 1993.

The 2nd Battalion, The Royal Ulster Rifles won the regiment's first battle
honour early in the war at the Belgian town of Louvain in defence of the Dyle
line in May 1940. Deployed across a wide front delineated by the railway and
centred on the rail station, the men held their position for several days. An enemy
attack seized one platform of the station, but the Rifles retained control of the
opposite platform – just 25 yards away – and of the subway and entrance.
Separated by barbed wire, and with showers of glass from the station's roof adding
to their problems, the two sides remained dead-locked until the British order to
withdraw came on 17 May.

The rigours of retreat were eased for a while by a five-day stop at Tourcoing on
the border, where Montgomery appeared to present decorations to the battalion,
including a DSO to the Commanding Officer. By the end of the month, the men
had been evacuated from Dunkirk.

The 2nd Ulster Rifles were to return to the continent on D-Day, where they
were followed that night by the 1st Battalion.

The 1st had started the war on the North-West Frontier dealing with the
aggression of the Fakir of Ipi. Returning to Britain, a rapid adjustment was made
to the 20th Century with a re-assignment as mechanized infantry. Having adapted
to this new function, the men were then switched to pack horses and mules for a
period of training in Wales, before being given yet another role as glider-borne
troops in the 6th Airlanding Brigade. It was in this capacity that they were finally
deployed, landing on the night of 6 June 1944 at Ranville.

Both battalions saw almost constant service for the first weeks of the European
campaign, with the 2nd Ulster Rifles leading Allied forces into the ruins of Caen,
the town that had delayed the advance for so long. Thereafter it progressed into

Belgium, with the Commanding Officer, Lieutenant-Colonel Harris meeting his French future wife en route.

The 1st Battalion, however, was withdrawn at the end of August 1944, having sustained 50% casualties. It returned some four months later to the river Meuse in response to the German counter in the Ardennes. Also on the Meuse was the 2nd, though the containment of the German offensive meant that neither battalion was called upon to fight.

A further airborne assault was staged in the crossing of the Rhine and, though stiff resistance made the operation less smooth than that on D-Day, with more than 250 casualties, the 1st Rifles made a major contribution to the action.

Both battalions fought on into Germany, where the 1st liberated 3,000 Allied prisoners of war from Stalag XI, whilst the 2nd staged a crucial amphibious assault on Bremen in the closing days: crossing 2,000 yards of artificially flooded countryside in Buffaloes, the men took the enemy by surprise.

Also active in the war against fascism were the 1st and 2nd Battalions of the London Irish Rifles, the territorial units of the regiment. The 1st London Rifles were in the British Expeditionary Force, and returned from Dunkirk to render valuable service in the dark days of the Battle of Britain. Perhaps most noteworthy was the success of 'A' Company in capturing intact a JU88 that had been forced down. Only two weeks old, the aircraft yielded valuable intelligence to British aviation experts, whilst the actions of Captain Cantopher in finding and removing two time-bombs on the 'plane earned him a George Cross.

The 2nd London Rifles formed part of the famous 38th Irish Brigade that fought in the Tunisian campaign. Both battalions served too in the Sicily and Italy campaigns. In the latter, the 1st experienced some of the worst fighting at Anzio, suffering 600 casualties. The consequent rapid turn-over of personnel – over 80% were replaced within the first month – made continuity of spirit particularly difficult.

The 2nd London Rifles were involved in the breaking of the Gustav Line, and later found a new role in Kangaroos.

Over 1,200 men of the Ulster Rifles and London Rifles died in the war.

The Royal Irish Fusiliers
(Princess Victoria's)

Principal Battle Honours 1939-45

St Omer-La Bassée – Bou Arada – Oued Zarga
Djebel Tanngoucha – Centuripe – Termoli – Sangro
Cassino II – Argenta Gap – Malta 1940

87th Foot raised 1793; 89th Foot raised 1793; these two regiments
amalgamated to form The Royal Irish Fusiliers (Princess Victoria's) 1881;
amalgamated to form The Royal Irish Rangers 1968; disbanded as 3rd
Battalion 1970.

The 1st Battalion, The Royal Irish Fusiliers was in the British Expeditionary Force, advancing on 12 May 1940 as part of the second line to take up a position at Arras. There a bombing raid cost the life of Captain Willie Scott, a veteran of the Great War, who had won a DSO at Cambrai in 1917.

Moving into Belgium on 17 May in time to cover the retreat, the battalion came under continual enemy fire and air attack. A stand was taken on the La Bassée Canal alongside an improvised unit of French troops, who matched the British for courage – the regimental history pays particular tribute to a French officer who took a damaged tank into the front-line to delay a Panzer attack, losing his life in his heroic action. Further French reinforcements saw the battalion's responsibilities reduced from 11,000 yards of front to 6,000 yards, but the position was ultimately untenable and the Irish Fusiliers were withdrawn for evacuation.

Difficult though the first experience of war with Germany had been, the 1st Battalion was to be even more sorely tested in Tunisia, where it served with the 38th Irish Brigade. Arriving in Algeria in December 1942, the men were immediately posted forward to the Bou Arada area, where they faced a paratroop brigade of the famous Herman Goering Division. Continual fighting through January was followed – after the German success at the Kasserine Pass – by a concerted enemy attack that was successfully countered and ultimately rolled back.

Further tough actions were fought at Djebel el Mahdi – where, at a cost of just 50 casualties, many more Germans were killed and 120 prisoners taken – and in the vital breakthrough at Tangoucha, which demanded several days of very determined attack.

Not granted the luxury of respite, the 1st Irish Fusiliers were soon in the thick of battle in Sicily. Expecting simply to consolidate at Centuripe, the 38th Brigade found itself called upon to join the as yet unresolved struggle to take the town. Further demands were made of the men in the crossing of the Simento.

The first battle honour to be won in Italy came at Termoli. Sent in to reinforce a bridgehead in the east coast town in October 1943, the battalion soon became embroiled in the effort to break through the German defences of the Winter Line. For two months heavy casualties – including the death of the Commanding Officer, Lieutenant-Colonel Beauchamp Butler – were incurred in a series of attacks on strong defensive positions that saw an advance through Sangro to the river Moro.

A period of recovery was terminated by a return to the front-line in the breaking of the Gustav Line. Thereafter the Italian campaign became one of constant patrolling and fighting, as the Allies pushed painstakingly northwards.

There was, however, the occasional lighter moment, as on All Fools' Day 1945 when all the officers of the Brigade arrived for a supposed party at the Irish Fusiliers. Suspecting the London Irish to be behind the spoof invitations that had been sent out, the Fusiliers retaliated by notifying the authorities that the London Irish had now left the town and their quarters could be re-assigned.

A final major battle honour was won at the Argenta Gap. By the time peace broke out, the Mediterranean campaigns had cost the battalion 280 dead and over a thousand wounded; 72 decorations for courage had been won, together with the tribute of Field-Marshal Alexander: 'The 1st Battalion of the Royal Irish Fusiliers is amongst the finest that it has been my privilege to command.' [1]

The 2nd Battalion was also involved in the Mediterranean theatre. Stationed in Malta at the start of the war, it served in the difficult and protracted siege of that island. The men left in June 1943, confident that the victory in North Africa safeguarded Malta's future. In September of that year, they were posted to another vulnerable island: Leros, in the Aegean. The following month saw a German invasion that took but a few days to destroy the defences. Amongst those killed was Lieutenant-Colonel M French; the survivors were taken prisoner.

[1] *Outline History of The Royal Irish Fusiliers* p.24

The Argyll and Sutherland Highlanders (Princess Louise's)

Principal Battle Honours 1939-45

Odon – Rhine – Sidi Barrani – El Alamein – Akarit
Longstop Hill 1943 – Italy 1943-45 – Crete
Grik Road – Malaya 1941-42

91st (Argyllshire) Highanders raised 1793; 93rd (Sutherland Highlanders)
Foot raised 1799; these two regiments amalgamated to form The Argyll
and Sutherland Highlanders (Princess Louise's) 1881.

The first battalions of The Argyll and Sutherland Highlanders to see active service were the territorial 6th, 7th and 8th in Northern Europe. Of these, 270 men of the 6th escaped from Dunkirk – though the battalion had suffered more than 400 casualties – and later re-formed as an anti-tank regiment. The 7th and 8th, however, were part of the 51st (Highland) Division, the most famous of the units left behind after Dunkirk to be killed or captured.

Soon after, in September 1940, Italian forces invaded Egypt from Libya, advancing some 50 miles to Sidi Barrani in a symbolic occupation of British-held territory. It was there three months later that the 1st Battalion, The Argyll and Sutherland Highlanders, were to win the regiment's first major battle honour of the war.

The British operation that was to become known as 'Wavell's Offensive' began at Sidi Barrani as it was to continue, with a complete rout of the Italians, the capture of large numbers of prisoners, tanks and guns, and the driving back of the enemy. The 1st Argylls, though suffering serious casualties, were in the forefront of the first Allied victory, and went on to assist the drive into Libya.

The offensive, of course, was not to prove decisive, for with the Italians in retreat, critical British forces were withdrawn from North Africa to pursue the doomed operations in Greece and Crete. Amongst them were the 1st Argylls, landing in Crete just one day before the German invasion commenced. With inadequate equipment, non-existent air cover and appalling standards of communication, the battalion's efforts were never going to be successful; when the order to evacuate came ten days after landing, the battalion was already carrying terrible losses. Of the 655 men who had been sent to the island, just 312 escaped, the remainder either killed or captured.

Returning to Africa to rebuild, the battalion served in Egypt, Eritrea and Palestine and in a support role at El Alamein. It was not until Sicily that it returned to front-line combat.

By this stage, further battalions of the regiment had arrived in North Africa to contribute to the war effort. The 7th Argylls, newly re-formed, arrived with the reconstituted 51st Division, landing in Egypt in June 1942 in time to participate in Montgomery's victorious operations.

At Alamein, the 7th achieved all its set objectives, including the taking of the hill designated Point 44 at Tel el Aqqaqir. When the enemy was finally cleared from the hill, a store of iron crosses was amongst the booty found. In a mock ceremony that displayed typical Army humour, the Commanding Officer was awarded this highest of German decorations.

In fact, Lieutenant-Colonel Lorne MacLaine Campbell had little need of such ersatz honours; he had been awarded a DSO in France in 1940, and received another for his part in the Alamein victory. The following year in Tunisia, he was awarded a Victoria Cross for his leadership in battle. Such an award is extremely rare for a commanding officer in modern times, and reflects a level of bravery that, as the citation states, 'can seldom have been surpassed in the long history of the Highland Brigade.'

In the second North African front, the 8th Argylls had landed in Tunisia and, together with the 1st and 7th, were to serve in Sicily and Italy.

Whilst most of the regiment's fighting was thus done in Europe and the Mediterranean, the 2nd Battalion had arrived in Malaya shortly after the outbreak of war, to engage in intensive training for a year before being thrown into action.

The battalion's task was to cover the British retreat from the Thai border. For the best part of a month, therefore, it engaged in a series of desperately hard delaying battles, fighting every mile of the way down the Malayan peninsula. On 7 January 1942, it found itself on the River Slim defending against a Japanese drive on Kuala Lumpur. By the end of the day, there were just three officers and 90 men left to withdraw to Singapore.

Even so, the 2nd Argylls were not yet beaten. Regrouping in Singapore, and bolstered by 200 Royal Marines, they returned to the mainland to cover the final retreat of the British forces. When the battalion itself withdrew, it did so to the sound of the last two surviving pipers playing a defiant 'Hielan Laddie'.

The same resolute spirit saw the Argylls fighting to the last against the invasion of Singapore; as the surrender was ordered, the Commanding Officer was preparing to re-engage with some 50 men he had gathered together. Those who survived the horrors of the jungle campaign were taken prisoner to face the even more horrific internment by the Japanese.

The Rifle Brigade
(Prince Consort's Own)

Principal Battle Honours 1939-45

Calais 1940 – North-West Europe 1940, 44-45
Beda Fomm – Sidi Rezegh 1941 – Alam el Halfa
El Alamein – North Africa 1940-43
Cassino II – Capture of Perugia – Italy 1943-45

Raised 1800; redesignated 3rd Battalion, The Royal Green Jackets 1958.

The first battle honour won by The Rifle Brigade commemorates one of the most celebrated actions of the war: the defence of Calais. Brigaded with the 2nd KRRC and 1st Queen Victoria Rifles, the 1st Battalion landed on 23 May 1940 intending to advance inland; in the event, the German offensive had already trapped them in the town, and the only option was to hold on for as long as possible.

Desperately outnumbered and out-gunned (a situation exacerbated by the early departure of a ship still half-laden with the Rifle Brigade's equipment), the Riflemen remained defiant for four days until the exhaustion of their stores of ammunition. The surviving defenders were captured, but their stand had tied up sufficient enemy armour to permit the evacuations from Dunkirk to proceed.

The 2nd Battalion had a happier entry into the war. Posted from India to Egypt, it served as a motor battalion in the 7th Armoured Division Support Group from the days of Wavell's offensive onwards. During that campaign the battalion, with the exception of 'C' Company who remained to guard prisoners, were in the force despatched to cut off the enemy retreat at Beda Fomm. The only British infantry at that battle, the Riflemen suffered losses of just three dead and four wounded, whilst taking 15,000 prisoners. The reaction to the victory was summed up in an officer's letter home:

'It is a great bit of luck to have been able to have a practice over or two, so to speak, with the Italians – what more delightful people to fight could there be?' [1]

'C' Company also had cause to thank the Italians: one prisoner was discovered to be a cook and was smuggled into the ranks as Rifleman Antonio to serve as chef to the Officers' Mess. Reports suggest that he was highly popular, if a little over-reliant on garlic.

The tide of the war, however, was about to turn, and with the withdrawal of the

2nd Battalion, it was left to the newly arrived and inexperienced 9th Battalion (a TA unit better known as 1st Tower Hamlets Rifles) to face Rommel. Caught by the German counter-offensive of March 1941, the battalion suffered over 300 casualties.

The 2nd returned to the front-line for Sidi Rezegh but was unsuccessful in its endeavours. Early in 1942 a new incarnation of the 1st Battalion arrived and served in the rearguard alongside the 2nd and 9th in the retreat from Gazala.

Badly damaged, the 9th was disbanded and used to reinforce the regular battalions, but in July 1942 the 7th (also known as the 1st London Rifle Brigade) was posted to Egypt, and at Alamein there were again three battalions of the regiment in action. The most spectacular contribution to that battle came from the 2nd Battalion who, under the command of Lieutenant-Colonel Vic Turner, led the famous assault on Kidney Ridge that proved so vital to the battle. Lt-Col Turner was awarded a Victoria Cross for his personal leadership.

On the other side of the North African war, the 10th Battalion – formerly 2nd Tower Hamlets Rifles – landed in Algiers in November 1942, and in the final stages of the campaign all four battalions fought together. (Rivalry, however, sometimes got in the way of regimental solidarity: soon after the arrival of the Desert Rats in the area, the pet pig of the 10th disappeared never to be seen again, believed to have been the victim of the Desert Rats.)

During the fighting in Italy, the 10th fought in the last phase of the struggle at Cassino and in the clearing of the Liri Valley. They were joined by the 2nd and 7th in the formation of a new brigade of Rifle battalions, fighting through the remainder of the campaign, though the role of mechanized infantry was for the most part abandoned as being inappropriate. The 10th was ultimately disbanded to reinforce the others.

The 1st and 8th Battalions meanwhile were involved in North-West Europe. The first months proved costly and to rebuild the numbers, members of the French and Belgian resistance movements were recruited in September 1944.

On VE Day the 7th became the first British unit to enter Austria, whilst the 8th was engaged in a dash to reach Denmark before the Red Army.

[1] Hastings *The Rifle Brigade in the Second World War* p.31

The Glider Pilot Regiment

Principal Battle Honours 1939-45

Normandy Landing – Pegasus Bridge – Merville Battery
Rhine – Southern France – North-West Europe 1944-45
Landing in Sicily – Sicily 1943

Formed 1941; disbanded 1957 on re-formation of new Army Air Corps.

The evolution of airborne troops in the British Army resulted in three new regiments being created during the Second World War. Of these, the Parachute Regiment and the SAS have received a popular acclaim normally accorded only to the most venerable of military formations; The Glider Pilot Regiment, however, has never received the recognition it so richly deserved.

The glider was conceived as an answer to the problem of carrying heavy equipment by parachute. Without needing the kind of prepared landing strips required by conventional aircraft, gliders could land jeeps and light artillery behind enemy lines, equipping a force of men more mobile and better armed than paratroops could hope to be.

The dangers inherent in such semi-covert action were starkly revealed in the first operation, staged in November 1942, nearly a year after the creation of the new regiment. Two Horsa gliders (constructed entirely of wood) were towed by Halifax bombers to Norway in an attempt to land troops near the Norsk Hydro plant, a key part of the German atomic weapons programme. One of the aircraft crashed into the mountains, both gliders crash-landed and those of the men who survived were executed by the Gestapo. It was not an auspicious start to a new regiment and a new kind of warfare.

Part of the problem was the irresolvable fact that gliders cannot act autonomously. Ever dependent on being towed into action, gliders and those who fly them are even more vulnerable to weather and enemy hostilities than are other aircraft. One can therefore only marvel at the courage and commitment of the pilots who flew their fragile craft to North Africa in anticipation of the invasion of Sicily in 1943. These flights, at the end of a tow rope, took some 12 hours to complete, under threat for much of that time from Luftwaffe attack.

That courage was rewarded, for the glider operation in the Sicily landing, though it did not go according to plan, was a major triumph for the new forces. Required to land at night on unsuitable terrain, with little time for preparation and with inadequate training facilities, the troops were asked to seize the Ponte Grande bridge leading to Syracuse – this town being the first target of the sea-borne invasion. The regiment's CO, Colonel Chatterton, refered to it as 'this frightening operation'. [1]

The arrival of the 1st Airlanding Brigade took the enemy by surprise. Despite poor weather that led to half the invasion force ditching in the sea and those who arrived being scattered across a wider area than anticipated, the bridge was successfully taken. And those troops who landed adrift of the target managed to convey the impression that a much larger airborne force was on the island, helping to confuse the enemy.

The pilots' role, of course, was not limited simply to transporting other troops. All pilots were, in addition to their primary function, trained infantrymen, able to fight after landing and to use all the equipment so critical to modern warfare.

The Sicily landings – the largest combined air and sea operation staged up till that point – can be seen as a trial run for the invasion of Normandy in 1944. Certainly for The Glider Pilot Regiment, North-West Europe was to be the major theatre of war, for which Sicily had provided vital training.

D-Day itself was preceded by an airborne assault on the night of 5/6 June. Gliders brought in the troops who captured Pegasus Bridge – the first piece of French soil to be liberated and scene of the regiment's most famous battle honour – and Melville Battery, an intense battle to knock out guns aimed at the beaches. Of the 196 pilots involved that night, 71 were to be reported as casualties.

The losses during the later struggle for Arnhem Bridge were even worse, as they were during Operation Plunder, which took the Rhine in March 1945, when 100 casualties were reported. The regiment ended the war with 551 fatalities from an outfit of little more than three thousand men. Its contribution, however, in an unknown and unprecedented field of war was immeasurable.

[1]   D'Este *Bitter Victory: The Battle for Sicily 1943* p.229

The Parachute Regiment

Principal Battle Honours 1939-45

Bruneval – Normandy Landing – Breville – Arnhem 1944
Rhine – Southern France – Oudna – Tamera
Primosole Bridge – Athens

Formed 1942.

The concept of parachute troops, operating behind enemy lines, was a new development in military thinking in the 1930s, and unsurprisingly, it was Germany who first explored the possibilities, with trials as early as 1937. Even less surprising is the fact that Britain did not take the idea seriously until Churchill came to power and demanded that attention be given to it.

Even so, the first British operation was not until February 1941 when 38 men were dropped in Southern Italy. Despite logistical problems, the mission was a minor success and temporarily achieved its objective – cutting water supply lines.

The first battle honour of what was to become The Parachute Regiment was won in the next operation, a full year later, when 120 men captured valuable radar equipment from a German station at Bruneval on the French coast.

Ironically, just as the British use of paratroops was getting into its stride, the German, who had pioneered it abandoned the technique. In the wake of the costly invasion of Crete, Hiter was moved to declare in the summer of 1941: 'The day of the parachutist is over. It is a surprise weapon and without this element there can be no future for airborne forces.' [1] The British were to prove him wrong.

On 1 August 1942 The Parachute Regiment was officially created to bring together the rapidly increasing numbers of parachute troops in the Army. New battalions were formed from existing infantry units, often keeping traces of their original identity: the 10th Somerset Light Infantry, for example, became the 7th (Light Infantry) Battalion, The Parachute Regiment, whilst the 10th Royal Welch Fusiliers became the 6th (Royal Welch) Parachute Battalion.

November of the same year saw the first use of parachutists in a combined operation with ground forces. As part of Operation Torch in French North Africa, the 1st Battalion landed at Souk el Arba, the 2nd at Depienne and the 3rd at Bône, ahead of the ground troops pushing back the Axis forces. The 1st and 3rd were both successful in destroying and disrupting enemy supply lines and in rejoining the main forces, but the 2nd were stranded when the land advance was unexpectedly delayed – a risk ever present in parachute actions. The battalion lost 16 officers and 250 men before it managed to reach its own lines.

Though they were not used in a parachute capacity again in North Africa, the men remained active and won a battle honour at Tamera as regular infantry.

During the Sicily campaign, their unique training was again employed to take strategic bridges south of Catania, to clear the path for the 8th Army.

Whilst the 2nd Parachute Brigade remained with the 8th Army in the advance through Italy, the majority of British paratroops were withdrawn from the campaign for the D-Day landings.

In fact, The Parachute Regiment was in action before the landings, dropping into France on the night of 5/6 June 1944. Brigadier Hill's words to the regiment before that drop could stand as a text for almost all the conflicts throughout the Second World War: 'Gentlemen, in spite of your excellent training and orders, do not be daunted if chaos reigns. It undoubtedly will.' [2]

It was indeed chaotic, but the regiment distinguished itself, securing the left flank of the British sector of the invasion. It was a far from straightforward action, particularly given the poor weather conditions, and 800 casualties were sustained in the first two days, whilst 1,000 men were separated from units in small disorientated groups.

One of the casualties of the operation was the Commanding Officer, killed along with more than 130 of his men in taking the village of Breville.

Breville was joined on the regiment's colours by battle honours won in Southern France, as part of the invasion there, and Athens, where the men of the regiment were involved in the civil war.

The most famous of all battle honours, of course, was awarded for the regiment's role in Operation Market Garden, the attempt to make a decisive breakthrough in the German defences. The plan was straightforward – whilst American airborne troops were dropped in to capture key bridges at Eindhoven and Nijmegen, British air forces would take the bridge over the Rhine at Arnhem. The British – the most forward of the units – were expected to hold for up to 48 hours whilst the land forces broke through the German army to link up.

The reality, of course, was very different. The staged landing over two days meant that only the 1st Parachute Brigade were available to storm the bridge on the first day, whilst the rest remained to guard the dropping area. The bridge was actually taken on the first day – 17 September 1944 – by the 2nd Battalion, but the German response effectively prevented reinforcements arriving. Meanwhile the second drop of men was delayed, whilst supplies were dropped wide.

More seriously, the ground forces failed to make the expected breakthrough and no relief was afforded the beleaguered airborne troops. The 2nd Battalion held the bridge for three days – longer than the entire Division was expected to hold out – but the effort was futile. By the time a withdrawal was ordered – on 25 August –

more than two thirds of the Division had perished.

Despite the disaster of Arnhem, parachute troops were again in the forefront during the advance into and across Germany, particularly in the victorious crossing of the Rhine in March 1945. For much of the campaign, however, the men found themselves in the ranks of the regular infantry.

[1] *Decisive Battles: The Turning Points of World War II* p.38
[2] Norton *The Red Devils* p.68

The Special Air Service Regiment

Principal Battle Honours 1939-45

North-West Europe 1944-45 – Tobruk 1941 – Benghazi Raid
North Africa 1940-43 – Landing in Sicily – Termoli
Valli di Comacchio – Italy 1943-45 – Adriatic

Raised 1941.

The third of the trio of related airborne regiments created in response to the new demands of modern warfare was the Special Air Service Regiment, formed in 1941 on the initiative of David Stirling. Then a lieutenant in the Guards Commando, Stirling arrived in the Middle East as part of the force intended to seize Rhodes, an operation quickly abandoned in the wake of the German offensive in the Balkans. Instead the Commando staged a series of seaborne raids against enemy targets in North Africa, none of which were successful.

While temporarily invalided, Stirling developed a new line of thinking. The value of such operations was unquestionable – the Italian and German forces in North Africa depended on air and sea supply lines in order to wage war – but the scale of the Commando raids, with around 200 soldiers involved in each, was wrong. Stirling argued that small groups of four or five men could take on sabotage attacks both more effectively and much more efficiently. In essence, he was calling for the introduction of guerilla tactics into the British Army, attacking by stealth and using a handful of men to tie up disproportionate enemy resources.

Fortunately Sir Claude Auchinleck, commanding the British forces in the Middle East, saw the strength of the argument, and in June 1941 Stirling was promoted to captain and authorised to recruit an establishment of seven officers and 60 men and to commence operations. The name was adopted to assist a piece of disinformation whereby the British were attempting to convince the Germans that a full parachute and glider brigade was operational in the area – Stirling's men became L Detachment, Special Air Service Brigade.

The first operations concentrated on enemy airfields and soon proved successful. Working with the Long Range Desert Group – whose more normal role was the provision of reconnaissance information – a group would drive through the desert, walk the remaining distance to the target and blow up aircraft, vehicles, fuel and ammunition dumps. It would then rendezvous with the LRDG to return to base.

Such raids, of course, were not only extremely dangerous, but demanded absolute fitness and commitment from the soldiers. Since the SAS depended on volunteers from other units, and since it required the best men available, there was sometimes an understandable reluctance from regiments to support the new outfit. As the successes mounted, however, permission was given to increase the strength, and recruits were also drawn from the French Free Forces and the Special Boat Section, the latter bringing an expertise that enabled the SAS to branch into sea-borne attacks.

In the first year of activity, this small force of 100 men accounted for the destruction of some 250 enemy aircraft. Apart from the obvious boost to army morale, this disruption of supply lines and diminution of German air superiority was of immense value in a conflict that depended above all on secure supplies.

In September 1942, for the first time, the GHQ Cairo intervened in operations and directed an attack on Benghazi by 200 SAS troops to coincide with similar assaults elsewhere. It was a disaster – the attack was expected and the SAS lost some 50 men. A side-effect of the official interest now being shown in the unit, however, was the recommendation by General Alexander (who had replaced Auchinleck) that the SAS should become a full regiment, with Stirling promoted to Lieutenant-Colonel.

The growth of the regiment continued despite the capture of its commanding officer during a reconnaissance patrol in Tunisia in January 1943, a growth assisted by the arrival of David Stirling's brother Bill at the head of a newly-raised 2nd SAS Regiment.

The move to Sicily reduced the scope of activities, the long slog of the war in Italy offering fewer opportunities for the free movement available in North Africa. Nonetheless valuable experience of operating in closer contact with conventional initiatives was gained.

This experience was to be employed in the assistance given to the Normandy landings. Much larger SAS teams, drawn from a combined Allied force now some 2,500 strong, parachuted into France ahead of the landings and, in conjunction with the Resistance, attacked railway lines, destroyed vehicles and engaged the enemy. Such operations continued through the advance into the Low Countries and Germany itself.

The success of the SAS can be gauged by the brutality with which captured men were treated by the Gestapo. As Eisenhower wrote to the regiment: 'The ruthlessness with which the enemy has attacked SAS troops has been an indication of the injury which you were able to cause to the German armed forces.' [1]

The success can also be seen in the fact that a unit that began as one man's inspiration at a time when the nation was facing its bleakest days, and that developed its tactics through improvisation on the battlefield, survived the end of the War to become one of the most celebrated of all regiments in the British Army.

[1] Strawson *A History of The S.A.S. Regiment* p.149

Royal Army Chaplain's Department

Established 1796.

A mongst the most famous men of the cloth who served with the army during the war was Father 'Dolly' Brookes, a Roman Catholic priest with the 1st Irish Guards. He later commented on the relationship of the padre and the soldier:

'The Military and Priestly life fit in well together as they both call for the same characteristics, perseverance, loyalty, courage and a deep regard for one's fellow men.' [1]

Indeed, contrary to some popular images, the key role of the chaplain was not at church parades, but in day-to-day contacts with individuals and small groups of men; here was embodied what Montgomery recognized as the great contribution that a padre could make – letting the soldier know that he mattered to God and that he was important.

This was perhaps most clearly seen in prisoner of war camps. Since army chaplains are officers (hence the unique title 'Department'), those taken prisoner by the Germans were automatically put in officers' camps. This led to the absurd situation where Reverend G F Miller found himself the senior of 31 chaplains in an oflag of just 1,200 officers. After much lobbying from within and political pressure from home, the padres were distributed more evenly amongst the stalags.

Even so, the chaplains' work was rendered difficult by their captors' distrust of anything that might raise morale, and all sermons were censored. Again, however, it was the informal discussion groups and the personal counselling that made the difference more than the official services.

As with other aspects of life as a prisoner of war, the situation was much worse in the Far East. The innate Japanese suspicion of Christianity meant that even when brief services were conceded, the full text was subject to censorship.

About those at liberty, tales of individual bravery are legion. Forbidden by the Geneva Convention to carry weapons, the chaplain regularly displayed the courage of the unarmed.

Most spectacularly this was seen in assisting the victims of war. In a battle during the Italian war in July 1944, when stretcher-bearers were unable to reach the wounded because of the dense enemy fire, Rev Paul Wansey of the 2nd Royal Fusiliers managed to bring in four wounded men on his own, receiving a Military Cross for his heroism. Rev Ronald Edwards of the 2nd/4th Hampshires was awarded a DSO for a similar action at the Gustav Line. But the padre was often a casualty himself: Rev H N Barratt of the Sherwood Foresters, for example, being killed by enemy shelling whilst conducting communion in North-West Africa.

There were many other roles the chaplain was called upon to fulfil, of which perhaps the most harrowing was the burial of the dead. Captain Henry Lovegrove, another recipient of the Military Cross, served with the Green Howards in France and is reported to have become a smoker for the first time in his life as he scoured the fields of Normandy for corpses to bury. [2]

In preparation for the D-Day landings, a Battle School was established in early 1944 for padres to gain basic training under simulated battle conditions. Its lessons, often with the accompaniment of live ammunition, undoubtedly proved of value to those who found themselves in the thick of conflict.

Amongst them was Rev J McLuskey who accompanied the SAS in a parachute drop near Dijon in June. He took with him the essentials of his calling – altar-cloth, cross, hymnals, prayer books and communion vessels – and held services with the men deep behind enemy lines, though we are told that the hymn singing was conducted *sotto voce*.

For the Normandy campaign too, the REME converted two three-tonner trucks to be used as mobile churches.

The attitude of the army to the message of Christianity was summed up by Rev Frederick Hughes, chosen by Montgomery as Senior Chaplain to the Eighth Army:

'The chaplains were never asked to harness the Christian Faith to military operations. Militant ranting was much disliked.' [3]

There were some, however, who found the contradiction between Christ's teaching and the actions of the army too much. As the King's Dragoon Guards were preparing to break out of Tobruk, its padre gave what was perceived as a particularly pacifist sermon. As the service ended Major Lindsay stood up and announced: 'King's Dragoon Guards . . . Attention! In spite of the sermon you have just heard, you will go out and smite the enemy hip and thigh!' [4]

This, however, was a rare incident and for the most part the 3,000 chaplains, together with the 640 Catholic priests, who served during the war spent their time professing their faith to men *in extremis*, finding a ready audience amongst those facing the ultimate horrors of war.

[1] Smyth *In This Sign Conquer* p.241
[2] see Hastings *Overlord: D-Day and the Battle for Normandy 1944*
[3] Smyth op. cit. p.234
[4] Mann *1st Queen's Dragoon Guards* p.403

Royal Army Service Corps

Corps of Waggoners formed 1794; known under various names until
Royal Army Service Corps 1918; re-named Royal Corps of Transport 1965;
amalgamated to form Royal Logistics Corps 1993.

The essential task of the Royal Army Service Corps during the war was, as ever, the provision of food, ammunition, petrol and – above all else – transport to the British army. Never the most glamorous of jobs, this nonetheless provided employment by the end of the war for a total of 335,000 men, a huge increase from the 10,000 members of the corps at the outset and some 10% of the whole army. Whilst the closely-related Movements Service of the Royal Engineers accounted for a further 180,000 personnel by 1945.

The central contribution made by transport was acknowledged by Churchill himself:

'Victory is the beautiful, bright coloured flower. Transport is the stem without which it could not have blossomed.' [1]

The range of transport provided by the corps demonstrates the truth of this claim: from the motorized support vehicles of cars, vans, motorbikes, lorries, ambulances, tank transporters and amphibian vehicles to the old-fashioned mule trains and pack-horses still so necessary in Italy, East Africa and Burma, the RASC facilitated every aspect of the army's mobility. It also provided trains and rolling stock for railways.

In addition to this land-based transport, the RASC was also responsible for the army's fleet of sea and inland vessels, ranging from ocean-going ships through harbour launches to canal boats and barges.

Yet even this was not the extent of the Corps' role, for there was still the air to be considered, and the RASC played a key part in the formation of the Glider Pilot Regiment, the Army Commandos and the Parachute Regiment; indeed Driver Evans was the first fatality of the Parachute Regiment. The Service Corps also dealt with the jeeps and armoured cars flown in by glider in airborne operations and provided supplies and support for such actions.

Whilst the introduction of airborne operations increased the roles of the corps, there was some lightening of the load in 1942 with the hiving off of the heavy motorized transport workshops to the newly-formed REME and of the stores depots for the same vehicles to the RAOC.

Perhaps the most spectacular of the RASC's projects was the construction of the underwater pipeline codenamed Pluto between Britain and France to assist Operation Crusader in 1944; some six million tons of petrol passed through the pipeline.

For the most part, of course, the men of the RASC were engaged in much more mundane though still often extremely hazardous activities. Amongst them was a company who spent two weeks in the trenches of Monte Cassino, emerging periodically to light the line of 1,600 smoke canisters that provided the cover for the third and final attempt to break through the German resistance.

For the men of the RASC, despite the corps' title, were not employed in a purely service capacity, but were also expected to join the front-line when necessary. Thus it was that 502 Company RASC, attached to 30 Armoured Brigade, found itself called upon to man the trenches at Geilenkirchen in order that hard-pressed infantry be allowed to rest prior to a new offensive. Members of the same company also took part in the liberation of Walcheren.

The confusion of war, however, meant that things were seldom straightforward. Typical of the experience of many was Driver Charles Brown [2]. Stationed at a secret fuel dump in Northern France in 1940, the first he knew of the German offensive was a single Luftwaffe bomb landing on the dump on 10 May, destroying three million gallons of motor fuel. With no fuel left to deliver, he was sent forward to join an artillery company as driver. Such was the chaos of the time that he never found the unit for whom he was intended, and spent the next three weeks driving through France and Belgium with no orders, before finding himself directed back to Dunkirk for evacuation.

During the second campaign in North-West Europe, 15% of the British forces were members of the RASC.

[1] *The Royal Corps of Transport* p.27

[2] see Harman *Dunkirk: The Necessary Myth* pp.76-77

Royal Army Medical Corps

Established as Medical Staff Corps 1855; subsequently re-structured as
Royal Army Medical Corps 1898.

It was widely expected in 1939 that the struggle against Hitler would be a repeat of the experience of The Great War, a prospect viewed with dread by not only the infantry but also the Royal Army Medical Corps. In the event, the horrendous levels of casualties in that earlier conflict were not even approached, at least so far as the British were concerned. To some extent, of course, the rapidity and fluidity of modern warfare ensured that fewer died in the pursuit of peace – only in the Soviet Union did the protracted slaughter of stalemate re-emerge – but credit is also due to the advances made in medical science.

The RAMC treated five million cases during the war, many of them hospitalized by disease rather than injury. In the 1943 Arakan campaign, for example, the rate of sick to wounded ran at one hundred and twenty to one; by 1945 the widespread use of the anti-malarial drug Mepacrine had reduced this ratio to six to one. (It should be noted that the drug's existence was not in itself sufficient to produce this transformation; officers were made responsible for their men's continued use of it, failure to do so becoming a punishable offence.) Even more significant was penicillin, discovered in the 1920s but only exploited fully in the '40s. It has been estimated that use of penicillin saved up to 15% of cases that would otherwise have proved fatal or necessitated amputation.

The medicines available to doctors had thus improved, and surgical techniques had also advanced since the Great War, but so too had the technology of armaments: new types of mines and weapons were producing new injuries. And though serious casualties might be fewer in number, the RAMC found itself in the position of having to chase after them – the static treatment centres of 1914-18 were shown to be out-dated as early as the retreat to Dunkirk. The doctors, surgeons and staff now had to move with the army, taking their medical stations with them.

Nowhere was this a greater problem than in North Africa, where the distances involved were enormous. In time, mobile Field Surgical Units were introduced and joined the Field Dressing Stations just behind the front-lines, with surgery being conducted in lean-to tents.

In a conflict as mobile as the desert campaign, however, being behind one's own lines did not always count for a great deal. One surgical unit found its position over-run by the Germans on four separate occasions, each time being subsequently retaken by the British. Through it all, operations continued, with only a muttered remark to the effect that visiting hours seemed to be somewhat lax.

The confusion was such that on one occasion a British Field Dressing Station was visited by Rommel, who – apparently unrecognized – was shown around, before making a hasty exit.

These stations treated enemy casualties alongside the Allied wounded, and there seems little doubt that the Geneva Convention was respected by all concerned. A characteristic example came with the withdrawal from Greece in 1941. Army doctors and nurses remained behind to treat the wounded who could not be evacuated, and were allowed to continue with their work by the Germans. With the collapse of Crete, more cases arrived and the two hospitals in Greece soon had 1,500 patients under care. Their situation was considerably easier than it had been in Crete, where a network of caves had to be pressed into service as a treatment centre.

One type of operation where the Geneva Convention was not applicable was the commando raid. Nonetheless each unit of 500 men was accompanied by one Medical Officer and nine other ranks, all fully trained as commandos. It was a medical orderly in one such action, Lance-Corporal H E Harden, who won the only Victoria Cross awarded to the RAMC in the war, for his sacrificial rescuing of the wounded under enemy fire.

The commando was but one of the innovations of the period. Even more spectacular was the Airborne Medical Services, formed in 1942, with a requirement for ultra-fit volunteers, amongst them 130 conscientious objectors. Landings by both glider, from Sicily onwards, and by parachute, as at D-Day, became an essential part of the war effort, ensuring that treatment was available from the outset of any combat.

The culmination of these operations came at Arnhem, where 588 members of the RAMC served. Almost all were to remain with the wounded and be captured, a fate common to so many in the Corps from the days of Dunkirk to the end. The service rendered in prisoner of war camps, with obvious lack of resources, was perhaps as important as any during the war, particularly in the appalling conditions of captivity in the Far East.

The most traumatic demand on the Corps came in the final advance into Germany in 1945 and the discovery of the Nazi death camps; it fell to the medical staff to attempt to treat tens of thousands of men, women and children dying of starvation, disease and brutality.

12,000 officers and 83,000 other ranks served with the RAMC during the war. 2,463 lost their lives.

Mention should also be made of two other vital medical units seeing service during the war.

The Queen Alexandra's Royal Army Nursing Corps had its origins in the post-Crimean army reforms and, as an auxilliary unit, made an invaluable contribution to the war effort.

Similarly the Army Dental Corps, formed in 1921, was an essential, if often unacknowledged, component in the army. Performing not only routine dental surgery, but also jaw surgery on the wounded – a particularly acute problem with the widespread use of mines – the ADC were a necessary addition to the modern fighting machine. In the Normandy landings there was one dental officer per thousand men, and by the time the campaign got into its stride the RAMC, ADC and Queen Alexandra's Royal Army Nursing Corps between them constituted 4% of the personnel.

Royal Army Ordnance Corps

Corps of Armourer-Sergeants formed 1858; evolved into Ordnance Store
Corps 1881; Royal Army Ordnance Corps 1918; amalgamated to form
Royal Logistics Corps 1993.

The challenges presented by the world's first fully mechanized war were
nowhere more pressing than in the ranks of the Royal Army Ordnance Corps.
In time, the creation of the REME – largely from within the RAOC ranks – was to
take some of the pressure off the Corps, but the first two years saw a rapid course
of education in the new warfare.

Problems were present from the outset in France. There was an acute shortage
of supplies and equipment (about which little could be done), there was a large
proportion of reservists whose enthusiasm was not always matched by familiarity
with the equipment they were being asked to deal with, and there was a distinct
lack of co-operation from the French hosts of the BEF. This meant that the depot
and workshops established in Nantes in 1939 were often inadequate: a tram depot
was assigned, but later reclaimed by the tram company, whilst other owners
disputed the commandeering of their land.

These difficulties were gradually ironed out, and with the establishment of a
second base near Rennes, the distances involved in servicing the army were
substantially reduced, but the experience of the first European campaign was far
from a happy one. Perhaps symbolic of the period was the fact that even though
most of the men were evacuated from St Nazaire, 50 were killed when the
Lancastria was sunk on its way home.

The other campaign of the era – in Norway – was also fraught with difficulties.
The shortage of equipment extended to a lack of camouflage clothes, in response to
which white sheets were acquired and local volunteers enlisted to sew them.

The lack of supplies and spares remained a pressing issue in North Africa.
Much of the equipment there was obsolete, and the situation was not eased by
the arrival of tanks from Britain that required modification for desert conditions.
The Corps' ingenuity was further called upon in modifying vehicles to enable
them to retrieve tanks and to take water supplies. 3,000 sun compasses were
also manu-factured for the campaigns, as well as tens of thousands of anti-tank
mines.

Other services provided by the RAOC during the conflict were less obviously
related to warfare, but still prerequisites of a modern army. Laundry plants, bath
units and mobile stores repair units – dealing with tents, furniture, cookers, lamps
etc. – were provided, whilst 1,000 Italian civilians were employed by the Corps in

clothing production, and a paint factory was established in Naples producing 500 tons of paint a week.

During the invasion of Normandy, the scale of the operation was exaggerated still further by the fear of chemical warfare being used by the Germans; in addition to the normal stores, anti-chemical provision had to be included.

The size of the Corps' activities can be gauged by its UK bases, which included accommodation for 250,000 vehicles and 58 million square feet of covered storage, including 10 million square feet for ammunition. Open storage far exceeded this total.

In common with other service units, the men of the RAOC were expected to serve as infantry when the situation required it. 788 casualties were sustained in Greece alone, part of the total of 5,000 in the course of the war.

Corps of Royal Electrical and Mechanical Engineers

Formed 1942.

During the first years of the war, responsibility for the army's vehicles had been handled by the Royal Army Ordnance Corps, but with the increasing mechanization of warfare, it soon became clear that a new unit was required to deal with the work. In 1942, therefore, the Royal Electrical and Mechanical Engineers was formed, drawing 95% of its officers from the RAOC, but also incorporating some personnel from the Royal Engineers and the Royal Army Service Corps. Amongst the latter was Major-General Bertram Rowcroft, the first director of the new service.

The principal tasks of the REME were the provision, storage, issue and repair of vehicles and spares, not only those used on the battlefield, but also the ever-more sophisticated equipment needed for anti-aircraft work, including radar, and the craft of the Army Air Corps. The basic operating structure was inherited from the RAOC and centred on Light Aid Detachments – recovery and repair units accompanying the front-line troops – and bigger base workshops to undertake work too large for the LADs.

The first major test of the corps came in the final phase of the North African campaign. During the course of Operation Torch and the subsequent campaign some 3,000 workers, both military and civilian, were employed. The scale and efficiency of the contributions was demonstrated in the final assault on Longstop Hill, where maintenance of the artillery facilitated a barrage so intense that enemy reports indicated a belief that the British were using automatic field-guns. Similar operations at an even greater level, such as those at Caen and at the crossing of the Rhine, were to increase the demands made on the engineers.

The conditions of North Africa and the distances involved made repair of tanks and armoured vehicles a constant problem, exacerbated by the journey necessary to bring the equipment to the theatre – tanks were frequently damaged in transit and had to be serviced before being issued.

The amphibious invasion of Sicily introduced a new task, that of waterproofing vehicles and guns, whilst five REME beach bricks were involved in the landing. Again these were functions later repeated on a larger scale, the REME making a vital contribution to the success of D-Day.

The terrain of Sicily and Italy was not well suited to accessible workshops, with most of the repair work having to be done in the field. It also inflicted heavy damage on the vehicles, to the extent that only some 25% of repairs were necessitated by enemy action; the remainder were attributable to mechanical failure and to conversion for more specialized functions.

The latter was another learning experience. As the campaign developed, tanks were required to be converted into Arks (the turrets removed and ramps installed to ford rivers) and Kangaroos (guns and turrets removed and seats installed to carry infantry into battle). In North-West Europe, the menagerie of adapted tanks was expanded to include Crocodiles with flame-throwers, Crabs with mine-clearing flails and Buffaloes, amphibious personnel-carriers.

The bocage countryside of Normandy produced conflict at often very close quarters, with the consequent difficulties of recovering damaged equipment. Even when they were retrieved, the close range of the fire meant that many were completely irreparable, though they could still be used to provide spares.

By the end of the war, the REME was 36,000 strong in North-West Europe, just under 5% of the British army, and had sustained 7,500 casualties, including 1,500 on the battlefield.

If conditions were difficult for the engineers in Africa and Europe, those in the Far East were often nigh-on impossible. There a sister service, the Indian Electrical and Mechanical Engineers, was formed with two thirds of its officers and artificers loaned from the REME and the remainder recruited locally.

The combination of a chronic lack of resources and an appallingly harsh environment meant that the vehicles of the forgotten army had to be constantly patched up and sent back into battle. There were few tanks involved in the campaign, but that simply made them all the more precious; some of those abandoned by the 7th Hussars in the retreat from Burma in 1942 were found when the ground was retaken two years later, repaired and pressed back into service.

The IEME also had the task of designing and manufacturing the portable equipment used during the Chindits operations.

Corps of Military Police

Military Mounted Police and Military Foot Police formed 1885; these two amalgamated to form Corps of Military Police 1926; amalgamated to form Adjutant General's Corps 1993.

The lot of the military policeman during the Second World War, far from being a happy one, was one of extreme danger, requiring a display of courage that was rarely equalled.

The despatch of the British Expeditionary Force to France in 1939 was the first time that this country had launched a mechanized army into battle conditions, and its operations were largely dependant upon the traffic management of the Military Police. The scale of this work is indicated in a contemporary report from the *Manchester Guardian*:

'Some 720 men of the Corps of Military Police have brought 25,000 vehicles many miles across country which they themselves had never seen until the day before the operation began.' [1]

And when the advance into Belgium and the subsequent retreat in the face of the blitzkrieg were ordered, the CMP were effectively in the position of first in, last out. Following in the wake of the vanguard of the 12th Lancers, the provost's task was to mark up the routes for the remainder of the army, and somehow to deal with the flow of refugees in one direction and soldiers in the other, along roads that were clearly inadequate for the demands placed upon them. In the retreat, it was the CMP's responsibility to regulate an even more chaotic traffic movement, and then to fight as infantry in the rearguard.

But perhaps the greatest contribution of all came on the beaches of Dunkirk; the success of the evacuation, the orderly nature of that operation, was a major victory for the Corps.

The more everyday aspects of the provost's role were also demonstrated during the BEF's time on the Continent. Military discipline was essential not simply for the smooth working of the army, but also for the maintenance of good relations between soldiers and civilians. In the light of the temptations put before enlisted men by the legendary hospitality of French culture – to say nothing of that of North Africa – this function was crucial, and in 1940 a Special Investigation Branch, a military equivalent of the CID, was established.

The early successes in North Africa, with the collapse of the Italian forces, created a new headache for the CMP: the responsibility for tens of thousands of prisoners. By now the Military Policemen had effectively become front-line troops, and the very fluidity of that front-line, together with the sheer distances involved in the campaign, meant that keeping soldiers in the right place was extremely difficult: stragglers' posts were established to direct lost troops back to their own lines.

By the time the fighting had moved to Italy, this was no longer a problem, but the absence of a coherent government in that country necessitated wide-spread anti-looting operations, whilst the break-through at Cassino, with 2,000 tanks and 20,000 other vehicles rushing forward, called again for skilful traffic control.

It was in Operation Overlord, however, that the provost's greatest challenge was faced and met. Firstly there was the scale of the operation with which it had to deal: hundreds of thousands of troops and vehicles and some three quarters of a million tons of stores had to be processed and directed. Then there was the fact that most of the equipment and stores came onto open beaches into a country that had suffered the deprivations of occupation for some four years: pilfering by civilians was compounded by soldiers dealing on the black market with army stores. And, of course, there were the enemy prisoners to administer.

Despite these problems, nearly a third of the 36,000 charges brought by the 10,000 provost active in the second North-West Europe war were concerned with absence; just 1,100 arose from drunkenness.

Again in Overlord, the CMP was amongst the first to see service, with the paratroops of the 6th Airborne Division Provost Company landing ahead of the amphibious forces. And though the popular image of the Military Police may not be as high as the Corps deserves, those involved in the fighting were always willing to pay tribute; in the words of Montgomery:

'The battle of Normandy and the subsequent battles would never have been won but for the work and co-operation of Provost on the traffic routes.' [2]

[1] Lovell-Knight *The Story of The Royal Military Police* p.23

[2] ibid. p.73

Royal Army Pay Corps

Army Pay Department (officers) established 1877; Army Pay Corps (other ranks) established 1893; these two amalgamated to form Royal Army Pay Corps 1920; amalgamated to form Adjutant General's Corps 1993.

Though not often called upon to serve in the front-line, the men of the Royal Army Pay Corps performed a vital part in the Second World War, as in previous conflicts. Ensuring that millions of conscripts stationed across the entire world were paid regularly, fairly and reliably produced immense logistical problems. It also demanded a large and efficient workforce: the Corps had a strength of some 1,800 in mid-1939, including more than 500 civilians; within 15 months it had grown tenfold.

The delayed start to the first campaign in Europe allowed the RAPC to establish a stable network of distribution of wages, and the rapidity of the German advance posed difficulties more to do with escape than operation. The evacuation, however, cost the Corps dear – most of the Command Pay Office in Rouen were amongst the 4,000 men who died when the SS *Lancastria* was sunk returning across the Channel. One paymaster who survived was fished out of the water still clutching 90,000 French Francs.

As the scale of the war spread, so did the demands on the distribution of pay. Local money could never be counted upon to retain its value. Apart from inflationary fluctuations, it was frequently the target of enemy action, seeking to destabilize the local economy, and it became necessary to introduce a new currency. A series of notes (in denominations of £1, 10s, 5s, 2/6d, 1s and later 6d) was introduced; stamped with the British Military Authority, the BMA notes were declared legal tender by the Army wherever it was operating. With the advent of the Americans, a new joint currency was introduced for Italy – the Allied Military Lire.

The scale of the RAPC's responsibilities is seen in the money issued by cashiers in North Africa: some £50,000 each week.

In the Far East, administration was even more awkward, a situation not eased by the destruction of the sterling reserve in the invasion of Hong Kong. Most of the RAPC men in Singapore, however, did escape from the colony, taking the Treasury Chest with them to Australia.

Greatest of all challenges perhaps came in the Chindits campaigns in Burma. Though undercover and in enemy territory, the Chindits still required money to pay local guides and to purchase food; appropriate funds therefore had to be dropped to the troops by air.

In addition to their regular duties, the men of the RAPC were also expected to be able to fight as infantrymen. Pay Officers in the UK served in the Home Guard, whilst those abroad were also available in an active capacity – men such as those in the Palestine Corps who formed a force of 60 officers and 600 men ready to fight.

Royal Army Veterinary Corps

Established as Veterinary Medical Department 1859; re-organized as Army Veterinary Corps 1903.

The nature of The Royal Army Veterinary Corps is evident from its name; less immediately obvious is the role it played in the Second World War, a conflict dominated by mechanization. The rapid expansion of the corps, however, demonstrated the continuing relevance of animals in war; at the outset it comprised just 85 officers and 105 other ranks, by 1945 a total of 519 officers and 3,839 other ranks had been involved, with 458 officers still serving.

The RAVC was to be faced with new challenges, but the first priority was something of a throwback to earlier times: the creation of the 1st Cavalry Division in Palestine, the last mounted front-line troops in the British Army. Even with a single cavalry division, the demands were substantial: 9,000 horses suitable for combat had to be located, trained and shipped overseas. The first element of this – finding the animals – was initially the responsibility of the Remount Services, but in 1940 this body was subsumed into the RAVC.

The 1st Cavalry Division, as mentioned elsewhere, was eventually mechanized in 1941 – thus bringing to an end the popular weekly gymkhanas at the veterinary base in Ramle – and thereafter the RAVC found itself chiefly occupied with the provision and care of animals for transport.

The Western Desert had no real requirement for beasts of burden, but the East African campaign saw horses, mules and camels used extensively, partly to traverse the mountainous terrain and partly to save on precious fuel. During the expedition, the shortage of medical support also gave the vets an opportunity to employ their skills on human patients.

Similar problems of terrain in Sicily and Italy, which made use of mechanized transport so difficult, brought horses and mules to the fore again in Europe. In many of the Italian battles, mule train was the only means available to carry supplies up hillsides and to ferry the wounded back down. By the end of the war, the 8th Army had some 7,300 animals on its strength, together with all the vets, farriers and associated trades required to maintain such an establishment.

The demands of the Far East were still greater. There the combination of jungle, forest and hills, together with the lack of resources available to the forgotten army made livestock critical to the war effort.

The first Chindits campaign in 1943 saw the troops advance into Burma with 1,000 mules, bearing such equipment as the men could not carry. The task of the vets was not simply the acquisition of the animals, but the preparation of them for such an unprecedented operation. It was a contribution that did not pass unappreciated by Brigadier Wingate:

'The great bulk of the mules reached the Brigade . . . in a raw, untrained and unhardened condition . . . . The labours of Captain Carey-Foster of the Veterinary Corps, whom I unlawfully placed in command, accomplished wonders.' [1]

The mules proved a valuable element in the campaign, though on the return journey the shortage of food led to a great many being slaughtered for their meat, with the consequence that the heavy equipment they were carrying, including radio sets, had to be abandoned. For the larger 1944 Chindits expedition, 250 bullocks were taken as food on the hoof, together with 547 horses and 3134 mules in a transport capacity.

One other lesson from 1943 had been learnt. Working in Japanese-held territory depended on remaining as far as possible invisible to the enemy. The braying of the mules had on more than one occasion proved a danger to the troops, a problem solved in 1944 by the removal of the vocal chords of the animals – a massive operation in itself.

Beyond these larger animals employed for carriage, the RAVC was also called upon to provide and train large numbers of dogs for use by the Army and the Military Police in a variety of roles: as guard dogs, messengers, trackers, patrolling and, increasingly important in modern warfare, detection of casualties and mines.

[1] Clabby *The History of The Royal Army Veterinary Corps 1919-1961* p.122

Army Educational Corps

Corps of Army Schoolmasters formed 1846; redesignated Army
Educational Corps 1920; amalgamated to form Adjutant General's Corps
1993.

Like so many of the corps providing support to the front lines, the Army
Education Corps saw a major expansion in its numbers and its scale of
operation during the war. In August 1940 it comprised just 113 officers and 238
instructors; during the winter of 1943/44, it had recruited and co-opted civilians to
bring that figure up to 4,000 lecturers providing 110,000 courses, lectures and
classes.

This level of educational provision for the armed services was unprecedented
and did not go unchallenged by some in the defence establishment, who could not
see the point of broadening the minds of conscripts. Nonetheless, the need for
recreational activities amongst the large numbers of troops waiting to be sent into
action, and for information about the issues behind and progress of the war, was
clear. 'The soldier who understands the cause for which he fights,' commented Sir
Ronald Adam, Adjutant-General from 1941 to 1946, 'is likely to be a more reliable
soldier than the one who doesn't.' [1]

The programme took some time to build up momentum. In September 1940, a
committee under Lieutenant-General Sir Robert Haining produced its report
Education in the Wartime Army, recommending that education be made available
in three key areas: humanities, utilities and arts and crafts. This instruction,
however, was to be provided on a voluntary basis outside normal hours. It was not
until Adam was appointed Adjutant-General that education became a regular and
compulsory part of service life: in particular, officers were made responsible for
leading their men in a discussion group for one hour a week as an integral part of
training.

These discussion groups were based around two series of pamphlets produced
by the Army Bureau of Current Affairs. *War* and *Current Affairs,* published
fortnightly on an alternate basis and providing basic digests on topics related to the
conduct of the war and to the wider social issues of the mid-20th century, were a
ground-breaking initiative. Backed up by films, portable exhibitions and later a
fortnightly publication *Map Review,* that illustrated the events of the previous two
weeks on a map of the world, they allowed access to knowledge for tens of
thousands who had missed out on formal education.

In September 1942, as the onset of winter reduced the time available for
training, the discussion hour was augmented by a further three hours a week: one

dedicated to a military subject, one to the individual soldier's own choice and the third to citizenship. It was the latter that was to make the greatest impact: a series of four books, *The British Way and Purpose,* was printed and became the foundation for ever more informed debate.

With the onus of leading discussion thus placed on the shoulders of ordinary officers, one of the key tasks of the AEC was to provide training courses for such men to acquire educational techniques.

These centrally co-ordinated programmes formed the bones of army education, but they were fleshed out by local initiatives. All available resources were exploited in the cause of advancing knowledge and raising morale, from serving and civilian experts on arcane subjects through to local art galleries, farms and factories; at one point in 1942 three symphony orchestras comprised of conscripts were functioning in Britain.

But the instability of service life – with units liable to sudden transfers halfway across the country – made such activities pointless to plan more than a few weeks in advance. In this context another of the Haining Committee's recommendations proved invaluable. Correspondence courses for vocational work were gradually established, covering professional skills and such subjects as foreign languages. By the end of the war, over 220,000 students – half of them from the army – had enrolled in these courses and the programme was so successful that it survived into peacetime.

Though much of this work was aimed at troops in Britain, similar schemes and materials were provided overseas. Here, particularly in the Far East, the literacy courses introduced in 1943 and the teaching of English were of especial value.

[1] White *The Story of Army Education 1643-1963* p.96

Pioneer Corps

First formed 1762, subsequently disbanded; Pioneer Corps formed 1939;
amalgamated to form Royal Logistic Corps 1993.

Unlike previous incarnations of Pioneer Corps, that of the Second World War
was fully combatant, an active force of – by the end of the war – more than
400,000 men.

Organized in companies of approximately 500 men with three officers, the
Pioneers were an integral part of the British Expeditionary Force, with some
18,600 men in France by the end of 1939, engaged upon dock-work and the
construction of railways, medical bases, depots and camps. The severity of that
first winter, however, had a devastating effect on what was essentially a body of
reservists, many of them elderly; 63 Company alone reported 86 men invalided out
by December 1939. Their place was largely taken by draftees and by the large
number of aliens who enlisted in the Corps.

Initially seen as unskilled labour, the first North-West Europe campaign was to
establish the Pioneers' credentials as a significant element in the army. Thousands
fought in the first campaign against Nazism and thousands were taken prisoner. Of
particular note were the 1,500 men of 5 Group who arrived in Boulogne under
Lieutenant-Colonel Dean on 20 May and spent five days holding off the German
onslaught whilst troops were evacuated from the harbour. By the time the
Pioneers' turn came to escape, just 600 were left.

It was with no exaggeration that Field-Marshal Lord Milne, appointed Colonel
Commandant of the Corps, paid tribute to his men in July 1940:

'You are not relying on the past alone; you are building up day by day a
tradition of esprit de corps and service to the country of which all ranks may be
proud, and your deeds during the past few weeks have been the admiration of the
whole world.' [1]

During the period when Britain itself was threatened with invasion, the Pioneers
again played a vital part, constructing Home Defence, fighting fires, laying mine-
fields and dealing with bombs. Nearly 15,000 Pioneers served during the London
Blitz alone.

By the end of 1940 there were over 100,000 men in the Corps in 263
companies, including 19 companies of aliens and 14 companies of conscientious
objectors serving in a non-combatant role.

Even with this strength, large numbers of local labourers were also used during
the North African wars. The building and repeated re-building of roads, railways
and water pipelines in the desert in some of the worst conditions possible called for

immense sacrifice by Pioneers and civilians alike. So too did the disastrous campaigns in Greece and Crete, which cost the Corps 80% casualties.

One of the problems of North Africa, however, led to an easing of the labour shortage. The large numbers of Italian prisoners taken demanded the construction of POW camps, but also provided new recruits: 66 Italian companies were formed in Africa, each some 200 strong under British guard.

The invasion of Sicily provided for the Corps, as for so many other units, a fore-taste of Overlord. 14 companies were amongst the first troops to land, providing ramps for men and equipment and building an airfield that was ready for use by the end of the second day.

On D-Day the tasks undertaken included unloading duties, the clearing of mines, building tracks for guns and armour, evacuating the wounded, burying the dead, guarding prisoners and fighting. As the lines of communication stretched, the work increased proportionately.

During the battle to cross the Rhine, the front-line nature of the Corps was particularly evident: Pioneers operated the boats transferring the troops, acted as stretcher-bearers, and provided transport and smoke companies. (This latter function had been introduced in 1941.) 252 men gave their lives in the struggle, some of the 3,500 British Pioneers to be killed during the war. A further 6,500 of other nationalities also died.

By the end of the war, the Pioneers had been joined by a million civilians under their command in Civilian Labour units. Their tasks centred on administering the two and a half million German prisoners in North-West Europe, and the further million in Italy.

[1] Rhodes-Wood *A War History of The Royal Pioneer Corps 1929-1945* p.72

Intelligence Corps

Formed 1940.

Though the Intelligence Corps did not officially come into being until after the return from Dunkirk, the function it was designed to fulfil was of course apparent before, and some 31 Field Security Sections – comprising 35 officers and 400 other ranks – served in the British Expeditionary Force.

Within six months of its birth, the new corps numbered just under 3,000 all ranks; by its peak, this had risen to more than 11,000.

The men were still organized as Field Security Units, though this title was somewhat misleading: their task was more concerned with counter-intelligence than with security.

Keeping track of the enemy's activities was an essential part of the war effort from the outset. During the 'Phoney War', for example, the border between France and Germany was not even sealed, despite the state of war that existed between the two countries; the consequence was an ever-present danger from enemy agents and from informers within the local population.

Similar problems were to arise wherever the Army was active, and even in many places where simply the threat of conflict might some time be realized, particularly in strategically sensitive areas such as the Middle East. The men of the Intelligence Corps were responsible for identifying and monitoring local situations.

The decentralized nature of this kind of activity inevitably meant that NCOs were given greater autonomy than in more regular units, often acting virtually alone, though often too in association with locally recruited volunteers. All the men were also trained as infantrymen.

In addition to these intelligence activities, the corps also provided some key elements in other unconventional ventures. Lieutenant-Colonel Patrick Clayton was one of the key figures in creating the Long Range Desert Group in North Africa – itself an important contributor to the establishment of the SAS – whilst Major F V Webster, as part of Z Force, spent most of the war with Japan deep in enemy-occupied Burma.

Army Physical Training Corps

Formed after the Crimean War as The Army Physical Training Staff;
retitled The Army Physical Training Corps 1940.

'There is only one standard of fitness,' commented Field Marshal Montgomery, the Colonel Commandant of the Army Physical Training Corps, 'the standard of Total War. We have got to make ourselves tougher than the Germans, and they are pretty tough. Besides, no man's brain is at its best unless he is physically fit.' [1] It is a perfect summary of the Corp's objectives during the war.

Bolstered by recruits from such civilian occupations as school teachers, athletes and coaches, the APTC grew from 280 members to 3,000 during the course of the war. Its front-line role was established at the outset when 39 instructors went to France in early 1940 to work with those in the field and on assisting those in convalescent centres. During the brief campaign, Staff Instructor Campbell became the Corps's first fatality, though the remainder of the men were successfully evacuated.

Although it specialized in teaching physical fitness, unarmed combat and battle training, the Corps also conducted much valuable research at its school in Aldershot. With the rise of mechanized warfare, techniques were developed for manhandling armoured vehicles and field guns out of ditches and across fallen trees, techniques that would be utilized by men in the heat of battle. Similarly the skills of landing from a parachute drop and of swimming with heavy equipment had to be explored, and the knowledge disseminated through the army.

Throughout a serviceman's career, the influence of the APTC could be felt. Potential recruits who had been turned down on medical grounds were trained at Physical Development Centres – some 60,000 of them during the war. When not actually fighting, soldiers still had to maintain a high level of fitness, and instructors were present on troop ships to co-ordinate recreational activities. And in many cases, therapeutic physical training was used as an essential part of the convalescent programmes employed for the wounded.

Much of this work was conducted at home, but APTC instructors were also involved wherever the army went. In Normandy in 1944, in particular, they were called upon to develop exercises to keep troops fighting fit and to assist in such essentials as the digging of trenches. Perhaps more welcome were the mobile games stores provided for some divisions – lorries laden with goal-posts, footballs, tennis nets and other equipment to help realize the army's long-standing love of sport.

[1] Oldfield *History of The Army Physical Training Corps* p.77

Army Catering Corps

Established 1941; amalgamated to form Royal Logistical Corps 1993.

Until shortly before the war, catering was an entirely decentralized affair, responsibility for feeding troops being devolved to regiments. Units were allowed 1/3d per soldier for a day's food, producing a somewhat unhealthy diet comprised mostly of pies, puddings and stews.

In early 1938, following a War Office report, Sir Isidore Salmon MP (the Chairman of the country's leading caterers, J Lyons & Co) became Honorary Catering Assistant to the Army. In this capacity, he introduced sweeping changes, insisting upon better diet, equipment and training, the latter centred at a new establishment at Aldershot. Cooks were also to be re-classified as tradesmen, giving them a higher status in the Army.

With conscription, large numbers of civilian chefs joined the ranks, bringing further improvements with them. In response both to the numbers involved and to the needs of a modern force, the Army Catering Corps was formed in 1941; within a short time, the ACC had a staff of 700 officers and 60,000 cooks.

The size of the Corps was essential for meeting the demands of a force that had long been accepted as epitomizing Napoleon's argument that 'an army marches on its stomach'. In particular the ACC faced a need to provide food for an enormous dispersion of units – anti-aircraft establishments throughout the country, and international commitments across the world – and of occasional concentrations, especially following the D-Day landings, of enormous numbers of troops.

In a highly-mobile war, the success of the new structure was such that it survived into peace-time.

Auxiliary Territorial Service

Formed 1939; disbanded 1954 following formation of Women's Royal Army Corps 1949.

The organized involvement of women in the work of the British Army pre-dates the Great War, with the establishment of the First Aid Nursing Yeomanry in 1909, to be joined during the war years by Queen Mary's Imperial Military Nursing Service. In 1938, however, the progress of women took a major step forward with the formation of the Auxiliary Territorial Service, the forerunner of the Women's Royal Army Corps.

Credit for the success of the ATS is due mainly to Dame Helen Gwenne-Vaughan, a veteran of the Great War and the first director of the new service. Under her tireless leadership, the nature and role of the ATS was outlined and, though she was to retire in 1941, to be replaced by Jean Knox and then Leslie Whateley, the massive development and expansion of the service would not have been possible without her work. As the war started, just under 17,000 women had joined and were ready to serve; at its peak, the ATS could claim some 212,000 members.

Much of the work in the first 18 months was centred on driving, principally at home, though some women did go to France with the British Expeditionary Force as drivers and telephonists, and a detachment was sent to the Middle East in 1940 to work in intelligence.

Initially a volunteer force attached to the Army but not subject to military discipline, the ATS suffered from a poor public image and was vulnerable to low morale. It was not until 1941 that a positive change was made. In April that year the government announced that numbers were to be substantially increased, that the service was to come under the jurisdiction of the Army Act and that, whilst women would only be employed on work 'for which they have a special aptitude . . . such work includes duties at searchlight and gun stations.' [1]

It was in this role that the ATS was really to make its mark. A chronic shortage of personnel at Anti-Aircraft Command had necessitated the employment of women on searchlight duties as early as 1940; within a couple of years, they had proved to be essential, with 56,000 women serving in integrated batteries. In November 1942 the first official regiment was formed, the 93rd Searchlight Regiment of the Royal Artillery, consisting of 1,500 ATS women under an RA Commanding Officer.

Though officially not expected to fire weapons, there is no doubt that self-defence demanded on occasion that action be undertaken, for anti-aircraft work was hazardous: in May 1942 the first ATS death in action was sustained, and by the end of the war some 389 had been killed or wounded, most whilst on AA duties.

The work of these batteries began to turn the tide of popular opinion, a cause undoubtedly assisted by the high profile given to Mary Churchill, the Prime Minister's daughter, who served in 481 Battery in Hyde Park. In early 1945 came an even more potent symbol of the increased stature of the ATS, with the commission as 2nd Subaltern of Princess Elizabeth, the heir to the throne, who was to become a driver.

But there was much more to the ATS's work than anti-aircraft and driving duties. With the expansion of 1941, given weight by the passing in 1942 of the National Service Act (No. 2), which brought conscription to women, a wide range of support functions could be and were undertaken. ATS members were employed as draughtswomen preparing maps, as film-makers, radar trackers, telephonists, despatch riders, wireless operatives and postal workers. The Royal Corps of Signals called upon the assistance of 11,000 women, the REME on 6,000, the RAOC on 22,500 and the RASC on 17,000. In almost every part of the vast support system necessary to back up a modern army, women were increasingly an everyday presence.

Mention too must made of the Middle East, perhaps the most demanding of all the challenges facing the service. 5,000 women, most of them local, served in the harsh conditions of North Africa and Italy, with some as far afield as Kenya, South Africa and India. Most spectacular in its breaking of stereotypical roles was an ATS unit under Junior Commander Goggin, who were the first Allied troops into Cremona, establishing temporary administration of the area and even taking the surrender of the German garrison.

Meanwhile, the First Aid Nursing Yeomanry continued to exist despite the emergence of the ATS. Unlike the newer formation, the women of the FANY were not restricted to non-combatant duties and were allowed to carry small-arms. Mostly employed as drivers, there were some notable exceptions: 40 women were sent to Finland to assist that country's resistance to the Soviet invasion, 39 others were sent undercover into occupied France (13 being killed), and many others worked in the Far East as wireless operators.

[1] Terry *Women in Khaki* p.119

THE
ROYAL AIR FORCE

The Royal Air Force

The ubiquity of the Royal Air Force during the Second World War was such that no single-volume account – much less this brief note – can hope to do full justice to its work.

The RAF went everywhere that the Army went: a list of all the encounters in which air cover and support was provided would produce a schedule of almost all the battle honours won by an Army regiment during the War. In addition, its role in civilian defence, in protecting shipping convoys and in offensive strikes against the enemy's heartlands – to say nothing of the Battle of Britain – makes the story of the RAF a particularly rich and full one.

Whilst therefore paying full deference to all sections of a service that numbered well over a million men and women by the end of hostilities, it is possible here only to sketch the broadest outline of some of the most significant and unique interventions of the Royal Air Force.

Fighter Command – The Battle Of Britain

In 1936, the Royal Air Force was restructured to create separate commands, allocated according to function, with the key operational branches being Fighter Command, Bomber Command and Coastal Command. Each was to play a vital part in the defeat of the Axis powers.

This new structure, however, was not without its limitations. British theories of aerial warfare in the pre-war years had been dominated by the potentially devastating power of bombing, and little attention had been paid to co-ordinating land and air forces. Certainly this was true in comparison with Germany, as the 1940 European campaign was to demonstrate.

The Luftwaffe, complete with dive bombers, was an integral part of the German military machine, co-operating closely with the tank and infantry advance. The RAF, on the other hand, never designed for front-line combat, found itself squeezed between on the one hand political pressure to become ever more involved, and on the other the simple recognition that there was little that could be done.

The possibilities that did exist were, of course, exploited. Bombing raids were undertaken, including an attack on two bridges at Maastricht that resulted in 100% casualties among the five bomber crews and the award of the RAF's first VCs of the War, to Flight Officer Garland and Sergeant Gray. And some vital protection was offered to the evacuees from Northern France. But for the most part, those taking a strategic overview saw that the RAF had everything to lose and little to gain from this battle; its time would come soon enough, for with the collapse of the BEF, 'the continued existence of the nation . . . depend[ed] on the Royal Navy and Fighter Command.' [1]

That was the view of Sir Hugh Dowding, the head of Fighter Command, and it formed the basis of his struggle with those politicians who wished to throw more and more squadrons into the fight as a symbol of Britain's commitment to her allies. His arguments against the depletion of scarce resources ultimately prevailed, but the North European campaign was very nearly fatal for the RAF: 959 aircraft never returned, including 453 Hurricanes and Spitfires – the most modern of British fighter 'planes – and the lives of 362 fighter pilots were lost.

The consequence was that in June 1940, a month before the Luftwaffe's offensive on mainland Britain commenced, there were just 331 Hurricanes and Spitfires available to defend the country.

Fortunately production was rising rapidly – within two months this figure had been nearly doubled – and the arrival of allied airmen and European refugees, particularly from Poland, built up the numbers of aircrew. Even so, Churchill's famous description of Fighter Command as 'The Few' owed more to fact than to propaganda.

The popular image of the Battle of Britain – of a thin sky-blue line of men protecting this country from invasion and occupation – was thus not far from the truth. And the stakes that were being fought for were understood on both sides. Churchill had told Parliament that 'the cause of civilisation itself will be defended by the skill and devotion of a few thousand airmen' [2], whilst Hermann Goering had spelt out the enemy objective:

'The Fuhrer has ordered me to crush Britain with my Luftwaffe. By means of hard blows I intend to have this enemy, who has already suffered a crushing moral blow, down on his knees in the nearest future, so that an occupation of the island by our troops can proceed without any risk.' [3]

What Goering did not seem certain of was quite what those 'hard blows' were going to be. The key target, of course, was the Royal Navy – without naval superiority, the invasion of Britain was clearly impossible – but the Navy was protected by the RAF, and triumph in the air had to precede victory at sea. How to achieve this ambition was fortunately not as easy to analyse at the time as it sometimes seems in retrospect.

The first enemy attacks, in mid-July 1940, were targeted directly at the Royal Navy and the Channel ports; it was only when that endeavour failed that the Luftwaffe, recognizing the role of the RAF, turned its attention to the mainland. Still the actual objective seemed unclear; whether it was a bombing campaign to weaken Britain's will to fight, or first and foremost an assault on the RAF itself.

Fighter Command had no such confusion; its target was clearly the bombers, not the fighters escorting them. An early casualty was the Stuka dive-bomber, supposedly one of the elite machines in the German arsenal and yet one which the RAF quickly defeated – it was withdrawn from the conflict within a matter of days.

It was on 13 August that the Luftwaffe switched its attack from the coast inland. Two days later three huge air formations flew across from continental Europe in an attempt to swamp the RAF's resources. In the first of the great engagements of the critical phase of Battle of Britain, all were repulsed, with the loss of 75 enemy craft to the RAF's 34. The Germans immediately tagged 15 August 'Black Thursday', while Churchill acclaimed it as 'one the greatest days in history' [4]. In retrospect, the most significant result of the day was not the losses but the fact that it persuaded the Germans that multi-pronged assaults were not going to be sufficient to overcome the RAF; thereafter the massed attacks, such as the 1,720 aircraft that headed for England the very next day, were to be more direct.

Within those figures for 15 August, the pattern of losses in the future had been set: fighter losses were roughly equal on the two sides, but in addition the RAF accounted for a substantial number of bombers.

Ultimately this steady erosion of the Luftwaffe's bombing capacity was to prove critical, but for some weeks the outcome of the Battle of Britain was far from certain. The relentless waves of German aircraft were largely contained by Fighter Command's efforts, but only at a terrible price. Ten days of combat in mid-August saw the loss of 154 pilots and 213 fighters; during the same period, only 63 replacement pilots were found and just 108 aircraft a week were coming out of the factories. Germany's losses were greater – 367 'planes – and its production was lower, but it had access to greater immediate resources and it was the RAF that was driven to the edge of desperation.

On 24 August the crisis deepened. The Luftwaffe assault on the RAF switched focus from the air to the ground: bases at Manston, North Weald and Biggin Hill were hit – in some cases repeatedly – and raids on Vickers' and Hawker's factories damaged production of new craft. The battle was turning in Germany's favour.

Had the Luftwaffe pursued the strikes against air-bases, it now seems certain that victory was achievable, if not inevitable. Yet another change of target, however, let the advantage slip from its grasp. On 7 September a major bombing raid on London inaugurated a new stage in the struggle. In retrospect it was the beginning of the end, though at the time it was still far from clear who had the upper hand: that night the signal 'Cromwell' was issued, indicating an imminent German invasion.

In the event, the change of tactic revived the aerial combats and, with the ground support system free to operate again, gave Fighter Command the opportunity to hit back at the bomber fleets. As far as the RAF and the British military and political leadership were concerned, the priorities were unchanged: the war in the air was of paramount importance, the defence of London less significant than the continued survival of Fighter Command.

Ten days of raids on London were steadily beaten back, reaching a critical peak on 15 September when 200 German bombers with a massive escort were confronted by 250 Spitfires and Hurricanes. The attack was repelled with 60 enemy losses to the RAF's 26; the earlier proportions were being restored.

The immediate damage to the enemy was greatly overestimated by the British – 15 September became adopted as Battle of Britain Day because it was erroneously believed to be the day of the Luftwaffe's greatest losses – but it proved to be sufficient. The attempt to break British control of the air during daylight hours had failed, and within two days Hitler had ordered that Operation Sealion, the proposed invasion of Britain be postponed; it turned out to be a cancellation rather than a postponement.

Raids on London continued, increasingly by night, but the immediate threat to the integrity of the British Isles had been removed. (The Battle of Britain did not officially end until 31 October – an arbitrary date, but a date of some kind was essential for the awarding of campaign medals and other official purposes.) By that time, the tally was 832 RAF fighters lost, compared to the Luftwaffe's 668 fighters and nearly 600 bombers.

The number of pilots killed was substantially lower: some 446 Allied pilots gave their lives in the struggle. This points to one of the crucial advantages that the RAF held over the Luftwaffe – that of fighting on home territory, with the consequence that a British pilot shot down stood a far greater chance of surviving and returning to his unit than a German pilot.

There were other factors that assisted the RAF victory. The German fighters had to escort much slower bombers at the cost of vital fuel and flying time, while the Luftwaffe as a whole was obliged to use unfamiliar French and Belgian air-bases, had a poorer rate of replacement craft from its factories and had no real answer to the British warning systems, both radar and the Observer Corps.

These were all contributory factors, but they were overshadowed in the public imagination – and indeed in fact – by the heroism of the aircrew themselves. Some 2,763 men are calculated to have served as aircrew in the battle, 2,316 of whom were British. Poland and New Zealand contributed more than a hundred men each to the effort and aircrew from Canada, Australia, South Africa, Czechoslovakia, Belgium and the USA also gave their lives. [5]

To these men can perhaps be attributed the turning-point of the Second World War, and possibly of the whole of the twentieth century.

If the premature abandonment of Operation Sealion was largely due to the efforts of Fighter Command, the contribution of Bomber Command should not be forgotten. Its target was the fleet of barges being assembled across the Channel to transport the would-be invasion force; in two weeks of raids during September

1941, the bombers of the RAF wiped out 12% of the barges and would undoubtedly have destroyed even more had the fleet not been dispersed. This early victory, however, gave no indication of Bomber Command's greatest campaign, yet to come.

Bomber Command – Area Bombing

In many areas of military thought in the years prior to the Second World War – in the use of airborne troops, the development of mechanised forces, combined air/land operations and so on – Britain lagged dangerously behind Germany. One significant exception, however, was the concept of aerial bombing.

The idea grew out of the experience of the Great War. The protracted trench stalemates, it was argued, were possible only because the factories of the warring nations, positioned well away from the front-line were safe from attack and could continue to produce the equipment necessary to perpetuate the conflict. New technology offered the option of strategic bombing that could destroy the enemy's industrial infrastructure and thus bring a speedy resolution to a war, without the necessity for full-scale land engagements.

For a nation reeling from the massive casualties of 1914-18, the claim that bombers could effectively win a war by their own efforts was a persuasive theory. One of its great proponents was Sir Hugh, later Lord, Trenchard, who became Chief of Air Staff in the '20s:

'It is on the bomber offensive that we must rely for defence. It is on the destruction of enemy industries and, above all, on the lowering of morale of enemy nationals caused by bombing that ultimate victory rests.' [6]

The second half of this equation – the deliberate targeting of civilians – remains a controversial development, though it too arose from the Great War. The Soviet revolution of 1917 held out the possibility that a war-weary population could be pushed into rising against its government and forcing an end to the conflict.

The political acceptability of such a strategy was in question even then, for though both sides anticipated bombing civilians, neither wished – at least on the western front – to be the one to initiate it, particularly in the wake of the international outcry at Guernica during the Spanish Civil War.

The Battle of Britain thus commenced in June 1940 with the Luftwaffe instructed to hit only military targets. Similarly, two months earlier the Air Ministry had issued its first directive to Bomber Command, specifying oil plants as the primary objective. It was not until 24 July 1940 that a stray flight of German bombers accidentally dropped its load on London, the first western city thus to be hit. The news was not welcomed in Berlin, where Goering issued a memorandum insisting that 'Luftwaffe High Command will itself undertake the punishment of each aircraft captain involved. They will be posted to infantry regiments.' [7] The British response was as immediate and unequivocal as Goering no doubt anticipated: on 27 July the RAF bombed Berlin, and the inevitable escalation began.

The problem for Bomber Command was that, despite widespread official endorsement of the theory of strategic bombing, the resources simply did not exist to put it into practice. The Berlin raid was a minor affair with little military value. Similarly the bombing of Munich on 9 November the same year – the anniversary of Hitler's 1923 putsch in that city – was essentially an exercise in propaganda. And the consequences of that raid illustrated the limitations of Bomber Command: in retaliation, the Luftwaffe bombed Coventry, killing 568 civilians; soon after an RAF attack on Mannheim (a city twice the size of Coventry) killed just 23.

Bomber Command was thus faced with a situation in which it represented Britain's only real front-line with the major enemy, was expected to make a significant contribution, and yet was unable to do so. There were various contributory factors: the aircraft at its disposal were inadequate to the task, the lack of fighter escorts meant that only night raids could be undertaken – at the expense of accuracy – and the sheer distance involved in reaching targets in Germany left the flights vulnerable. (The Luftwaffe, of course, had airfields just across the Channel from which to operate.)

The result was a disastrous start to a campaign intended to bring German industry to its knees. During 1941 it was estimated that only 20% of British bombers got within five miles of their targets, whilst 700 aircraft were lost that year. Even more alarming was the fact that casualties were higher amongst aircrew than they were amongst German civilians. A strategy that was designed to reduce loss of life was proving very expensive.

The first stage of the offensive reached a tragic climax on 7 November 1941. Of 400 aircraft that left for Germany that night, 37 failed to return. Within that operation, the raid against Berlin provided a terrible microcosm of the problems of Bomber Command: 169 airplanes set out for the city, only 73 actually participated in the attack, and 21 were destroyed. Nine enemy lives were lost, compared to 120 British aircrew.

Changes were clearly needed as a matter of some urgency, and fortunately they were made. February 1942 saw the introduction of a new navigational system, Gee, which made some improvement (though less than was initially hoped) to accuracy, whilst around the same time the first Lancasters came off the production lines and into service. The Lancaster, of course, was rapidly to become the most famous and successful of British craft.

Perhaps even more significant was the appointment of Air Marshal Arthur Harris as Commander-in-Chief of the Command on 22 February 1942, a man committed to the principle of strategic bombing. 'There are a lot of people,' he remarked, 'who say that bombing cannot win the war. My reply is that it has never been tried yet.' [8]

Harris took over a force of only some 250 serviceable medium and heavy bombers, whose efficacy was already being called into question. He also, however, inherited an Air Staff Directive of 14 February that gave scope for a renewal of the Command:

'[It] has been decided that the primary object of your operations should now be focussed on the morale of the enemy civil population and in particular, of the industrial workers.' [9]

The new objective recognised the simple fact that, with no other way of hitting Germany, the efforts of Bomber Command needed to be more effective. Harris certainly agreed and began a more coherent campaign of what was to become known as area bombing, striking directly at civilian centres. Through March, April and May, a steady escalation of assaults hit medium-sized towns – Essen, Kiel, Lubeck, Rostock – selected as much for their lack of defences as for their strategic importance. The results were mixed, initial impressions of major success being balanced by the failure to substantially disrupt normal life.

The Luftwaffe responded in similar fashion, with raids on equivalent British towns: Exeter, Bath, York and Canterbury. But with the energetic Harris at the helm, Bomber Command was at last acquiring the tools to tackle the tasks assigned to it, and was beginning to believe that this exchange of sorties was a battle that could be won. It was a belief that Harris was determined to impress upon the enemy in as emphatic a manner as possible.

On 30 May 1942 he launched Operation Millennium, the first raid involving more than a thousand bombers, against Cologne. It was a courageous decision, for it called upon not merely the entire front-line of Bomber Command's crew and craft, but also upon the reserve, drawing in even the flying instructors; a failure that night could have proved fatal to the Command itself. But Millennium was not a failure: 1,500 tons of bombs were dropped on Cologne, producing fires that raged across 600 acres of the town, whilst RAF losses were below the 'acceptable' level of 5%.

In terms of the objectives set, it has to be conceded that in the long term no apparent loss of German morale could be detected, but the effect on that of the Allies was immense. For if nothing else, Millennium was an inspiration at a time when it was desperately needed. That month had seen Rommel launch a major offensive in Africa, British troops abandon Burma to the Japanese, the fall of the Phillipines and the low point of the Battle of the Atlantic. The fact that Bomber Command was seemingly coming into its own was the only good news available.

To hammer the point home, a similar sized operation was staged over Essen just two days later, and again on Bremen later in June. The military effectiveness of these attacks was even more qualified than that of Millennium, and no more raids on this scale were to be launched, but they did much to assist the cause of Bomber Command in gaining allocation of British resources.

The case was strengthened in August 1942. Churchill returned from his Moscow summit with Stalin having promised that, in the absence of a second land front in Europe, Bomber Command's activities would be stepped up in an attempt to divert German forces from the Soviet Union. The number of raids increased through the second half of 1942 and into 1943.

The campaign was not without its critics. Reservations on morality remained, and there were those who called for area bombing to be supplanted, or at least augmented, by precision bombing of key enemy installations. Some such raids were in fact carried out with some success. In March 1942 the Renault factory outside Paris was hit by 470 tons of bombs with the loss of just one 'plane and minimal French civilian casualties. May the following year saw the famous dambusters raid against the Mohne and Elder dams, to be followed in August by an attack on the V1 and V2 factories on the Baltic.

Harris was not enthusiastic about such actions, dismissing as 'panacea targets' those installations that some argued were so crucial to the German war machine that their removal would cripple the enemy. In effect he was discounting Lord Trenchard's first objective – of destroying the enemy's industry – and focussing almost entirely on the assault on German morale.

His case was initially supported by the fact that the necessary accuracy was still far from achievable. The introduction of the Pathfinder squadrons in August 1942 – light aircraft that preceded the bombers and marked the target – together with the development of better navigational aids was to remedy the situation over a period of time, but even when a 1944 analysis showed that 95% of bombs were within three miles of their target, Harris was still not convinced of the value of precision bombing.

By 1943 area bombing had become an even more significant strand in the Allies' war plan. The turning of the tide in the Soviet Union and in North Africa made the demand for a second European front even more urgent; in the absence of an invasion, Bomber Command was that front.

For four months in Spring 1943, a concerted campaign was waged against towns in the Ruhr, the industrial heartland of the Third Reich. If some of the towns the previous year had been relatively 'soft' targets – poorly defended and vulnerable – this was certainly not true of the Ruhr. Over 18,000 sorties were made, with losses to the RAF of around 5%, though many more aircraft that managed to return were damaged.

The fruits of these endeavours are difficult to calculate with any degree of accuracy. The same could not be said of Hamburg, hit by a series of raids in July. In the unprecedented fire-storm that ensued, 60% of Hamburg homes were burnt out, with civilian casualties estimated at between thirty and fifty thousand dead and a similar number wounded. Less than 3% of aircraft failed to return. Even allowing for damaged craft, the ratio of British to German casualties was spectacularly redressed from the dark days of 1941.

The Hamburg fire-storm was as much the product of the prevailing weather conditions and of town planning as it was of the incendiaries dropped; it could not be repeated at will, as the protracted assault on Berlin and other cities between November 1943 and March 1944 was to show. Massive damage was done, but civilian casualties were significantly lower than they had been in Hamburg. Even worse was the fact that the Luftwaffe was beginning to find ways of repelling the RAF incursions; the loss rate was creeping beyond the acceptable 5% level – up to nearly 6.5% in the raids on Berlin and reaching a disastrous 12% on the night of 30 March 1944. That night over Nuremburg marked the end of what was later known as the Battle of Berlin.

There were to be further examples of area bombing – the horrors of Dresden in February 1945 chief amongst them – but essentially Nuremburg ended the era in which Bomber Command was considered to be the Allies' front-line. The D-Day landings would soon supplant the Command as the key to the war against Germany; thereafter, although Harris and others would still consider area bombing of crucial importance, their voices were increasingly unsupported by the politicians, people and Chiefs of Staff.

In retrospect the campaign can be seen to have failed in its stated objectives. In December 1943 Harris wrote to the Air Ministry that 'the Lancaster force alone should be sufficient but only just sufficient to produce in Germany by April 1st 1944 a state of devastation in which surrender is inevitable.' [10] Such a claim was a long way wide of the mark.

German infrastructure and industry were not destroyed, or even – as far as one can judge – severely affected. Within four days of the bombing of Dresden, the rail system in the town was reported to be working again, and elsewhere output of war machinery continued to grow apace: both tank and aircraft production rose by nearly two thirds during the course of 1943, and both were to rise further in 1944. This should not have been entirely surprising to the British: after the bombing of Coventry – one of the worst raids suffered by a British city – factory production had been restored within five days.

The same comparison could perhaps have been made with regard to civilian morale. The London Blitz, though admittedly not on the scale of the devastation wreaked on Hamburg and Dresden, had created a sense of communal spirit that introduced a new phase in the language. The German population responded in like manner; morale may have been dented, but it was resilient, and the spirit of the people was never broken.

These lessons could perhaps have been learnt from the experience of being bombed by the Luftwaffe, but Harris' comment that a full-scale campaign of bombing had never been tried was undoubtedly true; it could have been that the key to success was quantity. This was an experimental form of warfare – a fact which some critics of the policy appear to forget, just as some later politicians have missed the key lesson that it is not possible to bomb a revolution into existence, nor to win a war from the air alone. What cannot be denied is that the intention in the upper echelons of Bomber Command to avoid the bloodbaths of the Great War was an honourable aim, even if it proved unachievable.

Despite all this, the record sheet was in no way one-sided; the successes of area bombing were significant and measurable. At the peak of the campaign, two million German men and women were engaged in the attempt to hold back Bomber Command, including some 900,000 anti-aircraft gunners. These were all combatants that the Allied armies did not have to face on the ground. And the weapons themselves were kept away from the battle-fields, something for which tank crews who had so often come under fire from anti-aircraft guns could be thankful.

Equally, though the RAF's raids on U-boats in dock had little effect, so massive were the defensive shelters, the relentless assault on Germany itself damaged the infrastructure of canals that were required to convey the deadly weapons to the seas. The fact that the U-boat campaign never regained its 1942 momentum in the last years of the war is at least partly thanks to the efforts of Bomber Command.

For British civilians, whose support of the Command was often less equivocal than that of some in authority, encouragement could be found in the fact that the Luftwaffe was increasingly forced onto the defensive. By 1944 bombers accounted for just 11% of German aircraft production and the ability to strike at targets in Britain was consequently reduced. By the end of the war, 60,000 British civilians had been killed by enemy bombing, compared to 600,000 Germans.

Beyond these considerations were two others that fall well beyond the remit of this book: the final judgement on the morality of the campaign, and the question of whether the focus on area bombing was to the detriment of more effective tactics.

There was undoubtedly a sense in the aftermath of the war that area bombing had been somehow inappropriate. Sir Arthur Harris, alone amongst the major commanders of British forces, was not awarded a peerage, and no campaign medal was issued for the men who had fought.

This last fact is particularly regrettable. A total of 47,293 members of Bomber Command were killed in action during the war; a further 8,000 or so were killed whilst training. The courage of those men and of those who survived can hardly be rivalled.

Coastal Command – The Battle Of The Atlantic

The third of the home commands of the RAF never achieved the public profile enjoyed by Fighter Command and Bomber Command. Even within the inner circles of those who decided the shape of the nation's armed forces, Coastal Command seldom seems to have been seen as a major priority, acquiring a status as something of a poor relation.

The fact that the Command made its major war effort in the Battle of the Atlantic did nothing to lift its public profile: after the drama of the Battle of Britain, a three-year long war ranging across thousands of square miles of ocean seemed sometimes unspectacular. The significance of that war, however, can only be equalled by Fighter Command's struggle.

With the defeat of the Luftwaffe, the invasion of Britain was put firmly off the agenda for the immediate future. The bombing raids on British cities were to continue for the duration of the war, but it was now evident that this tactic alone was not going to be sufficient in itself. Instead Germany's attention turned to the possibility of blockading this country. With mainland Europe by now in the enemy's hands, the Atlantic appeared as the only open route into the country, the only line of communication through which supplies of raw materials and fuel could pass. Control of the seas was evidently the key to the nation's ability to prosecute the war, indeed to survive.

The danger on the seas had been apparent from the outset. The first month of the war had seen Germany destroy 53 vessels representing just under 200,000 tons of shipping. It was a total not immediately sustained, but by late-1940, the monthly average was up to 425,000 tons and starting to look critical. Against this threat, one of the central elements in the British defence was Coastal Command.

Created in the re-structuring of the RAF in 1936, Coastal Command was charged with reconnaissance duties and the provision of escorts for shipping, effectively coming under dual command of the Royal Navy. Under-funded and under-equipped, however, it could make little difference to the attacks on British and Allied shipping; when the attacks stepped up in summer 1940, there was no response available, and for two years, it was evident that Germany held the initiative.

There were, of course, some successes. In March 1941 an assault on the enemy base at Brest saw a Coastal Command 'plane torpedo the battle-cruiser *Gneisenau* and put it out of action for eight months. It was an action followed up by other attacks on surface ships.

To be successful, however, these attacks depended on dangerously close encounters with the enemy – on one occasion, a 'plane returned with a length of ship's mast attached to it – and were ultimately to prove too expensive. In 1942 Coastal Command could claim to have destroyed 45 ships, but at the cost of some

251 aircraft. Even in victory, there was a heavy price to be exacted. The 'plane that hit the Gneisenau was shot down; the pilot, Flying Officer Kenneth Campbell, was posthumously awarded the Victoria Cross.

In any case, the German surface-fleet, like the Luftwaffe, was only a part of the problem. The real key to the German offensive was the U-boat fleet under the command of Admiral Dönitz. And here neither Coastal Command nor any other Allied force was making much progress. By the end of 1940, U-boats had sunk more than two and a half million tons of shipping (some 585 ships) with losses of just 32 vessels. Coastal Command had suffered the loss of more than three hundred aircraft.

By 1942 the situation had deteriorated still further. That year nearly eight million tons of shipping were destroyed and serious doubts surfaced about whether Britain could survive this slow starvation of its industry and people.

This was, as noted above, a time when Bomber Command was beginning to make its mark and attracting the attention of politicians and military strategists alike. Meanwhile Coastal Command was still suffering from neglect. With the official entry of the United States into the war, the area for which the Command was responsible stretched still further, and the aircraft to respond were simply not made available. The Halifax, for example, a good long-range bomber that had been used in attacks on Germany since April 1941 and could have conquered the distance work of the Battle of the Atlantic, was seen as the property of Bomber Command, who were reluctant to share its benefits. (Coastal Command, on the other hand, contributed its aircraft to Operation Millenium.)

There were other logistical problems. The primitive radar of the early days of the war was inadequate, whilst the prime problem of detecting the surface movement of U-boats at night was not properly addressed until mid-1942, with the introduction of the Leigh Light – a carbon arc lamp linked to a bomber's radar system that illuminated the target. In June 1942, the new apparatus was tried out with a hit on an Italian submarine; the following month it scored its first U-boat kill.

This breakthrough, whilst offering no magic formula for winning the war, combined with innovations in tactics, technology and training to make a crucial difference at a sensitive time. The amount of shipping hit by Germany in 1942 was worryingly high, but the year's figures conceal a significant shift in the balance of war. During the first half of the year, only 21 U-boats were sunk, none of them victims of Coastal Command; in the second half, 65 were sunk, 15 of them by Coastal Command.

The battle was by no means over – indeed November 1942 was the second worst month for shipping losses in the war – but the corner was beginning to be turned. The encounters between packs of U-boats and Atlantic convoys began to see decisive interventions by Coastal Command.

The vital month was to be May 1943. That month a total of 41 U-boats were sunk, 16 of them by Coastal Command. On 24 May, Admiral Dönitz himself noted this trend in his War Diary and commented: 'The enemy air force played a decisive role in inflicting these high losses.' [11]

The same day he abandoned the attacks on convoys, effectively conceding defeat in the Battle of the Atlantic. The U-boat threat was broken – by 1944 the tonnage of shipping sunk by the U-boat fleet was less than 3% of 1942's figures. Britain – a country whose existence has throughout the modern era depended on trade, a nation of shopkeepers – had faced the strangulation of its trade routes and had found the resources to survive.

Even more, the defeat of the German threat at sea facilitated the landings at Normandy: the long-awaited European land war was not possible until the waves had been secured. Often uncelebrated, Coastal Command's contribution – a contribution that also included mine-laying and the escorting of convoys to the Soviet Union – can scarcely be over-valued. By the end of the war, it could claim 188 U-boat kills and the destruction of 343 enemy ships.

Middle East Command

Two of the key problems facing Coastal Command – its low priority in the allocation of resources, and the vast area for which it was responsible – were also common to Middle East Command.

As its name suggests, Middle East Command was not a structure based on function – as were the Home Commands – but on its field of operations. With its central base in Egypt and with various smaller bases and training establishments throughout the region, the Command was expected to cover the whole of North and East Africa, the Middle East and the Mediterranean: a total of four and a half million square miles. In this context, the lack of modern equipment and aircraft at the outset of hostilities was painfully apparent.

There was another, unique problem for the Command. The entry of Italy into the conflict effectively closed off the Mediterranean and necessitated the development of an alternative supply route to service the bases. The logistical problems were enormous and it is a tribute to the skill of the RAF engineers and technicians that they were overcome at all, let alone with the speed and efficiency that was displayed. A depot was constructed at Takoradi in the Gold Coast, and further stop-over points between there and Egypt, providing a lifeline strung out across the width of Africa; a journey of some 3,700 miles was needed to bring in supplies, spares and replacement craft, but the Takoradi route was to prove critical in keeping the Command in action.

The role of Middle East Command bore little resemblance to those of the Home Commands. The key was co-operation between the RAF and the Army, for the desert wars and the expeditions beyond North Africa were essentially land conflicts, with a subsidiary requirement for air support. In October 1940 Anthony Eden, then War Secretary, visited Egypt and reported back that: 'Liaison between the Army and Air Force is excellent and the RAF are giving support for which no praise can be too high within their limited resources.' [12]

This co-operation was not always achieved ungrudgingly, but nonetheless it was to be a common feature through the next few years, and the RAF was to make an essential contribution to the victories that were won.

The first of those victories was the virtual elimination of the Italian air force. The twin campaigns in Libya and Eritrea that destroyed Italy's African power base were characterized by total Allied air superiority (with the South Africans in particular evidence in the latter operation). The success of the North African offensive resulted in the destruction of 58 Italian aircraft to the RAF's 26, with a further 1,200 enemy craft captured on the ground. Thereafter the Italian air force was to play no further part in the war.

But there were signs elsewhere that more difficult challenges would have to be met. In October 1940 Italy invaded Greece and, though the Greeks were initially reluctant to accept Allied soldiers into the country for fear of dragging Germany into the conflict, Middle East Command did supply five squadrons to assist the expulsion of the intruders.

By March 1941, with the German threat looming ever larger, ground troops and more 'planes were rushed in. Some 200 RAF aircraft, most of them elderly reserve vehicles, were flown to Greece; in response, the Luftwaffe put together a force of 1000 'planes. The result was inevitable – in the German invasion the following month, 209 RAF craft were lost, leaving nothing with which to defend Crete when that island too came under attack.

The German army, of course, had also arrived in Africa by this stage, and the ground gained from the Italians was rapidly retaken. Despite the damage inflicted on Middle East Command in Greece, the battle in the air was not all one-sided; around Tobruk during the eight-month siege of the town, the Allies maintained air superiority, whilst bombing raids on Tripoli and Benghazi did much to disrupt the enemy's supply lines.

Much of the struggle in North Africa was as dependent on supplies as it was on military offensive, and perhaps the most significant part played by the RAF during 1942 was its bombing raids that helped denude the Afrika Korps of fuel and equipment in the lead-up to Alamein. A further function was added that year with the use of Hurricanes as fighter-bombers, playing a direct part in battlefield encounters and effectively becoming a British equivalent of the feared German dive-bomber.

It was the war on supplies, however, that produced the most celebrated of the RAF's endeavours in the Mediterranean theatre. Malta had a strategic value to the

Allies that was almost incalculable: it lay directly on the key lines of communication between the southern Italian ports and Tripoli, posing a threat to enemy shipping, and it provided the Allies with a naval base in the heart of a hostile sea. It was not therefore that the island came under heavy enemy pressure almost from the outset.

While this pressure was applied by the Italians, it was containable; the arrival of the Luftwaffe in Sicily in 1941 transformed the situation. By the end of that year, up to 200 German aircraft a week were attacking Malta, in constant combat with a handful of Hurricanes and, later, a few precious Spitfires. April 1942 saw more than 6,000 tons of bombs fall on the island, but it was at a cost to the Luftwaffe of 379 aircraft, a tally that included 122 shot down by anti-aircraft guns despite strict rationing of ammunition. This was the peak of the siege, but Malta remained the heart of a desperate battle until the victory at Alamein began the final push against the Axis.

The heroic defence of Malta – by civilians as well as by all three Services – took on an almost mythic dimension. Less vaunted was one of the RAF's most spectacular successes: the saving of Iraq. Also of strategic significance, Iraq was of value not only as an oil-producer in its own right, but as the gateway to the oil-fields in Iran and as the path into Egypt. The coup staged by the pro-German Rashid Ali in April 1941 was thus of great concern to the Allies.

The battle for control of the country was fought at the RAF's Flying Training School at Habbaniya. An Iraqi force numbering some 8,000 men and equipped with artillery, machine guns and armoured vehicles, including some light tanks, besieged the base. The 2,000 residents inside, reinforced by a few hundred infantry from the King's Own Royal Regiment, could muster only a couple of antique Howitzers and 64 obsolete aircraft, hastily fitted out to carry bombs, against 50 or so enemy craft. Despite the odds, five days of virtually non-stop fighting saw not only the successful defence of Habbaniya, but the driving off of the enemy.

On 6 May an attack was made from the base, taking the fight to the enemy and effectively bringing to an end the rebellion that had threatened British interests. At a time when Greece and Crete were falling, and Rommel was driving the Allies back in North Africa, the heroism of the staff and pupils of Habbaniya was a welcome triumph in the region. It was also typical of many of the minor but significant encounters that characterized so much of the war.

[1]   Taylor & Moyes *Pictorial History of the RAF: Volume 2 1939-1945* p.6
[2]   Churchill *The Second World War: Vol II* p.263
[3]   Keegan *The Second World War* p.91
[4]   Hough & Richards *The Battle of Britain* pp.184 & 191
[5]   RAF Battle of Britain Museum figures, quoted ibid. p.191
[6]   Ellis *Brute Force* p.166
[7]   Gelb *Scramble: A Narrative History of The Battle of Britain* p.229

[8]   Keegan op. cit. p.421
[9]   Terraine *The Right of the Line* p.474
[10] ibid. p.555
[11] ibid. p.449
[12] ibid. p.313

BIBLIOGRAPHY

GENERAL

Of the legion of books written on the British armed forces and on the Second World War, the following have proved especially helpful:

Aitken, Leslie *Massacre on the Road to Dunkirk* (London, William Kimber, 1977)

Ansell, Colonel Sir Mike *Soldier On: An Autobiography* (London, Peter Davies, 1973)

Barthorp, Michael *The Armies of Britain 1485-1980* (London, National Army Museum, undated)

Bates, Peter *Dance of War: The Story of the Battle of Egypt* (London, Leo Cooper, 1992)

Churchill, Winston S *The Second World War* (London, Cassell & Co, 1948)

Cole, Sir David *Rough Road To Rome: A Foot-Soldier in Sicily and Italy 1943-44* (London, William Kimber, 1983)

Cox, Geoffrey *A Tale of Two Battles: A Personal Memoir of Crete and the Western Desert* (London, William Kimber, 1987)

Decisive Battles: The Turning Points of World War II (Leicester, Windward, 1986 - author uncredited)

Deighton, Len *Blood, Tears & Folly: In the Darkest Hour of the Second World War* (London, Jonathan Cape, 1993)

d'Este, Carlo *Decision in Normandy: The Unwritten Story of Montgomery and the Allied Campaign* (London, Collins, 1983)

d'Este, Carlo *Bitter Victory: The Battle for Sicily 1943* (London, Collins, 1988)

Ellis, John *Cassino, The Hollow Victory: The Battle for Rome January-June 1944* (London, Andre Deutsch, 1984)

Ellis, John *Brute Force: Allied Strategy and Tactics in the Second World War* (London, Andre Deutsch, 1990)

Ellis, Major L F *Victory in the West Volume 1: The Battle of Normandy* (London, HMSO, 1962)

Ellis, Major L F and Lieut-Colonel A E Warhurst *Victory in the West Volume 2: The Defeat of Germany* (London, HMSO, 1968)

Forty, George *Desert Rats at War 2: Europe* (Abingdon, Purnell, 1977)

Fraser, David *And We Shall Shock Them: The British Army in the Second World War* (London, Hodder and Staughton, 1983)

Glover, Michael *The Fight for the Channel Ports – Calais to Brest 1940: A Study in Confusion* (London, Leo Cooper, 1985)

Grant, Ian Lyall *Burma: The Turning Point* (Chichester, Zampi Press, 1993)

Harmam, Nicholas *Dunkirk: The Necessary Myth* (London, Hodder and Stoughton, 1980)

Hastings, Max *Overlord: D-Day and the Battle for Normandy 1944* (London, Michael Joseph, 1984)

Horrocks, Sir Brian with Eversley Belfield and Major-General H Essame *Corps Commander* (London, Sidgwick & Jackson, 1977)

Humble, Richard *Crusader: The Eighth Army's Forgotten Victory November 1941 - January 1942* (London, Leo Cooper, 1987)

Karslake, Basil 1940, *The Last Act: The Story of British Forces in France after Dunkirk* (London, Leo Cooper, 1979)

Keegan, John *The Second World War* (London, Hutchinson, 1989)

Laffin, John *Scotland The Brave: The Story of the Scottish Soldier* (London, Cassell & Co, 1963)

Macksey, Kenneth *Crucible of Power: The Fight For Tunisia 1942-43* (London, Hutchinson, 1969)

Macksey, Kenneth *A History of the Royal Armoured Corps and its Predecessors 1914 to 1975* (Beaminster, Newtown, 1983)

Macksey, Kenneth *Commando Strike: The Story of Amphibious Raiding in World War II* (London, Leo Cooper/Secker & Warburg, 1985)

Maule, Henry *The Great Battles of World War II* (London, Hamlyn, 1972)

Mercer, Derrik (ed.) *Chronicle of the Second World War* (London, Longman, 1990)

Morris, Eric *Circles of Hell: The War in Italy 1943-1945* (London, Random House, 1993)

Murphy, John *Dorset At War* (Sherborne, Dorset Publishing Company, 1979)

Neillands, Robin *The Desert Rats: 7th Armoured Division 1940-1945* (London, Weidenfeld & Nicholson, 1991)

Noonan, Miles *Tales From The Mess: A Military Miscellany* (London, Hutchinson, 1983)

Parrish, Thomas (ed.) *The Simon and Schuster Encyclopedia of World War II* (New York, Simon and Schuster, 1978)

Paul, W Pratt *The Lowland Regiments: Lions Rampant* (Aberdeen, Impulse Books, 1972)

Perrett, Bryan *At All Costs! Stories of Impossible Victories* (London, Arms and Armour, 1978)

Richardson, General Sir Charles *Flashback: A Solddier's Story* (London, William Kimber, 1985)

Slim, Field-Marshal Viscount *Defeat Into Victory* (pbk edn, London, Papermac, 1986)

Verney, Major-General G L *The Desert Rats: The History of the 7th Armoured Division 1938 to 1945* (London, Hutchinson, 1954)

Weinberg, Gerhard L *A World At Arms: A Global History of World War II* (Cambridge, Cambridge University Press, 1994)

THE ROYAL NAVY

Bassett, Ronald *Battle-Cruisers: A History 1908-1948* (London, MacMillan, 1981)

Grenfell, Russell *Main Fleet To Singapore* (pbk edn, Singapore, Oxford University Press, 1987 - orig pub 1951)

Hay, Doddy *War Under The Red Ensign: The Merchant Navy 1939-45* (London, Jane's, 1982)

Hoyt, Edwin P *The U-Boat Wars* (London, Robert Hale, 1985)

Jones, Geoffrey *The Month of the Lost U-Boats* (London, William Kimber, 1977)

Middlebrook, Martin *Convoy: The Battle for Convoys SC.122 and HX.229* (London, Allen Lane, 1976)

Pope, Dudley *The Battle of the River Plate* (revised edn, London, Alison Press/Secker & Warburg, 1987 - orig pub 1956)

Tute, Warren *The True Glory: The Story of the Royal Navy over a Thousand Years* (London, MacDonald, 1983)

Warren, CET and James Benson *Above Us The Waves* (London, George Harrap, 1953)

THE ARMY

Much of the information on the Army is drawn from the official and unofficial histories of the regiments involved and from Regimental Handbooks. The authors of these works are often uncredited and for ease of reference, books on specific regiments are therefore listed here in Army List seniority:

The Household Cavalry At War: First Household Cavalry Regiment Colonel The Hon Humphrey Wyndham (Aldershot, Gale & Polden, 1952)

The Household Cavalry At War: Second Household Cavalry Regiment Roden Orde (Aldershot, Gale & Polden, 1953)

The Royal Horse Guards R J T Hills (London, Leo Cooper, 1970)

The Story of The Royal Dragoons 1938-45 J A Pitt-Rivers (London, William Clowes & Sons)

The Royal Dragoons R J T Hills (London, Leo Cooper, 1972)

Second To None: The Royal Scots Greys 1939-1945 Lt-Col R M P Carver (Regimental publication, 1954)

The Royal Scots Greys Michael Blacklock (London, Leo Cooper, 1971)

The Regimental History of 1st The Queen's Dragoon Guards Michael Mann (Norwich, regimental publication, 1993)

I Serve: Regimental History of the 3rd Carabiniers (Prince of Wales's Dragoon Guards) (regimental publication, 1966)

The First And The Last: The Story of The 4th/7th Royal Dragoon Guards 1939-1945 Major J D P Stirling (London, Art & Educational Publishers, 1946)

Change and Challenge: The Story of the 5th Royal Inniskilling Dragoon Guards General Sir Cecil Blacker (London, William Clowes, 1975)

The Queen's Own Hussars: Tercentenary Edition (London, 1985)

4th Hussar: The Story of The 4th Queen's Own Hussars 1685-1958 David Scott Daniell (Aldershot, Gale & Polden, 1959)

A Short History of the 9th Queen's Royal Lancers 1715-1949 Major Hanwell (Aldershot, Gale & Polden, 1949)

The 10th Royal Hussars in the Second World War 1939-1945 compiled by a regimental committee chaired by Brigadier D Dawney DSO

The 10th Royal Hussars Michael Brander (London, Leo Cooper, 1969)

The 11th Hussars Richard Brett-Smith (London, Leo Cooper, 1969)

The History of the XII Royal Lancers (Prince of Wales's) Volume II Captain P F Stewart (London, Oxford University Press, 1950)

History of the 13th/18th Royal Hussars (Queen Mary's Own) 1922-1947 Major-General Charles H Miller (London, Chapman & Bradshaw, 1949)

A Brief History of the 13th/18th Royal Hussars (Queen Mary's Own) (regimental publication)

Emperor's Chambermaids Lieutenant-Colonel L B Oatts (London, Ward Lock, 1971)

The History of 15th/19th The King's Royal Hussars G Courage (Aldershot, Gale & Polden, 1949)

A Short History of the 15th/19th The King's Royal Hussars ed. Major J S F Murray (Aldershot, 1964)

History of The 16th/5th The Queen's Royal Lancers 1925-1961 Brigadier C N Barclay (Aldershot, Gale & Polden, 1963)

The 17th/21st Lancers R L V ffrench Blake (London, Hamish Hamilton, 1968)

To The Green Fields Beyond: A Short History of the Royal Tank Regiment (London, regimental publication, 1965)

42nd Royal Tank Regiment 1938-1944 (London, private publication)

A History of the 44th Royal Tank Regiment 1939-1945 A G Brown, K C E Dodwell, F E Honniball and G C Hopkinson (Bristol, 1965, Old Comrades Association)

50th Royal Tank Regiment: The Story of a Regiment (50RTR Old Comrades Association)

Battle Thunder: The Story of Britain's Artillery Kenneth Brookes (Reading, Osprey, 1973)

Gunners At War 1939-1945 Peter Mead (London, Ian Allan, 1982)

The Royal Engineers Derek Boyd (London, Leo Cooper, 1975)

The History of British Army Signals in the Second World War Major-General R F H Nalder (London, Royal Signals Institution, 1953)

Brief History of The Grenadier Guards 1656-1949 Captain F Martin (Aldershot, Gale and Polden, 1951)

The Coldstream Guards 1920-1946 Michael Howard and John Sparrow (London, Oxford University Press, 1951)

'No Dishonourable Name': The 2nd and 3rd Battalions Coldstream Guards 1939-1946 ed. D C Quilter (London, William Clowes and Sons, 1947)

The Scots Guards (The 3rd Guards) Anthony Goodinge (London, Leo Cooper, 1969)

A Short History of the Scots Guards 1642-1962 ed. Major John Swinton (Aldershot, 1963)

History of the Irish Guards in the Second World War Major D J L Fitzgerald (Aldershot, Gale & Polden, 1949)

The Micks: The Story of the Irish Guards Peter Verney (London, Peter Davies, 1970)

Welsh Guards At War Major L F Ellis (Aldershot, Gale & Polden, 1946)

Welsh Guards: A Short History of their Achievements (Colchester, Benham & Company, 1946)

The Welsh Guards John Rentallack (London, Frederick Warne, 1981)

The Royal Scots (The Royal Regiment) A M Brander (London, Leo Cooper, 1976)

The Queen's Royal Surrey Regiment (London, Malcolm Page, undated)

The Queen's Royal Regiment (West Surrey) Jock Haswell (London, Hamish Hamilton, 1967)

A Short History of The Buffs, Royal East Kent Regiment (3rd Foot) Brigadier E Foster Hall (London, Medici Society, 1950)

The Story of The Queen's Own Buffs, The Royal Kent Regiment Gregory Blaxland (no publishing details)

The King's Own Royal Regiment (Lancaster) (The 4th Regiment of Foot) Howard Green (London, Leo Cooper, 1972)

The King's Own Royal Regiment (Lancaster) IV Foot (Morecambe, c1959)

The History of The Royal Northumberland Fusiliers in the Second World War Brigadier C N Barclay (London, William Clowes and Sons, 1952)

The Royal Northumberland Fusiliers (The 5th Regiment of Foot) Basil Peacock (London, Leo Cooper, 1970)

History of The Royal Warwickshire Regiment 1919-1955 Marcus Cunliffe (London, William Clowes and Sons, 1956)

Always A Fusilier: The War History of The Royal Fusiliers (City of London Regiment) 1939-1945 C Northcote Parkinson (London, Sampson Low, 1949)

The Royal Fusiliers (The 7th Regiment of Foot) Michael Foss (London, Hamish Hamilton, 1967)

The Story of The King's Regiment 1914-1948 Lieutenant-Colonel J J Burke-Gaffney (Liverpool, Sharpe & Kellet, 1954)

A Short History of the Regular Battalions of The King's Regiment (Manchester & Liverpool) Lt-Col R P Macdonald (Aldershot, Gale & Polden, 1962)

The Royal Norfolk Regiment 1919-1951 P K Kemp (Norwich, Regimental Association, 1953)

The History of The First Battalion, The Lincolnshire Regiment in India, Arakan, Burma and Sumatra September 1939 to October 1946 (Lincoln, 1949)

The History of The Second Battalion, The Lincolnshire Regiment in North-West Europe 6 June 1944 to 8 May 1945 (Lincoln, c1949)

The Devons: A History of The Devonshire Regiment 1685-1945 Jeremy Taylor (Bristol, White Swan, 1951)

The Suffolk Regiment 1928-1946 Col W N Nicholson (Ipswich, East Anglian Magazine, undated)

The Suffolk Regiment Guthrie Moir (London, Leo Cooper, 1969)

The History of The Somerset Light Infantry (Prince Albert's) 1919-1945 George Molesworth (regimental publication, 1951)

The Somerset Light Infantry (Prince Albert's) Hugh Popham (London, Hamish Hamilton, 1968)

A History of The East Yorkshire Regiment (Duke of York's Own) in the War of 1939-1945 P R Nightingale (York, William Sessions, 1952)

The East Yorkshire Regiment (The 15th Regiment of Foot) A J Barker (London, Leo Cooper, 1971)

A Short History of the Prince of Wales's Own Regiment of Yorkshire (XIV and XV Foot) 1685-1966 ed. Major H A V Spencer (undated)

The Bedfordshire and Hertfordshire Regiment G W H Peters (London, Leo Cooper, 1970)

Come On Tigers: The Royal Leicestershire Regiment compiled Major A D Chilton (Morecambe, Morecambe Bay Printers, 1955)

The Royal Leicestershire Regiment (17th Foot): A History of the Years 1928 to 1956 ed. Brigadier W E Underhill (regimental publication, 1957)

The Story of The Green Howards 1939-1945 Captain W A T Synge (Yorkshire, regimental publication, 1952)

The Green Howards (The 19th Regiment of Foot) Geoffrey Powell (London, Hamish Hamilton, 1968)

A Short History of XX The Lancashire Fusiliers Major-General G Surtees (London, Malcolm Page, 1955)

Regiment of the Line: The Story of XX The Lancashire Fusiliers Cyril Ray (London, B T Batsford, 2963)

A Soldier's History: The Royal Highland Fusiliers (Princess Margaret's Own Glasgow and Ayrshire Regiment) (Glasgow, University Press, undated)

The 6th Battalion, Royal Scots Fusiliers 1939-46 (Ayr, undated)

The History of The Cheshire Regiment in the Second World War Arthur Crookden (Cheshire, regimental publication, 1949)

The Red Dragon: The Story of The Royal Welch Fusiliers 1919-1945 Lieutenant-Commander P K Kemp (Aldershot, Gale & Polden, 1960)

A Short History of The South Wales Borderers, 24th Foot, and The Monmouthshire Regiment (Regimental Committee, undated)

Borderers in Battle: The War Story of The King's Own Scottish Borderers 1939-1945 Captain Hugh Gunning (Berwick-upon-Tweed, Martin's, 1948)

All The Blue Bonnets: The History of The King's Own Scottish Borderers Robert Woollcombe (London, Arms and Armour, 1980)

The History of The Cameronians (Scottish Rifles) Vol III: 1933-1946 Brigadier C N Barclay (London, Sifton Praed, undated)

The Royal Inniskilling Fusiliers in the Second World War Sir Frank Fox (Aldershot, Gale & Polden, 1951)

An Outline History of The Royal Irish Rangers (27th [Inniskilling], 83rd and 87th) 1689 to 1969 (Armagh, Trimbles, 1969)

Cap Of Honour: The Story of The Gloucestershire Regiment (The 28th/61st Foot) 1694-1950 David Scott Daniell (London, George G Harrap & Co, 1951)

The Worcestershire Regiment 1922-1950 Lieutenant-Colonel Lord Birdwood (Aldershot, Gale & Polden, 1952)

History of The East Surrey Regiment Volume IV: 1920-1952 David Scott Daniell (London, Ernest Benn, 1957)

The East Surrey Regiment (The 31st and 70th Regiments of Foot) Michael Langley (London, Leo Cooper, 1972)

The History of The Duke of Cornwall's Light Infantry 1939-1945 E G Godfrey & R F K Goldsmith (regimental publication, 1966)

The Duke of Cornwall's Light Infantry R F K Goldsmith (London, Leo Cooper, 1970)

The Duke of Wellington's Regiment (West Riding) (London, Malcolm Page, undated)

The Story of The Border Regiment 1939-1945 Philip J Shears (London, Nisbet & Co, 1948)

A History of The Royal Sussex Regiment: A History of The Old Belfast Regiment and the Regiment of Sussex 1701-1953 G D Martineau (Chichester, Moore & Tillyer, undated)

Regimental History of The Royal Hampshire Regiment: Volume Three 1918-1954 David Scott Daniell (Aldershot, Gale & Polden, 1955)

The Royal Hampshire Regiment (37th/67th Regiments of Foot) Alan Wykes (London, Hamish Hamilton, 1968)

History of The South Staffordshire Regiment Colonel W L Vale (Aldershot, Gale & Polden, 1969)

The Staffordshire Regiment (The Prince of Wales's) Information Handbook (London, 1973)

A Short History of The Dorsetshire Regiment 1702-1948 (Dorchester, Henry Ling, c.1948)

The South Lancashire Regiment (The Prince of Wales's Volunteers) Colonel B R Mullaly (Bristol, White Swan, 1952)

The Welch Regiment 1719-1960 (London, Malcolm Page, undated)

The Black Watch Philip Howard (London, Hamish Hamilton, 1968)

A Short History of The Loyal Regiment (North Lancashire) (London, Malcolm Page, undated)

The Oxfordshire & Buckinghamshire Light Infantry Philip Booth (London, Leo Cooper, 1971)

The Essex Regiment 1929-1950 Colonel T A Martin (1952, regimental publication)

The History of The Sherwood Foresters (Nottinghamshire and Derbyshire Regiment) 1919-1957 Brigadier C N Barclay (London, William Clowes & Sons, 1959)

The Story of The 2nd Battalion The Sherwood Foresters 1939-1945 Captain John W A Masters (Aldershot, Gale & Polden, 1946)

The Loyal Regiment (North Lancashire): The 47th and 81st Regiments of Foot Michael Langley (London, Leo Cooper, 1976)

The Northamptonshire Regiment Michael Barthorp (London, Leo Cooper, 1974)

The History of The Northamptonshire Regiment 1934-1948 Brigadier W J Jervois (Regimental History Committee, 1953)

The Royal Berkshire Regiment (The 49th/66th Regiment of Foot) Frederick Myatt (London, Hamish Hamilton, 1968)

The History of The Royal Berkshire Regiment (Princess Charlotte of Wales's) 1920-1947 Brigadier Gordon Blight (London, Staples Press, 1953)

The Queen's Own Royal West Kent Regiment 1920-1950 Lieutenant-Colonel H D Chaplin (London, Michael Joseph, 1954)

The Queen's Own Royal West Kent Regiment: The Dirty Half-Hundred (The 50th/97th Regiment of Foot) Roger Holloway (London, Leo Cooper, 1973)

History of The King's Own Yorkshire Light Infantry Vol VI: 1939-1948 Brigadier G F Ellenberger (Aldershot, Gale & Polden, 1961)

The King's Own Yorkshire Light Infantry (The 51st and 105th Regiments of Foot) Leonard Cooper (London, Leo Cooper, 1970)

The History of The Corps of The King's Shropshire Light Infantry Volume 3: 1881-1968 (regimental publication)

The King's Shropshire Light Infantry (The 53rd/85th Regiment of Foot) J R B Moulsdale (London, Leo Cooper, 1972)

The Middlesex Regiment (Duke of Cambridge's Own) (The 57th and 77th of Foot) Gregory Blaxland (London, Leo Cooper, 1977)

A Brief History of The King's Royal Rifle Corps 1755-1948 (Aldershot, Gale & Polden, 1948)

Swift and Bold: The Story of The King's Royal Rifle Corps in the Second World War 1939-1945 ed. Major-General Sit Hereward Wake and Major W F Deedes (Aldershot, Gale & Polden, 1949)

The Story of The Wiltshire Regiment (The 62nd and 99th Foot): 1756-1959 Colonel N C E Kenrick (Aldershot, Gale & Polden, 1963)

The Wiltshire Regiment (The 62nd and 99th Regiments of Foot) Tom Gibson (London, Leo Cooper, 1969)

History of The Manchester Regiment First and Second Battalions 1922-1948 Lieut-Commander A C Bell (Altrincham, John Sherratt and Son, 1954)

The North Staffordshire Regiment (The Prince of Wales's) (The 64th/98th Regiment of Foot) Hugh Cook (London, Leo Cooper, 1970)

The York & Lancaster Regiment Donald Creighton-Williamson (London, Leo Cooper, 1968)

The Story of The Durham Light Infantry Captain E W Short (Newcastle upon Tyne, J & P Bealls, 3rd edition)

The D.L.I. At War: The History of The Durham Light Infantry 1939-1945 David Rissik (Liverpool, Charles Birchall & Sons, 1953)

The Highland Light Infantry (The 71st Highland Light Infantry and 74th Highlanders) L B Oatts (London, Leo Cooper, 1969)

Queen's Own Highlanders (Seaforth and Camerons): A Short History (Inverness, Highland Printers, 1961)

Glory of The Gordons W Pratt Paul (Inverness, 1966)

Queen's Own Cameron Highlanders: A Short Regimental History Lt-Gen Sir Spencer Ewart, re-edited Lt-Col R D M C Miers (Inverness, Northern Counties Newspapers, 1948)

Whatever Men Dare: The Queen's Own Cameron Highlanders ed. Major N C Baird (Morecambe, 1953)

The Royal Ulster Rifles Vol III: 1919-1948 Charles Graves (Yorkshire, regimental publication, 1950)

The Royal Ulster Rifles 1793-1960 Lieut-Col M J P M Corbally (Glasgow, Paramount, 1960)

Outline History of The Royal Irish Fusiliers (Princess Victoria's) (Aldershot, Gale & Polden, 1955)

The Royal Irish Fusiliers 1793-1950 Marcus Cunliffe (London, Oxford University Press, 1952)

The Argyll and Sutherland Highlanders Douglas Sutherland (London, Leo Cooper, 1969)

Fighting Highlanders! The History of The Argyll and Sutherland Highlanders P J R Mileham (London, Arms and Armour, 1993)

The Rifle Brigade in the Second World War 1939-1945 Major R H W S Hastings (Aldershot, Gale & Polden, 1950)

Jackets of Green: A Study of the History, Philosophy and Character of The Rifle Brigade Arthur Bryant (London, COllins, 1972)

The Red Devils: The Story of The British Airborne Forces G G Norton (London, Leo Cooper, 1971)

Men of the Red Beret: Airborne Forces 1940 - 1990 Max Arthur (London, Hutchinson, 1990)

A History of The S.A.S. Regiment John Strawson (London, Secker & Warburg, 1984)

In This Sign Conquer: The Story of the Army Chaplains Brigadier The Rt Hon Sir John Smyth (London, A R Mowbray, 1968)

D Day to VE Day with the RASC (Aldershot, Gale & Polden, 1946)

Royal Army Service Corps: The Transport Corps of the British Army (Glasgow, Paramount)

The Royal Corps of Transport (Glasgow, Paramount, 1968)

Surgeons In The Field John Laffin (London, J M Dent & Sons, 1970)

The Royal Army Medical Corps Redmond McLaughlin (London, Leo Cooper, 1972)

History of the Royal Army Ordnance Corps 1920-1945 Brigadier A H Fernyhough with Major H E D Harris (London, RAOC)

Craftsmen of the Army: The Story of the Royal Electrical and Mechanical Engineers Brigadier BB Kennett and Colonel J A Tatman (London, Leo Cooper, 1972)

The Story of The Royal Military Police Major A V Lovell-Knight (London, Leo Cooper, 1977)

'The Historical Connection: The Fortunes of War' Brigadier L G Hinchliffe *Royal Army Pay Corps Journal Volume XXX No. 153* (Spring 1979)

The Army Veterinary and Remount Services in the 1939-45 War (London, War Office, 1961)

The History of The Royal Army Veterinary Corps 1919-1961 Brigadier J Clabby (London, J A Allen, 1963)

The Story of Army Education 1643-1963 Colonel A C T White (London, George G Harrap, 1963)

A War History of The Royal Pioneer Corps 1939-1945 Major E H Rhodes-Wood (Aldershot, Gale & Polden, 1960)

British Military Intelligence Jock Haswell (London, Weidenfeld & Nicholson, 1973)

History of the Army Physical Training Corps Lieutenant-Colonel E A L Oldfield (Aldershot, Gale & Polden, 1985)

The Army Catering Corps (1965)

The Army Catering Corps (Sutherland, Method, 1980)

The Women's Royal Army Corps Shelford Bidwell (London, Leo Cooper, 1977)

Women In Khaki: The Story of the British Woman Soldier Roy Terry (London, Columbus, 1988)

F.A.N.Y. The Story of the Women's Transport Service 1907-1984 Hugh Popham (London, Leo Cooper/Secker & Warburg, 1984)

THE ROYAL AIR FORCE

Gelb, Norman *Scramble: A Narrative History of The Battle of Britain* (London, Michael Joseph, 1986)

Guedalla, Philip *Middle East 1940-1942: A Study in Air Power* (London, Hodder and Staughton, 1944)

Hough, Richard & Denis Richards *The Battle of Britain: The Jubilee History* (London, Guild, 1970)

Taylor, John W R and Philip J R Moyes *Pictorial History of the RAF: Volume 2 1939-1945* (London, Ian Allan, 1969)

Terraine, John *The Right of the Line: The Royal Air Force in the European War 1939-1945* (pbk edn, London, Sceptre, 1988)

INDEX OF BATTLE HONOURS

This index covers only the major battle honours, those that the regiments concerned adopted as part of their banners.

Key to abbreviations used in this index

E Surr R	The East Surrey Regiment
E York R	The East Yorkshire Regiment (The Duke of York's Own)
Gliders	The Glider Pilot Regiment
Glosters	The Gloucestershire Regiment
Gordons	The Gordon Highlanders
Green Howards	The Green Howards (Alexandra, Princess of Wales's Own Yorkshire Regiment)
Gren Gds	Grenadier Guards
Greys, The	The Royal Scots Greys (2nd Dragoons)
HLI	The Highland Light Infantry (City of Glasgow Regiment)
IG	Irish Guards
KDG	1st King's Dragoon Guards
Kings	The King's Regiment (Liverpool)
King's Own R	King's Own Royal Regiment (Lancaster)
KOSB	The King's Own Scottish Borderers
KOYLI	The King's Own Yorkshire Light Infantry
KRRC	The King's Royal Rifle Corps
Lan Fus	The Lancashire Fusiliers
Leicester R	The Royal Leicester Regiment
LG	The Life Guards
Lincoln R	The Royal Lincolnshire Regiment
Loyal R	The Loyal Regiment (North Lancashire)
Manch R	The Manchester Regiment
Midd'x R	The Middlesex Regiment (Duke of Cambridge's Own)
Norf R	The Royal Norfolk Regiment
North'd Fus	The Royal Northumberland Fusiliers
North'n R	The Northamptonshire Regiment
N Stafford R	The North Staffordshire Regiment (The Prince of Wales's)
Para	The Parachute Regiment
Ox & Bucks LI	The Oxfordshire & Buckinghamshire Light Infantry
Queen's R	The Queen's Royal Regiment (West Surrey)
R Berks R	The Royal Berkshire Regiment (Princess Charlotte of Wales's)
REKR	The Buffs (Royal East Kent Regiment)
R Fus	The Royal Fusiliers (City of London Regiment)
R Hamps	The Royal Hampshire Regiment
RHG	The Royal Horse Guards (The Blues)
Rifle Bde	The Rifle Brigade (Prince Consort's Own)
R Innis Fus	The Royal Inniskilling Fusiliers

R Ir Fus	The Royal Irish Fusiliers (Princess Victoria's)
Royals, The	The Royal Dragoons (1st Dragoons)
RS	The Royal Scots (The Royal Regiment)
R S Fus	The Royal Scots Fusiliers
R Sussex R	The Royal Sussex Regiment
RTR	Royal Tank Regiment
R U Rifles	The Royal Ulster Rifles
RWF	The Royal Welch Fusiliers
R W Kent R	The Queen's Own Royal West Kent Regiment
SAS	The Special Air Service Regiment
Seaforth	Seaforth Highlanders (Ross-shire Buffs, The Duke of Albany's)
SG	Scots Guards
Sherwood For	The Sherwood Foresters (Nottinghamshire and Derbyshire Regiment)
Shrops LI	The King's Shropshire Light Infantry
S Lan R	The South Lancashire Regiment (Prince of Wales's Volunteers)
S Stafford R	The South Staffordshire Regiment
Suffolk R	The Suffolk Regiment
S Wales Bord	The South Wales Borderers
Warwicks	The Royal Warwickshire Regiment
Welch R	The Welch Regiment
WG	Welsh Guards
Wilts R	The Wiltshire Regiment (Duke of Edinburgh's)
Worc R	The Worcestershire Regiment
W York R	The West Yorkshire Regiment (The Prince of Wales's Own)
York & Lanc R	The York and Lancashire Regiment

THE BATTLE HONOURS

Aam	Dorset R
Aart	RS
Abyssinia 1940	RTR
Abyssinia 1941	R Sussex R
Adriatic	SAS
Advance on Tripoli	KDG, The Royals
Advance to Florence	16/5L
Akarit	Green Howards, R Sussex R, BW, Midd'x R, Seaforth, Camerons, Argylls, 2 Gurkhas
Alam El Halfa	The Greys, 4H, R Sussex R, KRRC, Rifle Bde
Alam Hamza	REKR
Aller	The Greys, 15/19H, E Lan R
Ancona	7H
Antwerp	Shrops LI
Antwerp-Turnhout Canal	Lincoln R, York & Lanc R
Anzio	Gren Gds, SG, IG, Queen's R, R Fus, Green Howards, Cameronians, DWR, Oxs & Bucks LI, Sherwood For, Loyal R, North'n R, R Berks R, KOYLI, Shrops LI, Midd'x R, Wilts R, N Stafford R, Seaforth, Gordons
Aradura	Norf R
Argenta Gap	The Bays, 4H, 16/5L, 9L, 10H, REKR, Lan Fus, R W Kent R, R Ir Fus
Argoub Sellah	KOYLI
Arnhem 1944	KOSB, Border R, S Stafford R, Dorset R, Para
Athens	Kings, Para
Beda Fomm	KDG, 3H, 7H, 11H, Rifle Bde
Belhamed	Bedfs & Herts R
Benghazi Raid	SAS
Bishenpur	W York R, 7 Gurkhas
Bologna	12L, 14/20H, 10 Gurkhas
Boulogne 1940	IG, WG
Bordj	16/5L
Bou Arada	R Ir Fus
Bourguebus Ridge	S Lan R
Bremen	The Greys, Warwicks, R S Fus, KOSB, Shrops LI, R U Rifles

Breville	Para
Brieux Bridgehead	Norf R, N Stafford R
Brinkum	Suffolk R
Bruneval	Para
Brussels	LG, RHG, WG
Buq Buq	3H, 8H
Burma 1942	7H, RTR, Cameronians, Glosters, KOYLI
Burma 1942-43	R Innis Fus
Burma 1942-44	DWR, Seaforth
Burma 1942-45	R Berks R
Burma 1943	N Stafford R
Burma 1943-45	RS, Lincoln R, Devon R, Suffolk R, Lan Fus, Border R, R Sussex R, North'n R Cameronians, S Stafford R, BW
Burma 1944-45	Norf R, S Wales Bord, Glosters, Worc R, E Lan R, Welch R, 6 Gurkhas
Burma 1945	Warwicks, E York R
Caen	13/18H, North'd Fus, Warwicks, Devon R, Lan Fus, RWF, S Wales Bord, KOSB, S Stafford R, Dorset R, Midd'x R, Manch R, N Stafford R, Seaforth, R U Rifles
Calais 1940	KRRC, Rifle Bde
Campoleone	Sherwood For
Canae	Welch R
Capture of Forli	Kings
Capture of Perugia	17/21L, Rifle Bde
Capture of Tobruk	Cheshire
Cassel	Glosters, Oxs & Bucks LI
Cassino	E Surr R, R W Kent R
Cassino I	Essex R, 2 Gurkhas, 7 Gurkhas
Cassino II	16/5L, 17/21L, North'd Fus, R Fus, Kings, Bedfs & Herts R, Lan Fus, R Innis Fus, DCLI, R Sussex R, R Hamps, BW, North'n R, R Ir Fus, Rifle Bde
Cauldron	North'd Fus, HLI
Centuripe	R Innis Fus, R W Kent R, R Ir Fus
Chindits 1943	Kings
Chindits 1944	King's Own R, Kings, Bedfs & Herts R, Leicester R, Lan Fus, Cameronians, DWR, Border R, S Stafford R, Essex R, York & Lanc R, 6 Gurkhas
Chor es Sufan	12L

Citta del Pieve	3H
Citta di Castello	3H
Cleve	Wilts R
Coriano	The Bays, 3H, 4H, R Fus, Sherwood For, 10 Gurkhas
Corinth Canal	4H
Crete	3H, Leicester R, BW, York & Lanc R, Argylls
Croce	Welch R
Damiano	R Berks R
Defence of Alamein Line	KDG, W York R, Essex R
Defence of Arras	WG, Wilts R, Manch R
Defence of Escaut	RS, Warwicks, Lan Fus, Glosters
Defence of Habbaniya	King's Own R
Defence of Kohima	R W Kent R
Defence of Rauray	Durham LI
Defence of Sinzweya	W York R
Defence of Tobruk	KDG, North'd Fus
Djebel	16/5L
Djebel Bou Aoukaz 1943	SG, IG, DWR
Djebel Kesskiss	Loyal R
Djebel Tanngoucha	R Innis Fus, R Ir Fus
Donbaik	RWF
Dunkirk 1940	4/7DG, 5InnisDG, 12L, Gren Gds, Coldm Gds, King's Own R, North'd Fus, R Fus, Lincoln R, Suffolk R, E York R, Bedfs & Herts R, KOSB, E Lan R, E Surr R, DWR, Border R, R Hamps, S Lan R, Loyal R, R Berks R, Shrops LI, Midd'x R, Durham LI, R U Rifles
Dyle	12L, R Berks R, Manch R, N Stafford R, R U Rifles
Egyptian Frontier 1940	7H, 11H, KRRC
El Alamein	LG, RHG, The Bays, The Royals, The Greys, 3H, 4H, 8H, 9L, 10H, 11H, 12L, RTR, Queen's R, REKR, North'd Fus, E York R, Green Howards, Cheshire, R Sussex R, BW, Sherwood For, R W Kent R, Midd'x R, KRRC, Durham LI, Seaforth, Gordons, Camerons, Argylls, Rifle Bde, 2 Gurkhas
El Hamma	The Bays, 9L, 10H

El Kourzia	17/21L
Enfidaville	Oxs & Bucks LI, Essex R
Falaise	The Greys, Suffolk R, R S Fus, Glosters, E Lan R, S Stafford R, S Lan R, Welch R
Falaise Road	BW
Fiesole	Loyal R
Flushing	RS, KOSB
Fondouk	16/5L, 17/21L, WG
Fontenay le Pesnil	Lincoln R, DWR, KOYLI, York & Lanc R
Fort Dufferin	6 Gurkhas
Garigliano Crossing	R Fus, R S Fus, R Innis Fus, North'n R, Wilts R
Gazala	The Bays, 8H, 9L, 10H, 12L, SG, E York R, Green Howards, Worc R, DCLI, Sherwood For
Geilenkirchen	4/7DG, 13/18H, Worc R, DCLI, Dorset R
Gemmano Ridge	Queen's R, Oxs & Bucks LI, KOYLI
Gheel	Durham LI
Goch	13/18H, Worc R, Gordons
Gothic Line	KDG, Gren Gds, RS, R Fus, Lincoln R, Leicester R, Cheshire, R Hamps, Sherwood For, Manch R, Camerons, 2 Gurkhas
Greece 1941	4H, RTR, KRRC
Greece 1944-45	KRRC, HLI
Grik Road	Argylls
Gueriat el Atach Ridge	Loyal R
Hamman Lif	WG
Hechtel	WG
Hill 112	The Greys, SCLI, Wilts R
Hochwald	The Greys, 15/19H, Shrops LI
Hong Kong	Midd'x R
Hunt's Gap	R Hamps
Ibbenburen	15/19H
Imphal	Devon R, Suffolk R, W York R, KOSB, Border R, North'n R, Seaforth, Gurkhas, 10 Gurkhas
Incontro	DCLI
Iraq 1941	LG, RHG
Irrawaddy	KOSB, 2 Gurkhas

Italy 1943	The Royals, The Greys, 11H
Italy 1943-44	KDG, Cameronians
Italy 1943-45	RTR, Coldm Gds, SG, Leicester R, R Innis Fus, E Surr R, Welch R, North'n R, Shrops LI, KRRC, Argylls, Rifle Bde, SAS
Italy 1944	LG, RHG, 3H
Italy 1944-45	16/5L, 7H, 9H, 12L, 17/21L, RS, Bedfs & Herts R, R Sussex R, Loyal R, 6 Gurkhas
Italy 1945	14/20H
Jitra	2 Gurkhas
Johore	Loyal R
Kasserine	17/21L
Keren	W York R, Worc R, HLI, Camerons
Kohima	RS, Queen's R, Norf R, Lan Fus, RWF, Worc R, Dorset R, S Lan R, R Berks R, Manch R, Durham LI, Camerons
Kournine	16/5L
Knightsbridge	The Royals
Kyaukmyaung Bridgehead	Welch R, 6 Gurkhas
Kyaukse 1942	7 Gurkhas
Lamone Bridgehead	9L, King's Own R
Lamone Crossing	The Bays
Landing in Sicily	Devon R, R S Fus, Border R, S Stafford R, Dorset R, HLI, SAS
Le Havre	S Wales Bord, Gliders
Liri Valley	16/5L
Longstop Hill 1943	E Surr R, Argylls
Lower Maas	5InnisDG, 8H, RWF, E Lan R, Welch R, Manch R
Madagascar	RWF, E Lan R, S Lan R, Seaforth
Malaya 1941-42	Leicester R, E Surr R, Argylls
Malta 1940	Manch R, R Ir Fus
Malta 1940-42	Devon R, Dorset R, R W Kent R
Malta 1941-42	King's Own R, Lan Fus, Cheshire, R Hamps
Maltot	Wilts R
Mandalay	Worc R, Dorset R, R Berks R, Camerons, 6 Gurkhas, 10 Gurkhas

Mareth	Gren Gds, E York R, Green Howards, Cheshire, Durham LI, Gordons
Marradi	N Stafford R
Maungdaw	W York R
Mayu Tunnels	S Wales Bord
Medenine	SG, Queen's R
Medicina	6 Gurkhas
Medicina	14/20H
Medjez el Bab	Lan Fus
Medjez Plain	Gren Gds, DCLI, R W Kent R, N Stafford R
Meiktila	W York R, Border R, 7 Gurkhas, 10 Gurkhas
Merjayun	The Greys, King's Own R
Merville Battery	Gliders
Mine de Sedjenane	York & Lanc R
Minturno	Green Howards, KOYLI, York & Lanc R
Mont Pinchon	4/7DG, 5InnisDG, 13/18H, Gren Gds, Coldm Gds, IG, WG, Warwicks, Glosters, Worc R, DCLI, Midd'x R, Wilts R
Monte Camino	KDG, Gren Gds, SG, Queen's R
Monte Ceco	DWR
Monte Chicco	6 Gurkhas
Monte Grande	Loyal R
Monte Ornito	CG, WG
Monte Piccolo	WG
Montone	King's Own R
Mozzagrogna	R Fus
Myinmu Bridgehead	Devon R, Border R, North'n R, 10 Gurkhas
Myitson	Glosters
Nederrijn	LG, RHG, 4/7DG, The Royals, 15/19H, DCLI
Neerpelt	IG
Ngakyedauk Pass	Lincoln R, KOSB
Nijmegen	Gren Gds, IG
Nofilia	The Greys
Normandy Landing	4/7DG, 13/18H, Warwicks, Kings, Norf R, Lincoln R, Devon R, Suffolk R, E York R, Green Howards, Cheshire, S Wales Bord, R Hamps, Dorset R, S Lan R, Oxs & Bucks LI, R Berks R, Shrops LI, R U Rifles, Gliders, Para

North Africa 1940	R Fus, S Stafford R
North Africa 1940-41	7H, Leicester R
North Africa 1940-42	3H, 8H, King's Own R
North Africa 1940-43	RTR, R Sussex R, KRRC, Rifle Bde, SAS
North Africa 1941	Bedfs & Herts R
North Africa 1941-43	KDG, The Bays, The Royals, 12L, SG
North Africa 1942	S Wales Bord
North Africa 1942-43	LG, RHG, 16/5L, 9H, 17/21L, R Innis Fus, E Surr R, North'n R
North Africa 1943	IG, R Fus, Lincoln R, Bedfs & Herts R, Leicester R, Loyal R, N Stafford R
North Arakan	Queen's R, Suffolk R, R S Fus, RWF, S Lan R, Wilts R, York & Lanc R, 2 Gurkhas
North-West Europe 1940	9L, 12L, 13/18H, 15/19H, RTR, Coldm Gds, RS, REKR,King's Own R, Warwicks, Norf R, E York R, Bedfs & Herts R, Green Howards, Cameronians, R Innis Fus, Glosters, Worc R, E Surr R, DCLI, DWR, Border R, R Sussex R, S Stafford R, S Lan R, Essex R, North'n R, R W Kent R, Shrops LI, KRRC, HLI, Gordons, Rifle Bde
North-West Europe 1944-45	LG, RHG, The Royals, 8H, 13/18H, 15/19H, RTR, Coldm Gds, SG, IG, RS, Warwicks, Norf R, Devon R, E York R, Leicester R, Green Howards, S Wales Bord, Cameronians, Glosters, Worc R, DCLI, DWR, Border R, S Stafford R, S Lan R, Essex R, North'n R, KOYLI, Shrops LI, KRRC, HLI, Gordons, Rifle Bde, Gliders, SAS
Norway 1940	IG, Green Howards, S Wales Bord, Sherwood For, KOYLI
Noyers	S Stafford R
Nyaungu Bridgehead	S Lan R
Odon	4/7DG, RS, Suffolk R, E York R, R S Fus, KOSB, Cameronians, HLI, Gordons, Argylls
Omars	R Sussex R
Oudna	Para
Oued Zarga	E Surr R, R Ir Fus

Ourthe	E Lan R
Palmyra	LG, RHG, Essex R
Paungde	7H, Glosters
Pegasus Bridge	Oxs & Bucks LI, Gliders
Pegu	7H
Pegu 1942	W York R
Pinwe	R S Fus, S Wales Bord, Glosters, E Lan R
Poggio del Grillo	7 Gurkhas
Primosole Bridge	Durham LI, Para
Proasteion	4H
Quarry Hill	SG
Rangoon Road	6 Gurkhas, 7 Gurkhas, 10 Gurkhas
Reichswald	RWF, E Lan R, Welch R, Oxs & Bucks LI, Manch R, HLI, Gordons, Camerons
Regalbuto	Devon R
Rhine	4/7DG, The Royals, 8H, 11H, 15/19H, RTR, Gren Gds, RS, Devon R, R S Fus, RWF, KOSB, Cameronians, R Hamps, BW, Oxs & Bucks LI, R Berks R, HLI, Gordons, Camerons, R U Rifles, Argylls, Gliders, Para
Rhineland	4/7DG, 13/18H, 15/19H, Coldm Gds, SG, IG, North'd Fus, Norf R, Lincoln R, Cameronians, DCLI, S Lan R, KRRC, Seaforth
Rimini Line	The Bays, 4H, 7H, Kings
Robaa Valley	REKR
Roer	8H, 11H, 13/18H
Rome	Cheshire, Wilts R, N Stafford R
Ruweisat	4H, 9L
St Omer-La Bassée	5InnisDG, Norf R, Cheshire, RWF, Dorset R, Camerons, R Ir Fus
St Valéry-en-Caux	DWR, Seaforth
Salerno	The Greys, Gren Gds, Queen's R, North'd Fus, R Fus, Lincoln R, Leicester R, Cheshire, R Hamps, Oxs & Bucks LI, Sherwood For, KOYLI, York & Lanc R, Durham LI
Sangro	Lan Fus, E Surr R, Essex R, R W Kent R, R Ir Fus

Santarcangelo	10H, 10 Gurkhas
Saunnu	10H
Schaddenhof	E York R
Scheldt	Leicester R, R S Fus, Cameronians, Manch R, HLI
Seine 1944	15/19H, Worc R, Wilts R
Senio Pocket	4H
Sferro	Gordons
Shweli	REKR
Sicily 1943	The Royals, RTR, REKR, E York R, Green Howards, Cheshire, Cameronians, R Innis Fus, S Stafford R, BW, R Berks R, KOYLI, Midd'x R, York & Lanc R, Seaforth, Gliders
Sidi Barrani	3H, 11H, Coldm Gds, North'd Fus, Leicester R, Camerons, Argylls
Sidi Rezegh 1941	7H, 8H, 11H, KRRC, Rifle Bde
Sidi Suleiman	3H
Singapore Island	Norf R, Suffolk R, Sherwood For, Loyal R
Sittang 1942	DWR, 7 Gurkhas
Sittang 1945	W York R, Welch R, 6 Gurkhas, 7 Gurkhas
Slim River	2 Gurkhas
Somme 1940	The Bays, 9L, 10H
Soulevre	LG, RHG
Southern France	Gliders, Para
Sully	S Wales Bord
Syria 1941	LG, RHG, The Royals
Tamandu	2 Gurkhas
Taukyan	Glosters
Tavoleto	7 Gurkhas
Tebaga Gap	KDG
Tebourba Gap	17/21L, R Hamps
Termoli	R Ir Fus, SAS
Tilly sur Seulles	Durham LI
Tobruk 1941	RTR, Coldm Gds, Queen's R, North'd Fus, Border R, BW, Essex R, York & Lanc R, Durham LI, SAS
Tobruk 1942	CG
Tobruk Sortie	King's Own R, Bedfs & Herts R
Trasimene Line	Kings, Bedfs & Herts R, R W Kent R
Trigno	REKR
Tuitam	10 Gurkhas

Tunis	KDG, The Bays, 16/5L, 10H, 11H, 12L, 17/21L, Coldm Gds, Bedfs & Herts R,BW, Sherwood For, Shrops LI, 2 Gurkhas
Tuori	Kings
Valli di Comacchio	10H, SAS
Venraij	Warwicks, Norf R, Suffolk R, Shrops LI
Villa Grande	Essex R
Villers Bocage	8H, 11H, Queen's R
Walcheren Causeway	HLI
Weeze	RWF, E Lan R
Withdrawal to Escaut	5InnisDG, 15/19H
Wormhoudt	Warwicks
Yenangyaung 1942	W York R, R Innis Fus
Ypres-Comines Canal	13/18H, RW, R S Fus, Oxs & Bucks LI, N Stafford R
Yu	North'n R
Zetten	Essex R

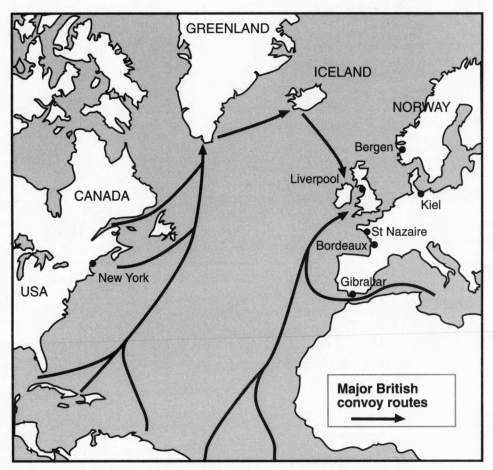

Map labels: GREENLAND, ICELAND, NORWAY, Bergen, Kiel, Liverpool, St Nazaire, Bordeaux, Gibraltar, CANADA, New York, USA

Major British convoy routes

The Battle of the Atlantic

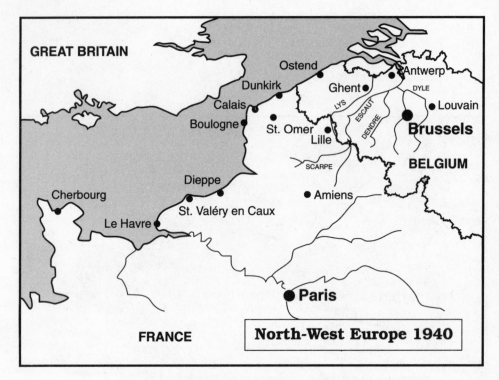

North-West Europe 1940

GREAT BRITAIN

Ostend
Dunkirk
Ghent
Antwerp
DYLE
Calais
LYS
Louvain
Boulogne
ESCAUT
St. Omer
DENDRE
Lille
Brussels
SCARPE
BELGIUM
Cherbourg
Dieppe
Amiens
Le Havre
St. Valéry en Caux

Paris

FRANCE

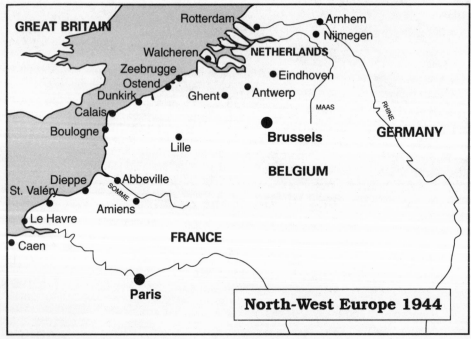

North-West Europe 1944

GREAT BRITAIN
Rotterdam
Arnhem
Nijmegen
Walcheren
NETHERLANDS
Zeebrugge
Eindhoven
Ostend
Dunkirk
Ghent
Antwerp
Calais
MAAS
RHINE
Boulogne
GERMANY
Lille
Brussels
Dieppe
Abbeville
BELGIUM
St. Valéry
SOMME
Le Havre
Amiens
Caen
FRANCE

Paris

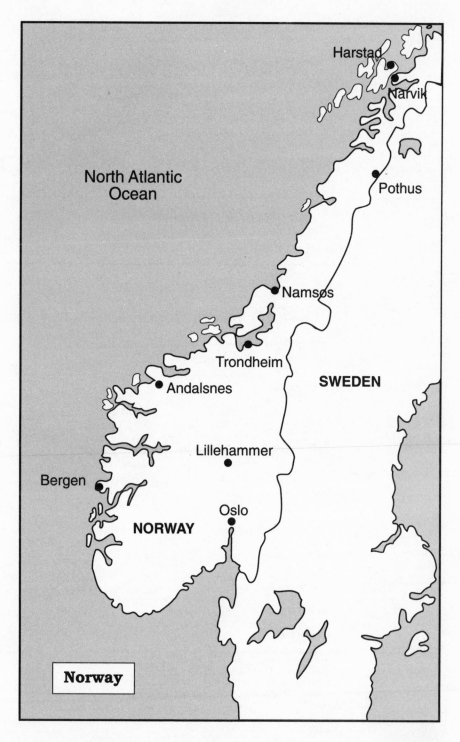

Harstad

Narvik

Pothus

North Atlantic
Ocean

Namsøs

Trondheim

SWEDEN

Andalsnes

Lillehammer

Bergen

Oslo

NORWAY

Norway

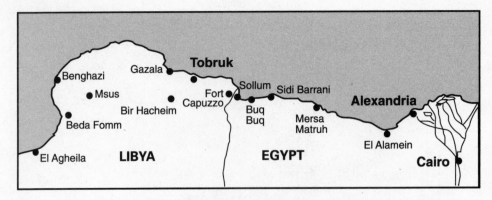

Western Desert

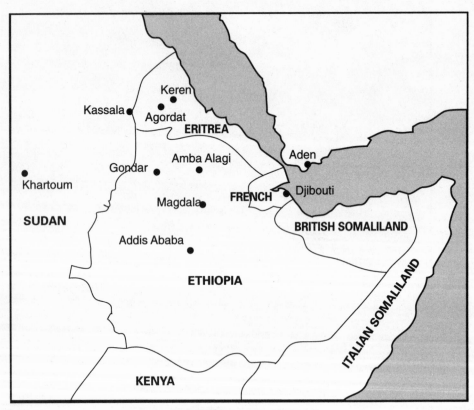

East Africa

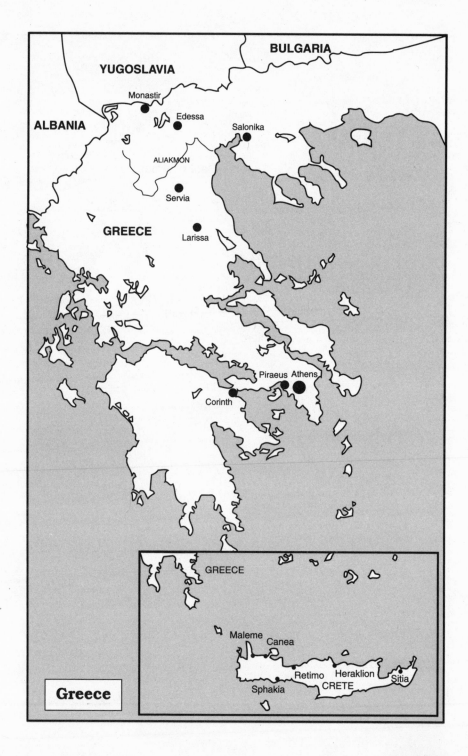

Greece

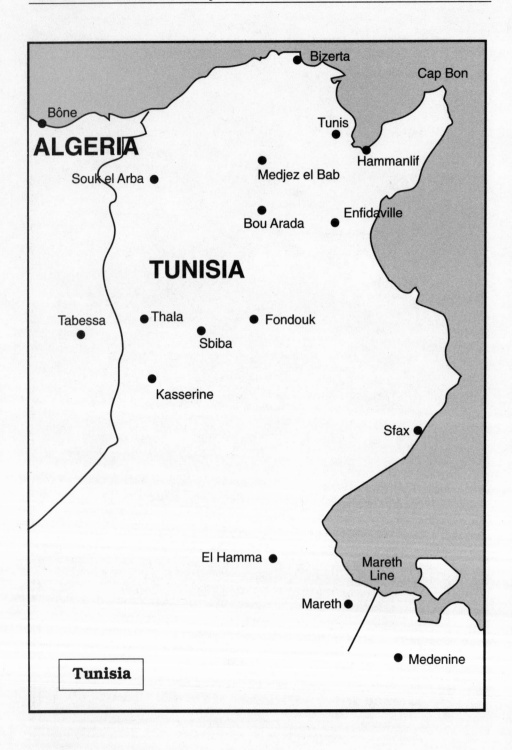

Tunisia

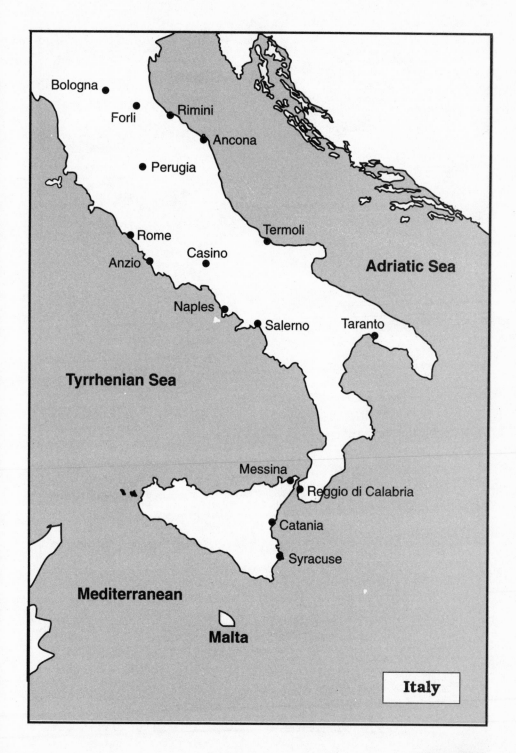

Bologna

Forli

Rimini

Ancona

Perugia

Termoli

Adriatic Sea

Rome

Casino

Anzio

Naples

Salerno

Taranto

Tyrrhenian Sea

Messina

Reggio di Calabria

Catania

Syracuse

Mediterranean

Malta

Italy

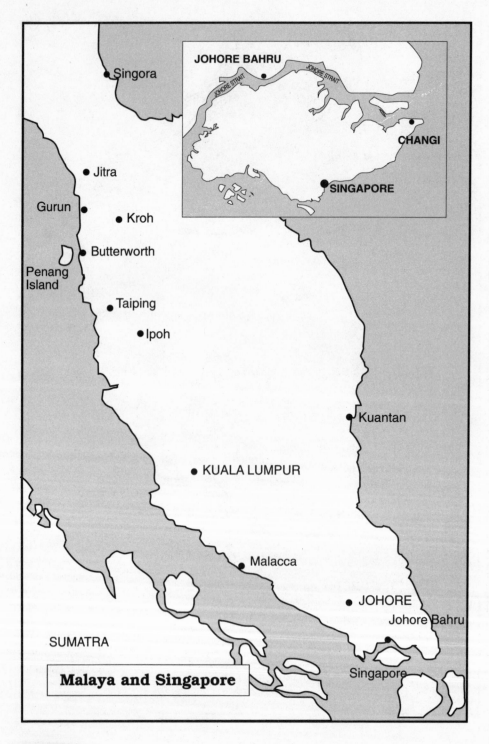

JOHORE BAHRU

JOHORE STRAIT

JOHORE STRAIT

CHANGI

SINGAPORE

• Singora

• Jitra

Gurun •

• Kroh

• Butterworth

Penang
Island

• Taiping

• Ipoh

• Kuantan

• KUALA LUMPUR

• Malacca

• JOHORE

Johore Bahru

SUMATRA

Singapore

Malaya and Singapore

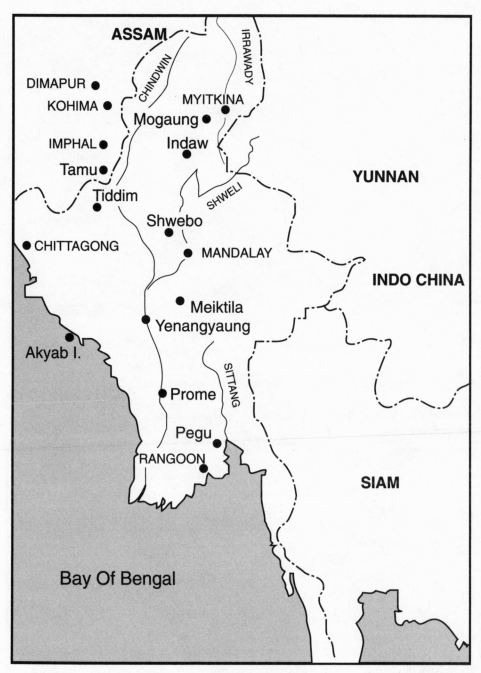

Burma

Fighter Command
The Battle of Britain

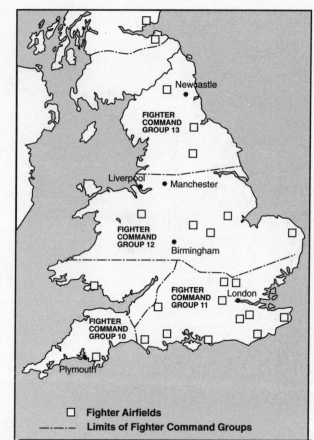

FIGHTER COMMAND GROUP 13

Newcastle

Liverpool

Manchester

FIGHTER COMMAND GROUP 12

Birmingham

FIGHTER COMMAND GROUP 11

London

FIGHTER COMMAND GROUP 10

Plymouth

☐ Fighter Airfields
—·—·— Limits of Fighter Command Groups

Bomber Command
Area Bombing

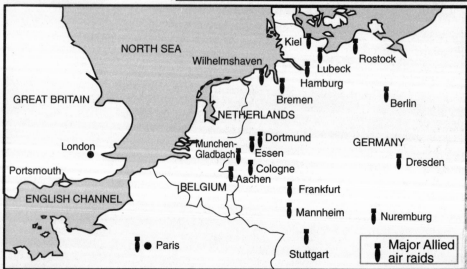

NORTH SEA

Kiel

Wilhelmshaven

Rostock

Lubeck

Hamburg

GREAT BRITAIN

Bremen

Berlin

NETHERLANDS

Dortmund

Munchen-Gladbach

Essen

GERMANY

London

Cologne

Dresden

Portsmouth

Aachen

ENGLISH CHANNEL

BELGIUM

Frankfurt

Mannheim

Nuremburg

Paris

Stuttgart

Major Allied air raids